CAMPFIRE COOKERY

CAMPFIRE COOKERY

ADVENTURESOME RECIPES *and* OTHER CURIOSITIES FOR THE GREAT OUTDOORS

SARAH HUCK

AND

JAIMEE YOUNG

PHOTOGRAPHY BY TARA DONNE
FOREWORD BY MELISSA CLARK

STEWART, TABORI & CHANG   NEW YORK

CONTENTS

Isn't it funny how you can know someone for years and yet never really know them?

Take, for example, my charming assistants and recipe testers Sarah Huck and Jaimee Young. I've had the pleasure of working closely with these two women for a combined period of eight years. Naturally, in that length of time I've learned plenty about them. First and foremost, I've learned that they have excellent palates. If ever I need to determine whether a dish needs a lift of lemon, a pinch of salt, or some other mysterious injection of flavor, I turn to them. I also know their specialties—Jaimee is an expert of flaky piecrust and Sarah has a remarkable way with salads and a special knack for grilling. I know that they are smart, funny, and exceptionally good cooks. Both start each workday with a cup of tea and by afternoon they start rummaging in my cupboards for a nibble of chocolate.

But I have to admit that until recently, I'd remained a bit in the dark about their more flamboyant sides. In fact, I have only just discovered them in these pages. Sure, there have been some clues—the Wilkie Collins novels and Girl Scout Guide peeking out of Sarah's tote bag, Jaimee's tipsy midnight Facebook postings, and both of them turning up to work on Monday morning looking a bit bleary and worse for the wear, smelling faintly of campfire smoke. So perhaps I could have guessed that there is more than meets the eye with this pair.

Still, when I read their mention of dining with Sartre or their list of suggestions to prevent nocturnal fairy visitations, I knew they had stepped over the line of reality. That is one of the things I love about this delightfully eccentric cookbook—its sense of fun, whimsy, and adventure. For though they may make moon-eyes at a flock of birds (or a gaggle of geese, bouquet of pheasants, pitying of turtledoves, et cetera), compose poems (and cocktails) in honor of fireflies, and jointly insist upon a "proper" cup of tea for their morning beverage (before telling your fortune from the leaves, of course), rest assured it is all said and done with a wink and a smile. I think.

One thing is for certain: These magnificent dishes will tempt even the most citified cook to venture out-of-doors and create a sumptuous meal over the open fire. Truth be told, you won't see me setting up a tent or unfurling a sleeping bag out in the bug- (and bear-) besieged woods anytime soon—but it's really not necessary to embark on a wilderness adventure in order to replicate Sarah and Jaimee's campy array of fireside goodies. Personally, my idea of a nature walk is a sidewalk stroll to my neighborhood farmers' market, but I can still look forward to trying out some of these recipes on my backyard grill. And this book will definitely be taken along on our family's next countryside jaunt, where we'll be trying out some of the baking techniques in the outdoor firepit. Because I may not always be clued in as to whether or not these two are pulling my leg—but I do know honest-to-goodness good food when I see it. Even when it's presented through a veil of smoke.

—Melissa Clark, New York, 2010

Camp (kamp) n.:
1. A place where people stay in tents.
2. Something that provides sophisticated, knowing amusement, as by virtue of its being artfully mannered or stylized, self-consciously artificial and extravagant, or teasingly ingenuous and sentimental.

Fire (fir) n.:
1. The phenomenon of combustion manifested in light, flame, and heat.
2. Burning intensity of feeling, ardor; liveliness of imagination, spirit.

NO ONE IN HER RIGHT MIND WOULD EMBARK UPON THE ADVENTURES WE HAVE SET FORTH IN THIS TOME.

But sometimes life's greatest adventures are a teensy bit practical and a whole lot fantastic. When asked why he decided to climb Mount Everest, the English expeditionist George Mallory is said to have replied, "Because it's there." His heroic feat was not time-saving, money-saving, or prudent; it was an act of free-spirited derring-do. It was the stuff of legends. And as all heroes know, creating something legendary is as simple as setting out to do it.

Which is why we knew if we were going to conquer the natural world, we'd have to do it with a skillet in our hands—because we're not the sort to go exploring on an empty stomach. Truth be told, our batterie de cuisine may have contained more than one skillet. It may even have contained more than one bottle of French Champagne (but not more than three; we were roughing it, after all). Frankly, we've never understood why outdoor holidays inspire austerity when nature itself is not austere—the panoply of stars, the patchwork of flowering meadows, the abundance of babbling brooks perfect for skinny-dipping. To our palates, this beauty is sheer inspiration for the dinner plate. We can think of no better way to pass our leisure hours than frolicking about the wilderness in pursuit of culinary delights that dazzle, food that is as much fun to prepare as it is extravagant to feast upon.

We hope this book emboldens one to embark on a premiere flight of fancy, where gastronomy and adventure intertwine in a most unexpected setting. For whether a cook makes one dish or one and twenty, this story is a fantastical romp: here is what one can accomplish when the culinary ideals of modern civilization meet the oldest cooking tool known to man—the open flame.

—SH & JY, May 2010

"O, FOR A MUSE OF FIRE,
THAT WOULD ASCEND
THE BRIGHTEST HEAVEN
OF INVENTION!"

—FROM **HENRY V**, WILLIAM SHAKESPEARE

CHAPTER ONE

KINDLING ONE'S FIRE

IT HAS ALWAYS BEEN THUS, OUR PRIMAL YEARN-ING FOR A HOT LICK OF FLAME TO SPARK THE BLAZE OF IMAGINATION. From the time of unceas-ing toil as hunter-gatherers (an era which forever echoes in our collective unconscious), it is the glow of the fire that is the zenith of what it means to be human. It is light, life, the promise of a hot meal and jovial companionship. If it is true that fire was a gift stolen from the gods by crafty Prometheus, then we do owe him a debt of honor. Or, if, as those more scientifically minded among us may believe, our ancestors first discovered open-fire cookery from the happy chance of a lightning bolt raining down upon a freshly killed beast, then we must all take a moment to marvel at our unbelievable luck.

Even today, there is nothing that so tempts the senses as a cooking fire. The sizzle of olive oil as it sputters off into the embers. The heady scent of merguez sausage as it sears over the flame's amber tendrils. Even the *rat-a-tat-tat* of popping corn makes an irresistible call to one's companions, inviting all to join in a ring around the campfire. It is still a beacon offering warmth, sustenance, and protection from the elements, but with a bit of practiced manipulation (and by following the helpful instruction herein), the fire may offer so much more. It may even offer chocolate cake.

But before one can get on with the fire-created delicacies of this book, it is important to master the intricacies of the flame: how to both kindle and douse it. To learn what measures to take to ensure the safety of one's companions and environment. For though fire is a beautiful force of creation, it is forever danc-ing on the edge of destruction. Perhaps that, too, is part of its tantalizing allure.

the well-stocked trunk

"She could not explain in so many words, but she felt that those who prepare for all the emergencies of life beforehand may equip themselves at the expense of joy."

—E. M. FORSTER

The hustle of preparing for camp is an exciting time, when one can dust off a well-worn steamer trunk, shine some silverware, and dutifully restock any tinctures or tonics that have dwindled since one's last foray into the wild, all the while bursting with holiday anticipation. One experiences great satisfaction in feeling well equipped to meet Nature's demands, whatever they may be.

But do remember that adventure is reliant on a certain measure of the unexpected, and one should never place such emphasis on accumulating the bare necessities that all opportunities for pleasures and thrills are stymied. For inspiration, please consult the following list of our personal camp essentials, some of which are indispensable (noted with an asterisk), others quite handy, and a few (or more) positively sybaritic. Certainly in the history of campfire cookery, one has made do with less. Perhaps, admittedly, even far less. But we'd rather not sally forth at all if it is meant to be a somber and sparse occasion; we suggest one always find room among one's requisites for those trinkets that are frivolous, wholly impractical, and most apt to yield impromptu joy.

As we are concerned primarily with the food and frolicking aspects of camping, we have chosen not to discuss sartorial needs or shelter and bedding. A good wilderness guide is sure to have plenty to say on such matters.

Assembling the Batterie de Cuisine

In French kitchens of high esteem, a workspace must be outfitted with a suitable *batterie de cuisine*, all the excellent tools and equipment that permit a kitchen to run as smoothly as a Swiss-made clock. In this regard, an outdoor kitchen is scarcely different, with the exception that one's necessary tools must include those that manage open fire. For clarity, we have divided these needs into three: cookery essentials, fire maintenance essentials, and items for tidy campkeeping.

COOKERY ESSENTIALS

★ **10-inch Cast-Iron Skillet with Lid:** One cannot go astray with cast-iron cookware (see The Incomparable Cast Iron, page 20). A skillet with a tightly fitting lid is just the thing for sautéing, pan-frying, steaming, and saucing.

★ **5-quart Dutch Oven with Lid:** Capable of holding greater volume than a skillet, the Dutch oven is ideal for soups, stews, braises, and roasts. One might fill it with water to boil at teatime or with cooking oil to fry breakfast beignets. It is important that it have a tightly fitting lid; the lids of camping-specific Dutch ovens have a lip (called a flange) to hold hot coals, supplying heat from above for baking breads, rolls, biscuits, and scones. One might also look for a camping Dutch oven with legs, so that it sits over, and not directly in, the coals when baking.

★ **Tripod Grill:** We are quite attached to our grill, a grate suspended on three legs via a pulley system. When placed over the fire for cooking, it allows excellent control, as one can bring the food closer to or further from the flame as desired. It also breaks down easily for automobile transportation.

★ **Grill Grate**: If one does not have the resources or space for a tripod grill, a collapsible grill grate can be used instead. A grate with legs that can be placed over the fire, it is wonderful for grilling or stovetop-style cookery; however, it does require greater attentiveness, since one cannot control the heat by adjusting the height as with the tripod grill.

★ **Short- and Long-Handled Stainless-Steel Tongs**: The shorter tongs help in tossing salads or turning food at close proximity; the long tongs are needed when one must reach something close to a scorching flame, such as when grilling meat or fish. We have also—somewhat inappropriately—used long tongs for rearranging logs on a fire. One finds tongs amongst the grilling tools at a hardware shop.

★ **Short- and Long-handled Stainless-Steel Mixing Spoons**: Use the short spoon for stirring ingredients off the heat and the longer spoon for stirring soups, stews, sauces, and risotto at a safe distance from the flame. One finds these spoons amongst the grilling tools at a hardware shop.

★ **Long-handled Stainless-Steel Spatula**: Ideal for flipping crumpets or pancakes at a safe distance from a scorching flame. Also excellent for stirring sautés and flipping fish. One finds these spatulas amongst the grilling tools at a hardware shop.

Metal Skewers: These sharp rods are just the tools for holding chunks of meats or fruit in place during open-flame roasting and for fondue dipping. One might even put the longer versions to good use in marshmallow toasting. Purchase an assortment of lengths and thicknesses.

★ **Mixing Bowls**: We like to use stainless-steel bowls in the wild, as they are sturdy and unbreakable (even when placed for short periods over the fire or used as a cake mold inside a Dutch oven). They also make excellent noisemakers to frighten away animals or in cases of sudden revelry. They are perfect for mixing salads, sauces, vinaigrettes, batters, and dough. Purchase an assortment of sizes.

★ **Cutting Boards**: For prepping food or letting it rest a moment after cooking. Although we prefer solid boards cut from hardwood or bamboo (a renewable resource), to conserve space, flexible plastic cutting boards can be rolled up and stashed in the trunk.

★ **Kitchen Knives**: We've seen so-called cooking professionals arrive at camp with enough knives in their kits to outfit a band of outlaws. We have found that a large chef's knife, a serrated bread knife, and a small paring knife are entirely sufficient for any kitchen needs.

Swiss Army Knife: The workhorse of the wilderness, this knife will do anything in a pinch, from slicing cheese to opening wine bottles to removing spinach from one's teeth. We've traveled with seasoned outdoorsmen who refuse to use any other knife in their outdoor kitchen.

Corkscrew: One must always, always carry into the wild a means for uncorking wine or other stubbornly stoppered spirits.

9-inch Round Cooling Rack: We use this to suspend fish or vegetables over simmering water for steaming—it fits inside the bottom of a cast-iron skillet. Since one has brought it along, it can also be used for cooling baked cakes, cookies, or scones.

Whisk: A fork serves adequately for the beating of eggs, vinaigrettes, and sauces, but we find nothing gives food the same airy loft as agitation by a whisk.

Stainless-Steel Ladle: One will be happy to have this along when dishing up soups, stews, or Turkish coffee. A tin cup can always substitute if it is desirable to conserve space.

Military Folding Table: We have prepped food upon a slab of shale and made a log of deadwood our dining table, but if one can spare the space, a folding table will facilitate cookery work and give one's party a place to display the ephemera collected during daily adventures.

Can Opener: Should one bring tinned foods on a holiday (they are, after all, indestructible and therefore lifesaving in instances of natural disaster), this will do the trick to pry them open.

Heatproof Rubber Spatula: One cannot discount the usefulness of this tool's flexible tip, which is the best choice for mixing cake batters. It can also scrape the last bit of food from hard-to-reach crannies in a pot, making for easier washing up.

Hand-Cranked Spice or Coffee Grinder: Freshly ground spices or coffee provide the most aroma and flavor. Often found at flea markets for a pittance, a hand-crank grinder will rise to the occasion without the need for newfangled electricity.

Basting or Pastry Brush: This brush is handy for slathering roasting meat with juices, or giving pastries a wash of cream before baking. Nylon-bristled brushes can be flammable; we suggest seeking out silicone varieties.

Instant-Read Thermometer: The woods might be filled with scavenging creatures that thrill to the taste of uncooked meat, but being civilized types ourselves, we always cook our meat and poultry to proper internal temperatures. An instant-read thermometer is an assured means of achieving this goal.

Bricks: Wrapped in heavy-duty foil, they can be used to weight down meat for searing. We also sometimes position several in a row to create a makeshift resting place for food. Do not heave bricks or stones at woodland creatures in an effort to frighten them away from camp; such tomfoolery is more likely to provoke than protect.

Hand-Cranked Ice Cream Maker: Anytime we have a scoop of fresh gelato in hand and the afternoon sun upon our backs, it is Rome all over again. And on a sweltering day at camp, when hiking seems too much of a bother, cranking ice cream always lifts the spirits.

Teakettle: While we personally find a Dutch oven boils water excellently, for some aficionados, teatime is not the same without the telltale whistle.

Kitchen Shears: Perfect for cutting through tough bones or cartilage in meat and fish, shears can also be used to cut kitchen twine or snip herbs. We always put a pair in our foraging basket, whether we are in search of greens, herbs, or wildflowers.

Thick Rope: Useful for stringing up food to keep it away from curious critters (and as a clothesline to dry damp clothing, rags, or linens). We have also found that a length of rope comes in handy at the most unexpected moments, such as when a companion accidentally stumbles into a crevasse.

✴ **Hatchet**: A sharp hatchet makes quick work of wood-cutting, so that one can sit fireside in short order.

Waterproof Matches: One will be happy to have purchased these special matches at an explorers' supply store when trying to construct a toasty fire in a relentless deluge of rain.

Coal Shovel: Essential for baking, which requires one to shuffle coals about the fire pit. It can also be used to adjust the position of logs upon the fire.

✴ **Metal Ash Bucket**: When the fire is raging, we fill this with water and keep it near at hand for emergencies; when we are ready to break down camp, we pour the water over the fire, scoop the ash into the bucket, and scatter the fully extinguished ash into the forest.

✴ **Heatproof Gloves**: We find we are always less skittish around a fire when outfitted in a pair of these burly suede gloves. While we would not recommend grabbing a blazing log with them, they are excellent for retrieving a hot pot or for shifting a cooking grate without burning one's hands.

Lightweight Foldout Saw: Some fear the mighty hatchet; for such a predicament, we suggest this tool, which can cut through medium-size pieces of dead-wood to be used for fuel.

Flint and Steel: A reliable, time-tested tool for igniting a flame, and one needn't worry about running out, as can happen with a box of matches. It does, however, require the addition of a scrap of linen or flannel and an old tea tin to make one's char cloth (see Igniting the Fire, page 24–25).

✴ **Water Spritzer**: Used to tamp down wayward flames; for style's sake, we like to recycle our old and empty perfume bottles (well-washed, of course, as any lingering alcohol would be quite flammable).

Plumbers' Candles: Long ago favored by plumbers to seal pipes, these candles boast a lengthy, hot burn. One can employ them for fire starting (their flame extinguishes less quickly than that of a match), or keep them on hand for any occasion on which one wishes to encourage a romantic ambience.

Chimney Starter: Should one be building a fire with lump charcoal, a chimney starter will aid speedy ignition.

Bits of Newspaper and Fluff: Take a moment to collect one's laundry lint, discarded newspapers, and other scraps of fluff from under one's bed. All will make excellent starter fuel for the fire.

TO ENSURE TIDY CAMPKEEPING
....

Vinegar Spritzer: We always bring a spritzer of vinegar water to keep our cutting boards and other surfaces free of contamination by toxic critters.

Hand and Dish Soap: Impeccable personal hygiene—in particular, frequent hand washing—and clean dishware are essential for preventing food-borne illness. For Nature's sake, do try to purchase nontoxic, biodegradable suds.

Icebox: A large airtight cooler fully stocked with ice will keep one's carefully selected meat, fish, and produce from spoiling. If possible, we recommend bringing three: one for meat, poultry, and fish; one for dairy; and the third for produce and beverages.

Five-Gallon Metal Bucket: We fill ours with hot water and use it for hand washing and dishwashing, as needed.

Garbage Bags: Always clean up camp carefully, making sure that every speck of paper, food, or other refuse goes into a bag and does not litter Nature's pristine floor.

Muslin Reusable Bags: We prefer to use these washable drawstring bags rather than plastic resealable bags whenever possible, as we find them more ecologically sound. They are particularly effective for the storage of fresh, uncut produce.

Rags: Consider the search for cleaning implements a perfect excuse to empty out one's wardrobe. That old gabardine blazer or cashmere muffler will make an excellent tool for cleaning camp.

Paper Towels: To be used sparingly; they are helpful for patting down freshly rinsed meat, draining fried foods, and cleaning up the occasional wine slosh.

Aluminum Foil: In addition to its usefulness in wrapping up leftovers, foil makes an excellent package for cooking food in the embers of a flame, as it will not melt.

Plastic Wrap: We try to use as little as possible, but it helps to keep bugs and other contaminants out of food.

Mason Jars or Other Airtight Containers: Reusable containers are an excellent way to store leftovers; we often bring our vinaigrette in a jar.

Suitable Sundries for Outdoor Dining & Living

In this section, we delight in all the nonessentials of campfire life. Not a single item upon this list is ever entirely necessary, and yet we are always glad to have them along with us, as they contribute inestimably to the domestication of our wilderness home.

Steamer Trunk: An investment that one will not regret, it is spacious enough for one's tools and other supplies, can be tightly shut for transport or at bedtime, and serves wonderfully as an improvised table or seat.

Lanterns: Should one need to venture into the dark depths of the forest after nightfall, a lantern's rays provide excellent illumination. We also use lanterns for shadow puppetry and *tableaux vivants*.

Parasol: When the noonday sun shines brightly, cultivate a delicate complexion under the shade of an elaborately designed, handheld umbrella.

Woolly Pendleton Blankets or Cheerful Quilts: Use one as a wrap on a chilly evening, to dry off post–river swim, or to protect clothing from damp grass during a meadow picnic.

Magnifying Glass: One will have greater success distinguishing the flora of the countryside with a magnifying glass. It is also useful for edible entomology (page 147) and for starting a fire by the heat of the sun. And it lends the bearer an air of authority and intelligence.

Foraging Basket: The open weave of a wicker basket allows greater air circulation, preventing fresh cuttings from wilting on a warm day; one can also use it to display fresh scones or biscuits upon the tea table.

Rucksack: A rucksack can be conveniently filled with nibbles, binoculars, guidebooks, first-aid materials, and other diversions that may be called for during the course of a hike.

Flask and/or Canteen: We usually bring two with us—one filled with water, the other with some type of tipple. The former will spare one from extreme thirst, the latter from low spirits.

Smelling Salts: We have witnessed companions fainting away—from heat exhaustion, from ghost story fright, from the sight of a spider—more times than we can count. A homemade box of salts will revive one quickly, without the need for unkind smacks upon the face.

Pocket Watch: Though we prefer to gauge the hour by the position of the sun (page 149), a pocket watch is indispensable when practicing the art of hypnosis (page 285). Children also find its shiny brightness attractive as a plaything.

Pen and Parchment: When inspiration strikes, one must always have a writing kit at hand for scribbling lines of poetry and prose, or for sketching a particularly striking vista.

Botanical or Other Field Guide: Nothing is more frustrating than spying a lovely bloom or colorful bird and being unable to call it by name. A well-respected guidebook is sure to enlighten.

Tarot Cards: When the sun lowers and the Great Outdoors wears a shadowy cloak, a mysterious reading of one's future will send shivers down the spine (page 258).

Pitcher for Bouquets: No need for cut-glass articles here—a rustic enameled tin is perfect for wild blossoms. It also doubles as an excellent container for lemonade or iced tea.

Bunting for a Festive Occasion: Suppose the group wishes to fête a member's birthday, or celebrate the survival of a particularly wretched monsoon? At times like these, we are always happy to pull a length of celebratory bunting from our trunk to string up between trees.

Lengths of Lace: We discovered a trick while out on safari in Africa, where the gnats swarm over one's luncheon with greedy ferocity: a bit of pretty lace swathed across platters of food keeps the insects at bay. It also makes for a highly attractive tablescape.

Whittling Knife: One might rely on a Swiss army knife for a stretch of meditative whittling (page 116), but one is less likely to suffer blisters and slip-ups with this specialized blade.

Playing Cards: A bit of friendly gambling is an excellent way to pass a rain-sodden day at camp. We are partial to games like whist, piquet, vingt et un, and baccarat.

One's Best Silverware: We would never subject our companions to the indignity of dining with disposable utensils. We are too fond of the authentic stuff, from its lovely patina to its dainty clink against the china, to its reassuring weight in the hand.

Excellent Reading Material: Never so domineering as to dictate what one ought to read in the outdoors, we shall only say that we are partial to ghostly tales, mythology, poetry, romance, history, and philosophy.

THE INCOMPARABLE CAST IRON

A cursory look at the recipes contained within this work will promptly show that when it comes to campfire cookery, we are staunch advocates of cast iron. It is simply the metal of choice for any outdoor outing. In the first place, no other material will withstand the torrid temperatures of the open fire. The cast-iron skillet or Dutch oven can be counted upon to sit directly in the embers—indeed, in the very flames—without suffering so much as a blemish on its pristine cook surface. So great is its mettle that one need only set out with a lidded cast-iron skillet and Dutch oven in order to meet all culinary needs. Within these vessels anyone can cook up anything, from a creamy fondue to a pine-smoked salmon to a buttery Madeira cake. Truly, it is a miraculous metal.

One must, however, take certain precautions in order to maintain the quality of one's cast iron. If it has not been preseasoned by the manufacturer, this must be done before its first use. This is a simple matter of gently cleaning the vessel with a mild detergent and cloth, rinsing it with water, then anointing it inside and out with cooking oil. Place the oiled cast iron in a low-temperature oven until dry and voilà! Seasoning is complete.

After using the cast iron, it's best to clean it with only a steel brush and warm water. Using detergent may rob the cast iron of its seasoning and allow rust to form. Alternatively, one may scrub it with a generous sprinkle of kosher salt to remove any crusty detritus. Always dry the cast iron thoroughly with a soft cloth or paper towel. Then, following a particularly vigorous scrub, anoint it once more with a swipe of cooking oil and dry it over the dying fire before stowing it for the night. With a little tender care, one's cast-iron skillet and Dutch oven will last and last—treasured heirlooms for generations to come.

Inspirational Objets d'Art: We love to take a pretty sculpted bust or palm-size painting along with us as a reminder that Art and Nature make sublime mates.

Binoculars: In addition to being a must-have tool for bird-watching, a set of binoculars can also help the user locate far-off familiar landmarks when lost.

Compass: Although one can be improvised with a simple sewing needle (page 80), if expense is no object, splurge on a well-made compass—it will never steer one astray.

Maps: Ideally, one's collection of maps will provide an accurate layout of the surrounding land, although attractive maps of other places can make inspirational place mats.

Linens & Colorful Textiles: Snip them into napkins, a tablecloth, or a makeshift apron; spread them upon the ground in lieu of a burdensome oriental rug; hang them over a clothesline for shelter—beautiful fabrics make a beautiful camp.

Snail Forks: Perhaps this seems one of our more fanciful items, but rest assured that it is an unrivaled means of wrenching a roasted snail from its snug shell (page 138).

Finger Bowls: Pretty little bowls for dipping one's fingers in after dining on cob corn or sticky teacakes make such a clever addition to the camp table.

Candlesticks: Though a blazing campfire should always remain one's main source of light, an extra candle or two upon the camp table lends a spirit of romance and drama.

Caviar Spoons: We once made the mistake of trekking into the wild with only teaspoons for the caviar; it led to unimpeded greed and overquick consumption of our caviar supply. These petite spoons provide modest portions and lend no unpleasant metallic tinge to our beluga.

Finest China: Whether one packs all one's plates, bowls, and saucers or simply one's favorite platter or teacup, china brings an air of elegance to the outdoors. Should one experience breakage, a tip: the sticky juice of garlic has adhesive qualities and can be employed in the temporary mending of glass and china.

Tea Service: What is teatime without one's sugar bowl, creamer, and teapot?

Champagne Bucket & Flutes: Our companions are always so pleasantly surprised when we pull these from our trunk the first evening at camp. While swigging from a coffee cup is not a criminal offense, a flute's shape is designed to retain the drinks' signature carbonation for as long as possible.

Thermos: When hiking over snow-capped peaks, a thermos filled with steamy campfire soup makes a most welcome lunch.

First-Aid Necessities

Ideally, one should never set out for a jaunt in the wilderness without one's personal surgeon, nurse practitioner, and friendly neighborhood apothecary in tow. However, for those occasions when medical professionals do not number among one's fireside guests, it is best to practice prudence (not to mention hospitality) by bringing along a fully stocked First-Aid Kit. We recommend a stylish valise in basic black or perhaps taupe, which will complement the other camping accessories, no matter what their color or design.

Oh, and the kit should contain the essentials of first aid as well! In addition to the obvious items one may need in the outdoors (sunscreen, insect repellent to ward off mini blood-sucking predators, antihistamine tablets in case of allergy, aspirins for the fuzzy head, bandages and cold packs for the light sprains and to soothe minor cuts and scrapes), one's valise should have enough room to carry a few necessities specific to a holiday around an open fire.

THESE INCLUDE

Spray-on Wound Cleanser: Give minor cuts or burns a gentle spritz of cleanser (no need to rinse) before bandaging. Keeping the wound clean right from the start promotes speedy healing.

Sterile Gauze Bandages: Fluffy cotton balls or adhesive bandages sometimes stick to minor wounds—especially burns—and could lead to further injury or scarring. Sterile gauze dresses wounds safely and effectively.

Pure Aloe Vera Gel: This is a natural way to sooth fire blisters or sunburn and other skin irritations. And it has a lovely aroma, too!

Hand Cream: A day spent with the hands over the fire can leave one's fingers as dry as an elephant's hide; rehydration is key.

Lip Balm: Scaly, flame-parched lips are no way to attract companionship. But do avoid flavored varieties—during one journey to the mangrove forests of Southeast Asia, a strawberry balm pulled from our pocket quickly drew a curious band of Silvered Leaf monkeys. Paying no heed to our protests, those nimble monkeys made off with our balm, and we were left indignantly damning their opposable thumbs but admiring their now oh-so-kissable lips.

Tweezers: One can use them to remove stubborn wood splinters (which, alas, abound fireside) or to groom brows, which seem to sprout, weedlike, in the fresh country air.

Saline Eyedrops: "Smoke Gets in Your Eyes" may be an enjoyable tune to warble around the fire, but it is less enjoyable when the lyrics are all too real. Bring along eyedrops to clear the windows to the soul.

firecrafting

The Anatomy of the Flame

To understand how, as Dante once scribbled, "from little spark may burst a mighty flame," it is necessary to turn to Science. Although the noble institution may possess its follies (oh, alchemy!), on the subject of fire, it is most reliable. From the gentle flicker of a candle to the towering blaze of a bonfire, all fires are created equally. Three things must be present to create the pure energy of fire: Air, Heat, and Fuel.

AIR

Just as we need oxygen to fill our lungs and keep us sprightly (or alive, for that matter), so, too, does a fire need oxygen to burn. When oxygen meets with a combustible material (fuel), and a source of ignition (heat), it bonds rapidly with the fuel, creating the light and warmth we identify as fire. Therefore, do not discount the importance of air to one's campfire—its role is pivotal, impacting the temperature of the flames, the speed at which the fuel will burn, and the ease with which one will be able to maintain or squelch a robust flame. Commit to memory this advisement; we will return to it more than once.

HEAT

Consider the crack of lightning that sets a forest aflame. It is precisely this quick flash of heat that one strives to achieve in the building of a campfire—on a drastically reduced scale, of course, confined only to one's cozy fire pit. Heat can be conjured through several means, including electricity, friction and sparking, and the energy of the sun.

FUEL

Of the three elements involved in creating a wood fire, fuel demands the greatest attention. In the wild, fuel-related inquiries abound: What sort suits one's purpose? What size and how much is needed? How might it be quickly secured? Each question is of paramount importance, and will be as much a constant companion on one's adventures as the fire itself.

If we should identify a single key quality for the cultivation of one's fueling skills, it would be patience. Many outdoorsmen have been burned, Icarus-like, after a botched attempt at building a fire too large, too quickly. Like the Great Pyramids of Egypt, superior fires require slow and careful construction (though, mercifully, less slave labor). The aim is to create enough energy with one's base level of fuel (tinder) to proceed to a slightly larger level of fuel (kindling), before crowning the flame with the dense, heavy logs that will burn longest and hottest. Haste, in this event, shall truly make waste—forge ahead too eagerly and one will likely suffocate the budding flame, only to be returned to square one, with fortitude waning and no fire to show for one's labor. In the interest of personal safety and air pollution prevention, we strenuously oppose toxic fire starter aids such as lighter fluid or, even more abhorrent, gasoline.

Tinder. This is one's first-level fuel. Tinder is material that is small and dry, and requires the least

Igniting the Fire

AT OUR CAMPFIRES, THE MOST COMMON STARTER IS THE FRICTION OF A STRUCK MATCH; HOWEVER, SHOULD CURIOSITY AND INDUSTRY REIGN, WE HIGHLY RECOMMEND THE EMPLOYMENT OF ANY OF THESE CLASSIC METHODS:

MAGNIFYING GLASS

After one has finished identifying all the flora and fauna in the field, it is gratifying to know that one's magnifying glass can be put to further use. In truth, any object with an intensified focal point will work to concentrate the sun's beams, including reading spectacles (not distance spectacles), the bottom of a glass bottle, or a pair of binoculars turned rearward.

Instructions:

1. On a clear and sun-drenched day, arrange a loose pile of tinder in the center of the fire pit.

2. Hold the glass several inches from the tinder. A bright white light should appear on the ground. This is one's concentrated sunlight. Twist and turn the glass until the point of light shines on the tinder.

3. Hold the lens steady (this is not work for a member of the party suffering from delirium tremens) for five to ten seconds. The tinder should ignite.

4. Blow gently upon the flame until the tinder catches.

FLINT AND STEEL

This method relies on the spark created when a hard material strikes against steel; it is the same basic principle that ignites firearms. The most popular material for striking is flint, though any stone harder than steel will do—one can enjoy similar success with bloodstone, agate, jade, quartz, or our favorite, diamond. (Consult a geologic scale that measures such things for other options.)

Instructions:

1. Before going camping, make a char cloth for the fire-starting kit: Set a scrap of linen or flannel aflame. Once it is burning well, transfer the cloth to an old tea tin and put the lid on to smother the flame. The resultant carbon on the cloth will ignite quickly upon contact with the spark.

2. Place a few bits of char cloth into the fire pit and scatter a loose bundle of tinder on top.

3. Hold the steel at an angle over the cloth. One can use an official, C-shaped fire steel or any old scrap of high-carbon steel, such as a metal file.

4. Strike a glancing blow with the stone upon the steel. It should spark briefly, but sufficiently to ignite the cloth.

5. Blow gently upon the flame until the tinder catches.

HAND-DRILL METHOD

This method has on its side the annals of history. It was the preferred fire-starting technique of primitive man, who did not enjoy the benefits of modern metallurgy and glasswork. Essentially, the friction of wood against wood can create heat enough to cause combustion. The nemesis of friction fire is moisture; procure the driest wood. We do not recommend this method for humid jungle adventures.

One can investigate several adaptations of this method: the fire-plow, bow-drill, and hand-drill method. We present only the latter as it can be used spontaneously and in an emergency.

Instructions:

1. Find a 2-foot-long, ½-inch-thick spindle of hardwood (such as oak). Whittle away any knobs that might irritate one's hands.

2. Secure a board of dry softwood (such as pine). Carve a small round depression on the top of the board near the edge.

3. Carve a ½-inch-wide, V-shaped notch adjacent to the depression. Cut the notch into the edge of the board all the way to the ground, so that the embers created will fall through it.

4. Place a leaf or piece of bark beneath the notch to catch the embers.

5. Arrange a loose pile of tinder in the center of the fire pit.

6. Burrow the spindle into the depression and roll it furiously between the hands until an ember is formed from the hot wood shavings.

7. Carefully transfer the ember to the fire pit and place it atop the tinder. Blow gently on the tinder until it ignites.

SPURNING SODDEN WOOD

Fire-fighting brigades arrive equipped with water for good reason: fire and water make abysmal playmates. By the same token, attempting to construct a fire with sodden or damp wood—tinder, kindling, or fuelwood—will lead to sorrow and gloom. The wood will smoke and smolder unbecomingly. One's eyes will redden, the lungs will cloud, the skin will parch, and the fire will, at best, sputter meekly before petering out entirely. Meanwhile, all those nasty smoke particulates have swarmed into the air, sullying our beautiful blue skies.

Obviously waterlogged wood can easily be avoided, whether foraging or purchasing it. A simple brush of the hand is typically sufficient to confirm the direst suspicions. Moreover, avoid wood that is green or freshly cut. Freshly cut wood is 50 percent water, and all that water must evaporate before the wood can flame. Ideally, firewood should have a water level of only 20 percent. It is for this reason that most commercial firewood is either *kiln-dried* (dried in an industrial kiln), or *seasoned*, meaning it has dried beneath the natural elements of air and wind for a period of six months to two years.

If, quite plausibly, one is collecting wood in nature, do not despair. Green wood can be identified by its flexibility; gather only wood that snaps and breaks readily. Moderately damp logs, sticks, and twigs may be split or whittled and the dry inner bits collected. We've discovered it also helps to remove the bark from twigs; bark tends to be a repository for moisture. Severely drenched wood, we regret to relay, remains a lost cause and is best cast aside.

heat and air to ignite. Any number of materials make excellent tinder, provided they are relatively shredded or fluffy, which allows for the maximum exposure to the air and ignition source. For example, leaves, as plentiful a gift as they are in nature, also happen to be flat and flimsy and frequently damp, making for poor tinder. Look for objects with the approximate thickness of a needle; our favorite sources include the curling, paperlike strips of cedar or birch bark (which also contain natural, flammable oils), pine needles, dry moss, thistle, cattail floss, milkweed fluff, the feathery tops of certain dead weeds, such as wild carrot or goldenrod, and the extremely fine fallen branches of dead trees or wild grapevines. If these are not available, one can also rely on dry, thin shavings from a larger piece of wood or, as a last resort, crumpled newspaper.

Kindling. As soon as one feels confident in one's glowing tinder, it is time to proceed to kindling. No thicker than a match, or at its largest, a nub of drawing chalk, tinder can consist of twigs, slightly larger splinters of bark, pinecones, or woodchips. So long as one can snap a bit of kindling with one's hands, it ought to perform its duty quite well. Although soft-wooded conifers such as pine, fir, spruce, and cedar tend to spark and burn too rapidly to provide good cooking logs, their keen flammability makes for wonderful kindling. Look for dead lower branches on these trees, or small chips of wood filled with sticky resin. As a cautionary measure, we occasionally divide our kindling into two groups, one smaller and one slightly larger.

Fuelwood. The largest pieces of wood required to feed a fire, fuelwood should not be confused with those grand, knotty stumps upon which one perches near the fire. Fuelwood logs need not possess great stoutness; in fact, larger logs will only serve to slow one's fire and the subsequent creation of the coals necessary for cooking. The best fuelwood will match the size of one's arm and no more. Should one be a strapping lad or lass with arms like cabin logs, we suggest one split the logs to a more manageable size, like that of a neighbor's wrist. Logs similar in diameter and length will burn most evenly. Deciduous hardwoods, like maple, hickory, beech, oak, elm, ash, mesquite, and gum tree will burn the longest and hottest.

A Word on Charwood

Alternately christened "natural lump charcoal" and "hardwood charcoal," charwood is in no away affiliated with noxious, chemical-filled charcoal briquettes. Charwood is simply as it sounds—irregular-shaped bits of wood that have been fired in a kiln until reduced to carbon. The process yields a wood that ignites with greater ease, burns particularly hot and steady, and produces less smoke and ash. And because it is merely a product of combusted hardwood, the cold ash can be collected at the fire's end and sprinkled merrily over one's garden compost back home. We do find it has some drawbacks, notably that, having already been burned, charwood has 60 percent less energy to contribute than firewood and is therefore inclined to be exhausted more quickly. We also miss the comforting aroma and crackle of standard wood.

How to Construct a Goodly Blaze

PUTTING ONE'S AFFAIRS IN ORDER

Although we know intimately the longing to gallop past the tedious minutiae of fire building and plunge headlong into the delights of cookery, one must remain sensible. Was Michelangelo's Sistine Chapel a slapdash affair? Did Paris advance heedlessly through the erection of Notre Dame? Certainly Rome was not built in a day. If history has taught us anything, it is that great art requires prudence. To organize oneself properly is to reap great rewards.

Investigate fire authorization. Whether setting out for a privately run campsite, a national park, a state forest, or one's own backyard, take a moment to determine any fire-building restrictions. Each site maintains its own regulations; fire privileges might be gratis or available for a sum, accessible with limitations or free of constraints. In some places, unfortunately, fires may be prohibited entirely. Rather than spoiling a journey with unanticipated disappointment, a distasteful confrontation, or an unexpected natural disaster, take a moment to communicate with one's local land manager prior to departure.

Be mindful of the weather. Sometimes, dear campers, a fire is not meant to be. Do not let hubris turn one into a tragic hero. Forewarning of weather that is excessively dry, hot, windy, or stormy can and should delay one's adventure. As we write this, we are reminded of an unfortunate incident that occurred some years ago to a supercilious Moroccan sultan we happened upon while trekking through the North African steppes en route to the Sahara. As one probably knows, this might well be one of the most dubious places on earth to build a fire, for here the implacable desert winds blow hot and dry across the grassland. Blessedly, although his entire party survived the inevitable blaze, their worldly goods did not fare so well. By the time we encountered them, all that was left of their caravan were the skeletal remains of a steamer trunk and an ornery, singed camel named Marrakesh.

Select one's wilderness residence carefully. Three points must be taken under consideration when putting up camp: where to designate one's sleeping arrangements, where to establish a food preparation area, and vitally, where to construct the fire:

> **Fire:** As this determination is most slavishly reliant on the conditions of nature, let us begin here. Look for an area on the ground where a fire appears to have been built before. If this succeeds, it will limit any further damage to wild vegetation. Soot, charred wood remains, and circular rock formations serve as valuable clues. If no evident area emerges, select a dry, even surface of earth or sand a good distance from buildings, flammable materials, overhanging branches, and ground roots. While some outdoor experts consider a slab of bare rock a worthy place for a fire, we shudder at the thought. Shale, streambed rocks, concrete, patios, and other stones are susceptible to explosion at high heat, and at the very least are destined to develop unsightly, long-lasting charring. Do not even entertain the notion of building a fire on grass or peat, lest one be prepared for the expression "spread like wildfire" to fall from the lips with distressing ease.

> **Sleeping Arrangements:** One's tent door or sleeping mats should be situated at least ten feet from the fire. Not only does this protect napping outdoorsmen from swirling embers and popping logs, it also creates a nice, airy plaza on which to socialize around the flame. Determine the prevailing wind and position the doorway to one's tent 90 degrees from it. The tent will remain toasty, while banishing smoke drift.

> **Food Preparation Area:** We do love the aroma of wood smoke, but cooking over a flame imbues the

A CONNOISSEUR'S GUIDE DE BOIS

Upon entering a forest, one can scarcely fail to be enthralled by the marvelous diversity of trees busily growing within. In addition to this being wonderful news for our ecosystem, it is also a fine treat for our stewpots; each wood boasts properties that will impart its own flavors, aromas, and propriety of use. We have laid out an array of options here and heartily recommend that one use this table for the *occasional* foray into the unfamiliar, as it will surely enhance the party's amusement.

However, we present this endorsement with one caveat: for everyday firewood cooking, we strongly encourage sustainability and the support of one's local wood economy. If purchasing wood from a local woodcutter, seek out tree varieties that grow most readily near at hand. One can also inquire at a local sawmill for leftover, untreated wood to make use of manufacturing waste. If collecting wood near one's campsite, make a habit of venturing away from the immediate vicinity—snatching the wood closest at hand will quickly strip the site and scar the land. And we never, ever advocate lifting an ax to fell a live standing tree. Rather forage for standing deadwood (wood from the forest floor is often too damp to burn properly). Treat a visit to the wild as one would tea with the Queen, and strive to be the most conscientious guest possible.

As for viewing this table, a few notes: "Flavor" refers to the nuances each wood provides one's cooking; "efficiency" to the wood's coaling quality, or ability to create long-lasting coal beds for cooking (which also makes them most environmentally sound); "usage" refers to each wood's ideal food complement, as well as any other practical items. We have intentionally omitted those woods that make a lovely fire but are not well-matched to cooking (unless one uses them primarily for kindling). These include resinous softwoods like pine, fir, and poplar, as well as the oft-sparking beechwood, the odiferous eucalyptus, and the poor-burning willow, juniper, and sycamore.

We favor dense woods like oak, maple, and birch for their heat and efficiency.

EFFICIENCY KEY		HEAT KEY	
Excellent	★ ★ ★ ★	Very High	🔥🔥🔥🔥🔥
Very Good	★ ★ ★	High	🔥🔥🔥🔥
Good	★ ★	Medium-High	🔥🔥🔥
Fair	★	Medium	🔥🔥
Poor	—	Medium Low	🔥

WOOD	FLAVOR	EFFICIENCY	HEAT	USAGE
Alder	Delicate, sweet	★½	🔥 (1)	Fish, pork, poultry, game
Almond	Nutty, sweet	★★★★	🔥🔥🔥🔥 (4)	All meats, flatbreads
Apple	Fruity, dense sweetness with hints of smoke	★★★★	🔥🔥🔥 (3)	Pork, poultry, excellent for smoking
Ash	Distinctive	★★★★	🔥🔥🔥🔥 (4)	Meat, fish; burns well, even when green
Birch (White)	Similar to maple	★★	🔥🔥 (2)	Pork, poultry; tends to burn quickly
Cedar	Smoky and aromatic	—	🔥 (1)	Fish, pork; good for smoking
Cherry	Mildly fruity	★★★★	🔥🔥 (2)	Pork, beef, poultry
Elm	Very smoky	★★	🔥🔥 (2)	Meat and fish; needs long seasoning and is very difficult to split
Grapevines	Aromatic, fruity, sweet, slightly tart	—	🔥🔥🔥🔥 (4)	All-purpose; great for kindling
Hickory	Strong, sweet, baconesque	★★★★	🔥🔥🔥🔥🔥 (5)	Pork, ham, beef; excellent for smoking
Lilac	Lightly smoky, floral	★★	🔥🔥 (2)	Seafood, fruits
Maple	Mellow, smoky, sweet	★★★★	🔥🔥🔥 (3)	Pork, poultry, game, vegetables, cheese
Mesquite	Rich, earthy	★★★★	🔥🔥🔥🔥🔥 (5)	Any meat, vegetables
Oak	Heavy smoke	★★★★	🔥🔥🔥🔥½ (4½)	All purpose; wood must be well-seasoned
Olive	High flavor and aroma	★★★	🔥🔥🔥🔥🔥 (5)	Baking, all meats
Orange	Citrusy, sweet	★★	🔥🔥🔥🔥 (4)	Fish, poultry, pork
Peach	Sweet, woodsy	★★	🔥🔥🔥 (3)	All-purpose
Pear	Sweet, fruity	★★★★	🔥🔥🔥 (3)	Pork, poultry
Pecan	Sweet, mild, hickorylike	★★	🔥🔥🔥🔥 (4)	All-purpose; good for smoking
Plum	Mild, sweet	★★	🔥🔥🔥 (3)	All-purpose
Walnut	Heavy; used alone can be bitter	★	🔥🔥🔥 (3)	Red meat and game; combine with milder woods

THE INVENTION OF THE MATCH AND THE ADVENT OF PHILLUMENY

Although evidence suggests that primitive forms of fire-lighting sticks existed in ancient Rome and China, it would appear that the modern, self-igniting match did not emerge until the nineteenth century, when a series of hazardous incarnations elbowed for dominance on the fiery world scene. The first, invented in the early 1800s by a Mr. Chancel of France, was a match ignited by dipping it in an asbestos bottle of sulfuric acid. Costly and dangerous, it was succeeded by the friction match, which was invented by one John Walker. The friction match contained such a potent mix of chemicals that it had a tendency to ignite with an explosion of hellish sparks and an ill odor, and was therefore dubbed the "Lucifer match." The next resounding failure was yet another French contribution: around 1830, the Frenchman Charles Sauria added white phosphorus in an effort to eliminate the Lucifer match's off-putting odor. This worked very well. But the phosphorus proved to inflict fatal bone disorders upon the workers in match-making factories.

As outdoor adventuresses dependent on fire, we remain gratefully indebted to Sweden for the patenting of the safety match. A mid-nineteenth-century endeavor, the familiar, red-tipped safety match is still in use today, and has, to our knowledge, eliminated a great majority of frightful physical or pyrotechnical mishaps in the well-lit Western world.

Perhaps in memoriam to the great carnage left in the wake of the match's evolution, the last century witnessed the rise of *phillumeny,* an art which entails dedication to the collection of matches, matchbooks, and matchbook covers.

food with smoke aplenty. Select an area upwind of the fire for storing ingredients to protect them from taking on overly pungent smokiness. If perishable ingredients are in tow (see A Prudent Note upon the Merits of Spoilage Protections, page 42), try to select an area free from direct sunlight, such as beneath a tree or under a rocky overhang.

If one has landed at a posh campsite with a clearing set out and a fire pit well in place, bravo! Work in these matters should be fairly straightforward. One's main task consists of situating the tent and food preparation area in thoughtful proximity to the fire.

Arrange a fastidious workspace. Though it may be amply awash with dappled sunlight and splendid birdsong, an al fresco kitchen remains a kitchen. We dedicate the first hour of our time at camp to establishing a culinary home that is tidy and organized. Consider it a sweeping sort of *mise en place* in the grand French tradition. Among the chief priorities:

๏ **Unpack:** Lay out the food, fire, and cookery equipment where they will be most useful. For example, set pokers, tongs, coal shovels, and cooking gloves near the fire pit, and relegate bowls and cutting boards to one's food preparation area (for a full list of suggested tools, consult The Well-Stocked Trunk, page 14). Find a large flat river rock or other stone to serve as a makeshift trivet for hot pots fresh from the fire. And don't forget to dig out any weatherproof matches (we find dipping regular match heads in melted wax or paraffin works wonders). Place imbibements everywhere, so that one's glass might never be fully drained; it's important that the wood remain dry, not the cook.

🌿 **Collect the firewood:** Send out a party in search of all the necessary firewood while daylight remains strong. We find this is also a supreme occasion to forage the property for any wild-growing culinary delights such as berries, herbs, or mushrooms. Once abundant fuel is gathered (our experience suggests thrice as much as one *thinks* one needs), chop it if necessary, separate it by size, and set each pile next to the fire pit.

🌿 **Prepare for unforeseen disaster:** Have ready a means of extinguishing fire, whether it is for a runaway flame or the close of one's weekend getaway. Water, dirt, and sand each tamp down wayward flames, though we place our greatest faith in water. While dirt and sand are reliable at snuffing out fire, embers below can continue to smolder, and a brisk wind following one's departure might result in an unintentional inferno. The exception to this rule is a grease or oil fire. Water is ineffective in extinguishing a grease fire; one can either suffocate the flame inside a pot by replacing its metal cast-iron lid (glass will shatter at high heat, one really ought not be so foolish as to cart glass cookware to the wild), or douse it generously with baking soda or kosher salt.

Construction of the Fire Ring

We love the perfect circular symmetry of the humble fire ring or pit. It speaks of civilization's greatest strides, from the invention of the wheel to the brilliance of Euclidean geometry to the gleaming curve of a newly minted coin. We also love that it is marvelously uncomplicated to construct one's own fire pit; it requires only a shovel and some well-shaped rocks.

Because we reside most of the year in urbane society, where one cannot go scrabbling over stone and creek before breakfast, we have also provided instructions for building a fire pit in one's own back garden. Delighting in one's rosebush from a nook at the kitchen window is well and good, but cooking over a backyard flame—bathed in the scent of wood smoke and surrounded by the blink of fireflies—can provide the most welcome respite from a week that is otherwise flooded with drudgery.

Bear in mind that a garden fire pit is a more permanent structure than one in the wilderness and therefore requires a tad more labor to construct. Note that it is also larger in size, as the rocks will line the inner, as opposed to the outer, perimeter.

THE WILDERNESS FIRE PIT

First, select a suitable site for the pit. It should be several feet away from flammable bushes, tents, or low-hanging branches.

Instructions:

🌿 Mark a circular area approximately four feet across. If building in a grassy knoll, use one's shovel to scalp the sod from the area. Try to do this in one piece so that the sod can be replaced when one breaks camp. Set the sod aside.

🌿 Unearth four to six inches of dirt from the scalped area, keeping the bottom and sides as level as possible; set it aside to replace at the fire's end. (The dirt also can be used as an emergency extinguisher.) This depression will protect the surrounding grass from rebellious flames.

🌿 Remove any parched grass, twigs, or leaves from the perimeter of the pit, then rim it with dry, flat-bottomed stones (avoid river stones, which might

WEATHER APHORISMS

It would seem a law of nature that upon venturing bravely into the wild, one will eventually cross a grizzled, wild-eyed recluse with a penchant for cryptic weather sayings. We met ours, an aging, laconic sea dog, one chilly autumn evening not far from the Bay of Fundy. After we had plied him with spiced rum round the fire, he abandoned his laconic ways and shared with us the following aphoristic gems, which we hope will be as true a guide for our readers' camping journeys as they have been for us.

> *Campfire smoke descends,*
> *Good weather ends.*
> *Red sky at night, sailors delight,*
> *Red sky in the morning, sailors take warning.*
> *When the sun sets bright and clear,*
> *easterly winds one need not fear.*
> *When clouds look like rocks and towers,*
> *the earth's refreshed by frequent showers.*
> *A wind from the south has rain in its mouth.*
> *When leaves show their undersides,*
> *be very sure that rain betides.*
> *If birds fly low, expect rain and a blow.*
> *When halo rings the sun or moon,*
> *rain or snow approaches soon.*
> *If a cat washes her face o'er her ear*
> *'Tis a sign the weather will be fine and clear.*

explode if overheated). Place the stones as close to the edge of the pit as one can manage; do not stack them unless it is certain they will remain stable.

- If the ground is excessively damp, line the bottom of the pit with green logs or a thin sheet of metal.

THE BACK-GARDEN FIRE PIT:

Before even lifting one's garden spade, contact the local authority on fire codes to make certain that constructing a pit is a lawful pursuit. Use these guidelines to determine the appropriate fire site, well away from sheds, topiaries, and other flame-susceptible objects.

Instructions:

- Thrust a dowel into the ground where the center of the pit will be. Tie a two-and-one-half-foot piece of string to the dowel (to make a five-foot pit) and pull it taut. Sketch the outline of a perfect circle with the dowel, following along with a sprinkling of flour to mark one's path.

- Use one's shovel to scalp the sod from the area.

- Unearth six to eight inches of dirt from the scalped area, keeping the bottom and sides as level as possible.

- Spread three to four inches of gravel into the bottom of the pit to facilitate drainage after a downpour.

- Top the gravel with three to four inches of sand. This will suffocate the fire before it can thread its way underground to the roots of one's beloved and stately elm tree.

Line the inside perimeter of the ring with stacks of bricks or landscaping stones (no river rocks) and continue arranging the stones to make a wall twelve to twenty inches tall and as perpendicular to the ground as one can manage. Leave periodic chinks in the wall for continued airflow in and out of the pit.

Laying the Fire

Now that one has completed the obligatory preparations, the time has come, as Robert Browning once rhapsodized, to "heap logs and let the blaze laugh out!" Dozens of fire-building techniques exist, most of which we simply cannot be bothered to try. Over the years, we have stood loyally by several of the reliable prevailing methods, which we now divulge. With any fire-laying method, it is important to remember two things: work at a tortoise's pace, building larger layers of fuel as the fire strengthens, and always arrange the twigs, sticks, and logs in a loose formation, so as to allow for the ample air circulation one's fire craves.

THE TEPEE METHOD

We rely on this method for a rapid flame. Because the heat is forced up to a single peak, it is an excellent choice for boiling water or quick skillet cookery. Before long, the tepee usually collapses into a mound of coals, at which point we usually begin arranging additional fuel onto the fire in an informal log-cabin style (see page 35).

Instructions:

Wedge a small, Y-shaped kindling stick into the ground to serve as support for the first layer.

Make a loose, fluffy ball of mixed tinder. Nestle the tinder slackly around the stick.

THE TEPEE METHOD

Prop the slenderest, shortest pieces of kindling around the ball of tinder in a small tepee shape, using the Y-stick for support. Do not neglect to leave a small opening of approximately eight inches through which one can light the fire.

Prop a second layer of slightly wider and taller kindling around the first layer in the same tepee formation. Remember to leave space between the sticks so that the fire can breathe.

Create a third layer using small fuelwood no thicker than one's wrist.

Light the fire; if a greater blaze is still desired, place several split logs around the third tepee layer. Beware that this will create a much taller flame.

Splitting Wood

OR, HOW TO BE A MASTER AXMAN

We heartily applaud anyone in possession of the wood-splitting spirit and assure such individuals that they are in excellent company. We do not doubt history's cup brimmeth over with notable woodsmen and women who took ax in hand, even if we've not the foggiest idea who they might be. It is a noble tradition. And as our master axman, Patrick, is fond of reminding us, self-cut wood warms twice.

Naturally, as with so many noble endeavors, like fending off a fleet of buccaneers or wrestling jungle cats, it is not without peril. An ax is a potentially mortal tool, and using one requires extraordinary sensibility. To avoid bodily damage, always work with a sharpened ax, which will afford the greatest control and precision; check also to see that the ax head is tightly secured. Relegate all companions, who will be eager to cheer one on, to a vantage point several meters or more away, as both a swinging ax and flying splinters constitute physical hazard. When finished using the ax, sheathe it. Do not it abandon it on the ground, where it might develop rust or nicks, or where some poor soul might stumble upon its blade; do not place it near the fire, where heat might soften the steel. Even if—understandably—one is compelled to pause in chopping for a glimpse of the rare orange-crowned warbler in flight, place the ax far from harm's way, such as beneath a log.

TO SPLIT A LOG

Find a small clearing free of branches an ax-length around (the combined length of one's arm and the ax). One can trim bush and branch to create this area, but if it requires chopping live trees, seek a different clearing. Hacking away at a live tree can lead to its untimely death.

Place the log upon flat, firm earth or a hard surface low to the ground, such as a large tree stump.

Stand squarely in front of the log. Seek out any cracks in the edges of the log; those are most vulnerable for splitting. Likewise, avoid troublesome gnarled knots. Fix the eyes on the spot where the blow will land, and do not divert the attention from that place.

Grip the knob of the handle with both hands firmly, but not tensely. Arms should be straight when swinging, so position oneself at a suitable distance from the log.

Bend knees slightly, then stand quickly, raise the ax, and bring it down with authority and swiftness. One will benefit more from assuredness than brute strength. The ax head and handle should be level when the blade strikes the log.

ADDITIONAL WOODCUTTING TECHNIQUES*

If felling a dead, standing sapling, always chop it close to the ground at an angle to the wood grain. Strike with the ax head directed away from one's body.

When cutting a dead branch from a log, if possible stand on the side of the log opposite the branch to provide a barrier between oneself and the ax (if the log is so large that this feels awkward, stand on the same side, but proceed carefully). Strike where the branch meets the log, hitting from the bottom upwards, rather than down through the joint.

To cut kindling from small lengths of split log, find a chopping block slightly below knee height. Hold the log along the side, so that fingers are far from harm's way. Grasp the ax closer to the ax head and swing with short, controlled strokes.

---

* Although intrepidness is a valuable quality in the outdoors, one might reasonably grow cold at the thought of wielding an ax. Fret not—wood can be split without it. One might purchase a wood-splitter's maul, whose wedged head is less inclined to stick, stubbornly and Arthurian-like, in the wood. Or place an aluminum felling wedge along the grain of the wood and hammer it in using another log or mallet. A lightweight, folding saw is also useful for cutting thick branches.

THE LOG CABIN METHOD

THE HUNTER'S FIRE

THE LOG CABIN OR CRISSCROSS METHOD

Our preferred method, the log-cabin fire, burns steady and hot. The elevated structure encourages the inhalation of air through the bottom opening and forces it through the top.

Instructions:

- Into one's fire pit, place two hefty, ankle-thick pieces of split fuelwood parallel to each other and eight to ten inches apart.

- Make a loose, fluffy ball of mixed tinder. Place the tinder between these lengths of fuelwood.

- Lay small kindling across the two heavy branches above the tinder, leaving approximately one inch between each stick for air circulation.

- Crisscross slightly heavier kindling on top of the first area, one inch apart, for a gridlike effect. If desired, repeat with a third layer of light fuelwood.

- Light the fire and add additional fuel as appropriate to the burgeoning flame; for example, if the tinder is spent before the kindling has sufficiently caught fire, add tinder gradually until the kindling is burning in full force. Once the fire is burning bright, heavier fuelwood can be added.

THE HUNTER'S FIRE

We rarely construct this fire, as it does not provide great warmth or conviviality. However, it is a useful technique to have in one's sack of cookery tricks, as its effectiveness does not rely on the use of a cooking grate or tripod grill.

Instructions:

- Into one's fire pit, place two hefty, ankle-thick pieces of split fuelwood next to each other, six to eight inches apart at one end and three to five inches apart at the other.

- Make a loose, fluffy ball of mixed tinder. Place the tinder between these lengths of fuelwood.

- Construct a small tepee fire around the tinder, between the logs.

- Light the fire and continue to slowly feed the tepee until it has broken into hot coals; spread the coals in a graduated fashion to create areas of greater or lesser heat, depending on one's cookery needs.

- Place cookware over the fire, using the logs as a platform.

Tending the Flame for Cookery

Like one's attic-confined aunt or the bumbling local vicar, fire cookery can be a bit of a loose cannon. One adventure might be kissed with cerulean skies and a warm breeze, while others reign arctic and blustery. One forest might teem with bone-dry kindling, while another proves exasperatingly verdant. The morning's blaze might scorch the pot, then snuff out mean-spiritedly at teatime without warning. As in life, the vicissitudes of fortune are wide and swinging. In this sense, outdoor cookery can require vast personal stores of daring and adaptability, as well as a readiness to bend to the whims of Nature. Be grateful for these hurdles—we promise that not only will they build the sort of character sometimes lacking in the civilized world, they will ultimately provide the merriest memories.

Moreover, scores of techniques and tools exist to help one along. Just as one can fiddle with the knobs and dials of the home stove, so, too, can one gauge and adjust the heat of open-fire cookery. In this section, we present various means of achieving successful fire control, whether cooking over flames or a bed of embers. We have even thoughtfully set out adaptations techniques for the backyard grill and indoor kitchen, should one aspire to an outdoor adventure from the home. Each method has advantages and drawbacks; we suggest experimenting until one hits on a system that feels most comfortable.

Which brings us to the most essential tenet of fire cookery: be attentive. Listen to the fire. Observe the food. Unlike at home, it is never wise to set a pot upon the flame, wander off for a dip in the spring, and return at the ding of an egg timer. No matter which techniques one applies, a fire's needs are always most readily ascertained if approached with calm vigilance.

Love the fire, and it will return the affection in kind.

USING A CHIMNEY STARTER

If one does select charwood over firewood, a charcoal chimney starter is an excellent tool for simplifying combustion. Fill the bottom of the chimney with a sheet or two of newsprint. Pile the charwood on top of the paper and place the apparatus inside one's fire ring. Ignite the paper and leave the chimney to its own devices. Once the coals have begun to glow and are lightly coated with ash, tip them out into the fire ring and add additional charwood or small lengths of fuelwood until the fire is burning at the desired pace and strength.

elevate the oven slightly above the bed of coals beneath to help prevent burning. If one's pot does not possess legs, one can fill the bottom of the pot with small stones and top them with a layer of foil before placing food in the pot. For steamed cakes and puddings in which the oven is filled with water and a smaller baking vessel nestled within, a folded tea towel may be substituted for the stones. This will help create an additional barrier between the food and coals.

&. Although by no means a firm rule, we find that a single ring of hot coals beneath the outer lower edge of the oven and a single ring of hot coals lining the lip of the lid approximates a temperature of 350 degrees. If we wish to reduce the temperature, we remove coals from above and beneath the oven. When we wish to increase the heat, we generally add coals to the top—a second ring approximates 375 degrees, and so forth. In baking over a campfire, one usually aims to add more heat (coals) to the top of the pot to prevent scorching the sensitive bottom, but use common sense, depending on what is in the pot.

&. To avoid patches of excessive or insufficient heat (which leads to disappointing food that is at once burnt and raw), rotate both pot and lid a quarter turn every ten minutes, or more frequently if your dish requires a shorter cooking time.

&. One fresh batch of coals typically retains heat for one-half to three-quarters of an hour. Do not neglect to replenish coals as needed to maintain even baking temperatures.

Advisement: When cooking (as opposed to baking) with our Dutch oven, we are partial to the live-fire method; alternatively, one can use the coal method. To achieve the high heat required for frying or boiling, all the coals should be underneath the pot. For roasting, the coals should be equally distributed at the top and bottom. For long-simmering stews and soups (which we also prefer over coals), pile more coals beneath and scatter only about one-quarter of the coals on top of the pot.

Judging One's Heat

Any number of factors might influence the heat of one's fire. The amount and type of fuel being fed to the fire (plenty of dense hardwood burns hottest), the amount of oxygen accessible to the fuel, the thickness of one's coal bed, the length of time the coals have spent burning away their remaining energy, and even altitude and weather conditions all influence heat.

In absence of a thermometer, this could pose terrible difficulties in determining when one has attained a proper cookery temperature. Fortunately, fire cooks are a clever lot, and strategies abound to combat this challenge. The chart below outlines some of these clues. Bear in mind that they are meant as guidelines; the degree of heat perceived does not necessarily correspond to a precise numerical temperature.* However, we do believe that the more attuned one is to these visual and sensory clues, the more culinary success one is bound to enjoy:

The Hand Method. Most popular among outdoorsmen, this method calls for one to suspend a hand approximately six inches over the coals or preheating

---

*To avoid delays in accurate temperature diagnoses, it is also crucial to let a fire burn for one-half to three-quarters of an hour ahead of time, whether one intends to cook over a live flame or a coal bed. Like an oven at home, fires need some time to build up sufficient heat. To prepare coals to support a baking endeavor, one should expect to burn more fuel and wait longer.

pan (if using live fire). Proceed to count the seconds one can remain in this position before drawing the hand away.

The Coal Method. This method demands a keen eye and is used for coal and ember cookery. One simply assesses the appearance of the coals. Coals can reach temperatures much higher than those stated in the chart on page 41 (we've been told as high as 700 degrees), so do not place too much emphasis on specific temperatures; in general, very hot or hot coals that are ash-covered and glowing are best for this type of cookery, particularly for baking.

The Live-Fire Method. Similar to the coal method, but one relies upon visual examination of the flames' action with respect to the cooking surface to reach a temperature conclusion.

Advisement: The more diminutive the piece of meat, the hotter a fire it can and should withstand. To ensure even cookery, do not prepare large, dense pieces of meat over the highest heat.

Advisement: Should a flame or bed of coals exceed the preferred temperature, a misting of water is an excellent means for disciplining errant flames. Just be sure to rinse the bottle thoroughly with suds before filling it with water—the lingering alcohol in perfume is remarkably flammable, as we discovered one luckless evening. Our eyebrows did not need plucking for some time.

Making Adjustments for Home Cookery

We hope that one might find the recipes provided in this book useful wherever one's gustatory adventures might lead. To that end, we have taken measures to see that each of these recipes can be easily adjusted for cookery at home, whether over a gas or charcoal grill on the back portico or in one's kitchen (baked goods being an exception).

If cooking over a stovetop, use a recipe's heat indications as a guide. For example, if we dictate that a dish should simmer, covered, over a medium-low heat, do precisely that at home.

If cooking over a gas or charcoal grill, again rely on the provided heat indications. Assume that all dishes require direct grilling, unless otherwise specified in a special advisement in the recipe.

Dousing the Flame

Parting is such sweet sorrow. And yet the inevitable moment arrives when an adventure must draw to a close. For us, this is signified by our final duty, performed after the last plate has been scoured, all wine dregs lapped up, and all trunks snapped shut. Then, we turn our attention to putting out the fire.

Though we have mentioned already the frightful tragedies that might visit those who do not properly douse a flame, it bears repeating: even should a fire appear as dead as day-old Champagne, neoclassical art, or Archduke Franz Ferdinand, it might conceal a still-vital force that awaits just one stray bit of dandelion fluff to kindle it anew. We hate to be a bore, but we implore all fire makers to take seriously the following instructions on fire extinguishment.

If one has planned wisely, only glowing coals and a bed of cinders will remain in the fire pit after cooking. If this is not the case and flames persist, use a large branch to stir the fire gently, scattering the coals and burning wood around the pit. Dip a switch of pine needles into a bucket of water and shake it over the coals, taking care to step out of the path of any steaming ash that this might rouse. Continue to douse the pit with water until most of the steam has dissipated and repeat this process until the telltale

THE JUDGMENT OF HEAT				
TEMPERATURE (°F)	HEAT LEVEL	HAND	COALS	LIVE FIRE
500 or more	Very high	1 second	Thin layer of white ash; glowing red	Flames above grill grate
500 to 450	High	2 to 3 seconds	Thick white ash layer; glowing red	Flames licking grill grate
450 to 400	Medium-high	3 to 4 seconds	Thick white ash layer; barely glowing	Flames occasionally licking grill grate
400 to 350	Medium	4 to 5 seconds	Solid gray ash-covered coals; not glowing	Flames just under grill grate
350 to 300	Medium-low	5 to 6 seconds	Not applicable	Flames well below grill grate
300 to 250	Low	6 to 7 seconds	Not applicable	Flames low and tame

hiss of smoke has vanished. Pass a few minutes reminiscing about the wonderful time one has just spent in the wild or trade impressions of the great cathedrals of Europe, then kneel before the coal bed and feel about for any lingering pockets of heat that would require more water.

Scoop the extinguished coals and ash into a pail and either take one last, invigorating walk deep into the forest to scatter the remains among the flora, or carry them home to enrich a backyard garden or compost patch. Wood ash contains useful salts, most importantly potassium carbonate (so-called potash) and will enhance the pH value of one's soil.

Before bidding a final farewell to the camp, cover the now-vacant fire pit area with dirt and replace any scalped grass, allowing nature to return to its pristine state.

A Prudent Note upon the Merits of Spoilage Protections

A feast-filled adventure in the Great Outdoors will make one feel like the emperor of all one surveys. Unfortunate be the monarchs for whom the thought of food poisoning hangs over the head like a sword of Damocles. Fear not, intrepid epicures! Such a harrowing impediment to carefree jollity may be banished by a modicum of forethought and planning.

To start, we recommend packing one's perishables in three separate coolers. We use one cooler exclusively for meats, poultry, and fish; another for milk, eggs, and butter; and the third for produce and chilled beverages such as soda water, juice, or Champagne. This way if by some unfortunate happenstance one's meat should go bad, it won't put off one's butter or bubbly (which would be too tragic for words).

Naturally, one must equip one's self with the finest coolers money can buy. At explorers' or camping specialty shops one may find coolers of the deluxe variety, which promise to keep the larder within fresh for up to six days. Why they haven't manufactured one that can last a full calendar week remains a tantalizing mystery—perhaps our more inventive readers might design one for market in the foreseeable future? One can dream. If one's finances permit the purchase of only a single deluxe cooler, do give priority to the storage of meats, poultry, and fish, as they should be the first concern in terms of spoilage protection. Let us be honest, shall we? The cooler full of Champagne will not last terribly long anyhow.

One may also wish to invest in reusable cooling packs as opposed to bags of ice. They will last longer, are lighter to carry, and are more portable than old-fashioned frozen water. If one does chill with ice, do remember to keep it contained in a sealed plastic bag or similar vessel, as food surrounded by damp, melting ice cubes is more susceptible to spoilage and contamination. Furthermore, do not make a habit of opening the cooler just to peer at its contents. A cooler can only do its work if the lid is kept closed. Open only as necessary, and be quick about it. To prevent potential food spoilage, a cooler should maintain a temperature of 41 degrees.

When stocking one's cooler, place the heavier items at the bottom and the lighter items at the top. This will prevent the contents from damage during travel. Also, give a thought to one's menu. Be prepared to serve such items as mussels or salmon fillets quite soon after making camp. No matter the quality of one's cooler, foodstuffs such as these have a fleeting freshness and are not the sort of pleasure one can reserve for later. Feast upon mussels now, for who knows what tomorrow may bring? For further information on the maintenance of seafood, Nature's most delicate offering, see Minding One's Fruits of the Sea, page 154.

Stratagems for the Thwarting of Curious Critters

The aroma of open-fire cookery is a temptress even more alluring than Cleopatra—it will certainly draw a number of rakish centurions to one's banquet bower, but it may attract asps (or other such fanged faunae) as well. To avoid such pesky visitations, strategy must be employed.

SNAKES

Though these slithering forest dwellers may feature prominently in one's nightmares, they are perhaps the last creature one need fear when enjoying an outdoor holiday in North America. The adage "it's more afraid of you than you are of it" is entirely apropos with respect to these cool reptiles. A snake simply will not strike unless frightened or provoked, so take care not to frighten or provoke it. Carry a battery-operated torch during moonlit strolls, lest one should inadvertently tread upon a wee serpent. Carry a walking stick and use it if one intends to overturn any rocks or old logs along the path. Should one spy a snake, take a quick moment to eye its coloring and abide by the phrase "red on yellow will kill a fellow, but red on black venom will lack." (If it is the former, retreat. Hastily.) And finally, keep one's ears alert. Aside from the occasional coral snake, copperhead, or moccasin, the primary venomous snake one might encounter on this continent is the rattlesnake. It will make itself immediately known by the sound of its rattle, an unmistakable racket like that of a furious infant shaking his silver-plated christening gift (a sound best avoided, no matter the source).

MOSQUITOES, TICKS & OTHER MINUSCULE MOTES

Nothing spoils an outdoor feast like these insupportable demons! Infuriatingly, these buzzing pests are attracted by both the sweet and savory flavors of the feast, as well as by the cheery beacon of the fire. A commonplace strategy for warding off these flying unmentionables is to burn citronella candles, the scent of which repels mosquitoes. While this does work, we cannot recommend employing it as one's primary defense, for the smell may clash with one's well-considered menu. Similarly, one may wish to arm one's self with a battery of insect repellents, and with this we can agree, so long as one chooses a salve or spray without a cloying scent or chemical toxicity. We would hate for one's appetite to be the principal casualty of the war on mosquitoes. It is whispered in some circles that a mix of pungent spices, such as allspice, rosemary, and cinnamon, sprinkled upon the skin might repel pests, but this sounds like a messy business. We generally employ a somewhat unorthodox precaution taught to us in the steppes of Eastern Europe. There, a kindly aged woman of Romany descent prescribed eating a whole clove of raw garlic just as the sun went down. Our meager language skills being what they are, we cannot say exactly what sort of bloodsucker the garlic was meant to protect us from, but we can attest that it worked a smashing success to thwart those nasty mosquito bites.

Chemical repellents are also an option when one wishes to ward off ticks. It's a good idea to keep one's trouser legs tucked into one's boots at all times, wear long sleeves, and keep one's neck covered—perhaps with an attractive feather boa if the weather is too temperate for a woolen muffler. We also recommend practicing the buddy system. Select one's most attractive companion (take heart, everyone has a different idea of what attracts, so everyone is bound to pair up by the feast's end) and search him or her for ticks. Allow the companion to return the favor. This can be a rather festive way to while away an hour or two before retreating snugly into one's bedroll.

COUGARS, MOUNTAIN LIONS & OTHER CATS OF THE WILDERNESS

As those of us who adore our domestic felines know, cats are charming predators, who, if offered a choice, prefer to stalk, pounce upon, and devour their dinner whilst it is alive. For this reason, they

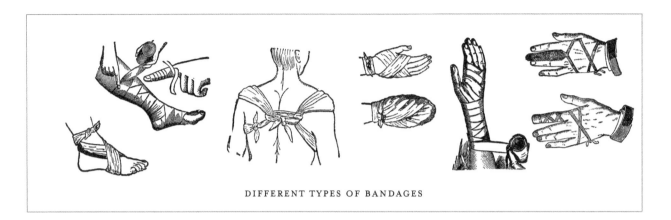

DIFFERENT TYPES OF BANDAGES

are not so much of a threat to the food at one's campsite. However, they can be a real bother when encountered on a nature walk. If one should happen upon a wildcat, experts say, it is best neither to crouch nor to look the kitty directly in the eye. Simply hold one's head high (averting the gaze so as not to show aggression) and back away slowly. We think it might also be helpful to offer up a silent prayer to one's deity of choice. Because, really, one's chances of surviving such an encounter are slim to none. The optimal stratagem here is to inquire of one's wildlife representative if mountain lions are common in the area. If the answer is in the affirmative, simply choose another venue for the outing.

BEARS, RACCOONS, OPOSSUMS, SQUIRRELS, CHIPMUNKS & FIELD MICE

We are not so different, we members of the animal kingdom. So many of us enjoy a bite of pleasantly charred steak, a mouthful of oaty porridge, a luxuriously sticky swipe from the honey pot. And though it may be our inclination to share these goodies with all creatures great and small, we must insist that urge be resisted. For though our tastes may be similar, our methods of eating may be very, very different and indeed are so incompatible as to gravely endanger the safety of the *Homo sapiens* members of the animal family. Raccoons may look like sweet and fuzzy little banditos and opossums like sleepy little interplanetary visitors, but both have claws and teeth more than sufficient to wreak grave damage (and which they are not too timid to use to raid our outdoor larder). And that squirrel or chipmunk may seem as if it's about to break into a cute little song with accompanying choreography, but we have seen such a creature send one of our companions to the emergency room with a mere flick of its tiny wrist and ill-timed extension of its talons. We've never actually heard of field mice hurting anyone, but still . . . do they not look a little shifty?

The most fearsome of these creatures is the bear. One must not trifle with a bear, as it will show no mercy in the pursuit of a good meal. And while we sympathize with this pursuit, we do all we can to thwart it. Firstly, all food for the wilderness feast must be locked up tight, secured with a sturdy rope or chain, and kept at least one hundred feet away from one's sleeping area. Do not secrete morsels in one's tent for a midnight snack. One's beauty sleep may be interrupted by a lumbering beast who thinks nothing of shredding one's bedroll in search of a macaroon. Indeed, it is wise, when spending a night under the stars, to eschew the use of any scented products that may normally be part of one's evening ablutions. Pity the vanity of our rouge-tressed camping companion, who once washed her hair in ginger-root shampoo! Her night was far from restful.

In addition to keeping one's food packs the prescribed distance from one's tent, it is also advisable that they be hoisted above the heads of prowling bears each night before lights-out. This can be accomplished by stringing one's pack between two sturdy tree branches by use of a rope and pulley, which can be purchased at most hardware or dry goods stores. Many campgrounds provide manmade enclosures with eaves meant to house heavier coolers and protect them from animal attack. Contact the campsite in advance to inquire whether these facilities are available.

"The guests are met,

the feast is set:

may'st hear

the merry din."

—FROM THE RIME OF THE ANCIENT MARINER, SAMUEL TAYLOR COLERIDGE

CHAPTER TWO

PREPARING FOR THE FEAST

IT IS SAID THAT IN ANCIENT ROME, TYPICAL BAN-
QUETS CARRIED ON FOR A GOOD TEN HOURS,
DURING WHICH TIME GUESTS ENJOYED A LAV-
ISH SPREAD OF DELICACIES LIKE CONGER EELS,
PEACOCK, FLAMINGO, AND BOAR'S HEAD. While
attendees lounged on couches, servants wandered
about playing lutes and passing out garlands of rose
petals to offset the effects of plentiful fig wine (er,
perhaps because the blossoms were distractingly
lovely?). Naturally, those crafty Romans did much to
give the event an air of impulsive debauchery, as if
one just happened to have an extra jug of pomegranate port lying about and thought it made a fine excuse
for an impromptu soiree.

Do not be fooled. Events of mythic proportions
entail preparation. And so it is in the Great Outdoors, which, if one tallies it up, is at least on par
with antiquarian tables. Consider: a feast in the Great
Outdoors might continue unabated for a weekend or
longer (take that, Nero!) and is rife with exotic edibles
of its own, such as venison, foraged snails, and rare
species of delicate fungi. And while it may be unlikely
that one might manage to employ a wandering lute
player, it is highly likely that one's friends will amble
about in search of another cask of fig wine.

Advance into the wild confident of one's place

in the annals of history; seize the opportunity to
adequately prepare. Many larder items can be made
in advance of a holiday, and many are the better for
it. Pickles, relishes, chutneys, and homemade spirits
enhance the dinner platter and improve with a few
weeks' aging; vinaigrettes are more flavorful when
the ingredients have married a day or two. Teatime
will be jollier if a party isn't waiting for the jam to
set. Companions will delight in hand-crafted foods
usually purchased at the grocer, like graham crackers,
marshmallows, mustard, and catsup. Moreover, an
afternoon spent at home creating small holiday treats
frees up feast days for the larger particulars, like setting up one's pig spit or trying on one's toga.

Above all, feel no pressure to overachieve. Frankly,
we find the opulence of Roman feasting a bit vulgar
(How those Italians struggle with restraint!). A special touch or two is all one really needs to impress
companions and elevate one's camp. Not to mention, stocking camp trunks with a few ready-made
vittles is the mark of a well-prepared adventurer. For
should one's flame fail to materialize or an excursion
be struck by inclement weather, one takes comfort
in knowing starvation is not nigh so long as a crisp
cracker and swipe of marmalade are at the ready. One
cannot say the same about a roast peacock.

CONDIMENTS

WE CANNOT THINK OF CONDIMENTS WITHOUT THINKING OF GEORGE BERNARD SHAW. Like Miss Eliza Doolittle, that humble cockney maid so intent on becoming a genuine lady, the condiment needs only firm tutelage to surpass its scrappy reputation. For while some might associate condiments with swift dining and lowly food cloaked in spicy sauce, we have always believed in their noble potential.

The vital rule for condiment making is strict adherence to quality and freshness. Use only the ripest, meatiest tomatoes for one's ketchup, and the most fragrant pears for one's chutney. And remember that the best condiments are a happy marriage of flavors—strive for perfect harmony. Taste them often and attentively during preparation, and allow one's palate to reign, even if it means straying a bit from the recipe. A splash of vinegar or pinch of spice might be just the thing to elevate one's common condiment to an entirely different class.

World's Fair Catsup

According to folklore, many foods have celebrated their birth at world expositions, including the ice cream cone, celery salt, and various brands of chewing gum and pancake syrup. Technically, catsup was not one of those foods. But our version should have been. It is a blue-ribbon recipe that forgoes the cloying stickiness of mass-produced brands. And because one's best recipes should always be shared, not hoarded, we will reveal that our secret is the use of perfectly ripe tomatoes, which add natural sweetness and increased pectin, Nature's thickening agent. Meaty tomatoes, such as plum or beefsteak, yield burger-worthy results (see our burger recipe, page 182).

PROVIDES APPROXIMATELY 2 CUPS

3 pounds ripe plum or beefsteak tomatoes

2 tablespoons extra-virgin olive oil

1 small onion, finely chopped

1 celery stalk, finely chopped

3 garlic cloves, finely chopped

1 teaspoon kosher salt

½ teaspoon paprika

¼ teaspoon ground cinnamon

½ teaspoon dry mustard

1 tablespoon tomato paste

⅓ cup firmly packed light brown sugar

⅓ cup cider vinegar

One 1-pint canning jar, sterilized (see The Successful Cannery, page 58–59)

1. Bring a large pot of water to a boil. Use a sharp knife to draw a small *X* in the base of each tomato. Working in batches, drop the tomatoes into the boiling water for 20 seconds. Remove with a slotted spoon; the skin should have a slightly wrinkled appearance and should be curling slightly at the incision. Peel away the loosed skin. Chop the tomatoes, removing and discarding the seeds along the way.

2. Heat the oil in a large skillet over a medium heat. Add the onion and celery and cook until softened,

about 7 minutes. Stir in the garlic and cook 2 minutes. Stir in the salt, paprika, cinnamon, mustard, and tomato paste; cook 1 minute. Stir in the tomatoes and increase the heat to medium-high. Simmer the tomatoes until they have almost entirely broken down, 10 to 15 minutes. Stir in the sugar and vinegar, and simmer over a medium heat until the mixture has a dry appearance, 30 to 40 minutes.

3. Pass the mixture through a food mill, or alternatively, puree it until smooth and strain through a medium-mesh strainer. Pour the catsup into the jar and seal, if desired; alternatively, let cool completely before chilling for up to 2 weeks.

The Colonel's Mustard

We met The Colonel one summer while exploring the nearly impenetrable jungles of Panama. A scruffy old fellow with an eye patch, snowy mop of hair, and fondness for military history, his origins were as enigmatic as his inexplicable limp. Local lore had it he was heir to a Viennese mustard empire that crumbled before he could take the throne.

Though we never did wrench a recipe from his hard-set jaw, we believe he'd enjoy the one we've created. Truthfully, it turns out that making mustard could hardly be easier; soaking the spicy seeds before pureeing mellows their flavor and improves the body of the mustard.

PROVIDES ABOUT 1 CUP MUSTARD

3 tablespoons yellow mustard seed

3 tablespoons brown mustard seed

⅓ cup white wine

¼ cup white wine vinegar

1½ tablespoons finely chopped shallot

¾ teaspoon salt, plus additional, to taste

Large pinch ground nutmeg

Small, clean jar

Place mustard seeds in a bowl. Add all other ingredients and stir to combine. Wrap the bowl tightly with plastic wrap and chill overnight. The next day, transfer the mixture to a blender; puree until it reaches the desired thickness, thick or smooth. Thin with water, if one needs it, to achieve the desired consistency. Transfer to a clean jar and chill for up to two weeks.

PICKLES & RELISHES & CHUTNEYS

THERE IS SIMPLY NO EVADING THE TRUTH ABOUT PICKLES, RELISHES, AND CHUTNEYS: IN THE CULTURE OF CONDIMENTS, THEY ARE THE UNDISPUTED BOHEMIANS. And not only because it seems we always turn to Parisian cigarettes and candlelit poetry readings after opening a jar of such preserves. It's also because they teem with the exotic, boast seasonings that range from sweet to spicy to tart, and conjure the richest results from the humblest ingredients. These are invaluable qualities in the wild (and in a bohemian). And though one can scarcely absorb culture through diet alone, we daresay that a nibble of pickled ramps or spoonful of apricot chutney might very well have one whistling Puccini and shedding a tear for Rodolfo and Mimi.

Spicy Dill Pickles

We enjoy a good visit to the cobblestone streets of the pickle district, where briny barrels overflow with petite gherkins, sweet slices of bread-and-butters, tart green tomatoes, and even the occasional tangy lime pickle from India. Though temptations abound, in the end we always return, like Odysseus, to our beloved: classic spears of crunchy dills. We spice our version with garlic, chile flakes, and peppercorns; one wishing for mellowness might leave any or all of them out. Always use the freshest cucumbers possible for the crispest results, and if one is able, purchase fresh dill that is going to seed (it will bear telltale yellow buds), as it boasts the most flavor.

PROVIDES 2 QUARTS DILL PICKLES

1 tablespoon whole coriander seed

2 teaspoons dill seeds

1 teaspoon mustard seeds

1 teaspoon red pepper flakes

6 black peppercorns

2 bay leaves

8 medium unwaxed kirby cucumbers, unpeeled (about 1¼ pounds)

1 small bunch fresh dill, cleaned and drained

4 garlic cloves, peeled

5 tablespoons kosher salt

5 tablespoons white vinegar

8 cups water

2 (1-quart) wide-mouth canning jars, sterilized (see The Successful Cannery, page 58–59)

1. In a small bowl, stir together the coriander, dill seeds, mustard seeds, pepper flakes, peppercorns, and bay leaves.

2. Under a warm running tap, scrub the cucumbers well with a vegetable brush. Transfer cucumbers to a large bowl of ice water and chill for at least three hours or overnight. (This is meant to refresh one's cucumbers as much as possible so that they will turn out nice and crunchy. One may skip this step if the need for pickles is dire.)

3. Drain the cucumbers and pat them dry. Trim off any stems at the place where they meet the cucumber (do not cut off the tip of the cucumber itself). Slice the cucumbers lengthwise into quarters; Drop them into a large, nonreactive bowl, such as ceramic, glass, or stainless steel. Sprinkle the spices, fresh dill, and garlic over the cucumbers.

4. Fill a small saucepan with 8 cups cold water; stir in the salt and vinegar. Bring to a simmer over medium heat and cook until the salt has dissolved, 2 to 3 minutes. Remove the pan from the heat and pour the hot brine over the cucumbers. One wants the pickles to remain submerged in the brine; weigh them down with a heavy plate or bowl. Leave them in a cool, darkish corner of one's kitchen for at least 24 hours and up to 48 hours. The longer they stand, the more pickled they will become. We suggest taking an occasional bite to see that they are pickled to one's tastes.

5. Pack the pickles upright into the jars, as tightly as possible, making sure to allow enough space at the top for the brine to completely cover the cucumbers. Ladle the brine, spices, and dillweed over the pickles, as needed, taking care to cover them completely. Discard any leftover brine. Screw the lids tightly on the jars and chill the pickles for up to one month.

Pickled Ramps

The first time we encountered wild ramps was on a woodland trek with a party of friends. We had paused for a spell beneath a shady maple when the fragrance of freshest onion tickled our nostrils. Naturally, our initial inclination was to suspect the lunch pail of an allium-loving companion. But after some surreptitious rooting for the source, we came upon a cluster of long, lilylike leaves that led to roots of pale, slender bulbs. Now, each spring when ramps proliferate, we crave their delicate flavor, which hovers between leek and garlic. We especially enjoy pickling them for the cocktail tray, but sliced bulbs and greens are put to good use in stews, sautés, and omelettes.

PROVIDES 1 SCANT QUART PICKLED RAMPS

2 pounds ramps

1 cup cider or red wine vinegar

2 tablespoons plus 2 teaspoons kosher salt

½ cup sugar

1 teaspoon mustard seeds

1 teaspoon fennel seeds

½ teaspoon black peppercorns

3 sprigs fresh thyme

2 bay leaves

4 whole cloves

One 1-quart canning jar, sterilized (see The Successful Cannery, page 58–59)

1. Trim the leaves from the tops of the ramps. (Rather than discard these greens, we suggest one reserve them for future use in omelettes, salads, or any other dish where chopped herbs might do.) Trim and discard the hairy bottoms from the ramps— these are suited only for the compost bin. Rinse the ramps well to remove any grit left behind.

2. Bring a pot of water to a boil over high heat. Tip in the ramps and cook until crisp-tender, 30 seconds to 1 minute, depending on the size of the ramps. Drain and rinse under a cold running tap to halt the cooking.

3. Stir together the remaining ingredients in the jar and add 1 cup water. Stir in the ramps. Screw the lid tightly upon the jar and chill for at least 2 hours or up to 3 months. The longer they stand, the more pickled the results.

Sweet Cucumber–Pepper Piccalilli

Should some great explorer ever stumble upon the fountain of youth made famous in the history of Herodotus, we suspect it will be tinged goldenrod with miraculous turmeric. Also nicknamed Indian saffron, both for its Asian pedigree and yellow coloring, this elixir of a spice is rumored to stave off all sorts of unpleasant maladies. Never ones to decline an opportunity for longevity, we like to slip a pinch of it into our pickle relish; its earthy, slightly peppery flavor is a pleasant foil to the condiment's sweetness. It also contributes a lovely hue. To avoid staining one's fingers, we advise delicate handling.

Spoon this relish over burgers, sausages, or sandwiches. We even like it atop the occasional pork chop.

PROVIDES APPROXIMATELY 1 PINT PICCALILLI

4 cups finely chopped, unwaxed kirby
   cucumbers, skin left on (1½ to 1¾ pounds)
1 cup finely chopped onion (about 1 medium)
½ cup finely chopped red bell pepper (about 1
   medium)
½ cup finely chopped green bell pepper (about
   1 medium)
1 tablespoon kosher salt
⅔ cup distilled white vinegar
½ cup firmly packed light brown sugar
1 teaspoon ground turmeric
½ teaspoon freshly milled black pepper
1 cinnamon stick
One 2-cup canning jar, sterilized (see The
   Successful Cannery, page 58–59)

1. Under a warm running tap, scrub the cucumbers well with a vegetable brush. Place the cucumbers, onion, and bell peppers in a large colander set over a bowl. Sprinkle 2½ teaspoons of the salt over the vegetables and toss to combine well. Let them stand for 3 hours, then discard any liquid in the bottom of the bowl.

2. Transfer the vegetables to a clean dish towel (we prefer towels cut from thin cloth, such as a flour sack). Bundle the vegetables tightly and squeeze them as strongly as one can manage, until no more liquid can be extracted.

3. In a small saucepan set over medium heat, stir together the vinegar and sugar until the sugar completely dissolves, 3 to 4 minutes. Stir in the vegetables, turmeric, black pepper, the remaining ½ teaspoon salt, and cinnamon stick; simmer until the liquid has evaporated and the relish is thick, 10 to 12 minutes.

4. Fill the jar with the hot relish and seal, if desired (see The Successful Cannery, page 58–59), or let cool to room temperature before chilling. Chilled, unprocessed relish will keep in an airtight container for up to 1 month.

Smoky Green Olive & Almond Relish

After one too many cocktail parties where the host dutifully passed about a platter of crackers thick with ho-hum black olive tapenade (which is so easy to mistake for caviar, leading to some disappointment), we decided it was high time a visionary took the matter in hand and transformed the ugly duckling into a swan. Our updated version is much accessorized—bright with green olives, smoky with African harissa, and crunchy with almonds. Delicious upon a Crisp Fired Cracker (page 73), we also serve it alongside Open-Flame Moroccan Merguez & Red Pepper Brochettes (page 172). One might even whisk it into a vinaigrette or toss it with potatoes or couscous.

PROVIDES APPROXIMATELY 1 PINT RELISH

2 cups pitted green olives, roughly chopped
½ cup finely chopped whole salted almonds
½ cup extra-virgin olive oil
1 tablespoon *harissa* paste (see Advisement),
   plus additional, to taste
Finely grated zest of 1 lemon

2 teaspoons freshly squeezed lemon juice, plus
additional, to taste

One 1-pint canning jar, sterilized (see The
Successful Cannery, page 58–59)

1. Tip the olives and almonds into the bowl of a food processor fitted with the blade attachment; chop finely. With the motor running, gradually add the oil and process until blended.

2. Scrape the relish into a bowl; stir in the *harissa*, lemon zest, and lemon juice. Taste and adjust the seasonings, if one desires. Spoon the relish into a jar and tightly screw on the lid. Chill for up to 2 weeks.

Advisement: A marvelous North African paste made of tomato, hot chiles, garlic, and spices, *harissa* has a fiery temperament suitable to its sun-baked origins. It is so tasty that we are hard-pressed to conceive of inappropriate uses; soups, salad dressings, marinades, dips, and sandwiches are all fair game. We suppose one must stop short of custards and delicate pastries, though the most adventurous among a party might enjoy a dab upon their s'mores.

Rhubarb Chutney

We have lovely childhood memories of clipping rhubarb stalks from the back garden and munching upon them raw and dipped in a bowl of sugar. In our mature years, we feel we've outgrown the need for unnecessary bellyaches, and now prefer the complex and worldly flavors of this piquant chutney, which is most excellent with Stone-Seared Cornish Game Hens with Bombay Spice (page 166). When foraging for rhubarb, do take care not to nibble upon the large, impressive-looking leaves, which are toxic, with or without extra sugar.

PROVIDES APPROXIMATELY 1 PINT CHUTNEY

½ cup finely chopped red onion

¼ teaspoon plus 1 pinch kosher salt

¾ cup firmly packed light brown sugar

¼ cup cider vinegar

1 tablespoon finely chopped, peeled fresh ginger

1 fat garlic clove, finely chopped

1 teaspoon ground cumin

1 teaspoon mustard seeds

½ teaspoon ground cinnamon

¼ teaspoon ground cloves

¼ teaspoon red pepper flakes

1½ pounds rhubarb, cut into ½-inch cubes
(about 4 cups)

¼ cup dried currants

One 1-pint canning jar, sterilized (see The
Successful Cannery, page 58–59)

1. In a saucepan over medium-low heat, combine the onion and the pinch of salt. Sweat the onions, stirring, until softened, about 3 minutes.

2. Stir in the sugar, vinegar, ginger, garlic, cumin, mustard seed, cinnamon, cloves, and pepper flakes. Bring to a simmer over medium-high heat and cook until the sugar has completely dissolved, about 2 minutes. Stir in the rhubarb and currants and simmer until the fruit is tender but not falling apart, 5 to 10 minutes.

3. Using a slotted spoon, remove the fruit, letting any excess juice drip back into the pan. Transfer the fruit to a bowl. Continue to simmer the juice until it is syrupy enough to thickly coat the back of a spoon. Pour the syrup over the rhubarb, making sure to scrape all of it from the sides and bottom of the pan. Stir in the remaining ¼ teaspoon salt. Transfer the hot mixture to the prepared jar. Seal, if desired (see The Successful Cannery, page 58–59), or let cool to room temperature, before chilling, tightly sealed, for up to 2 weeks.

Apricot & Cherry Chutney

It would be all too tempting to allow our friends and acquaintances to believe that our pairing of apricots and cherries is pure ingenuity, created in mad-scientist fashion during a spontaneous afternoon cooking frenzy. Alas, we confess that the truth is simply a matter of botanical research. The apricot and cherry are both members of the genus Prunus; therefore, they share a number of genetic traits, primarily deliciousness. Here we've combined them with spicy ginger and fragrant cardamom (which happen to share a family tree of their own) for an ancestral reunion of flavors. Serve this with Stone-Seared Cornish Game Hens with Bombay Spice (page 166) or grilled pork tenderloin.

PROVIDES APPROXIMATELY 1 PINT CHUTNEY

⅓ cup finely chopped onion

½ teaspoon plus 1 pinch kosher salt

½ cup firmly packed light brown sugar

¼ cup honey

¼ cup white wine vinegar

1 teaspoon finely chopped, peeled fresh ginger

1 garlic clove, finely chopped

1 teaspoon ground cardamom

½ teaspoon freshly milled black pepper

1¼ pounds firm, ripe apricots or peaches, pitted
  and cut into ¼-inch cubes (about 2½ cups)

½ cup dried tart cherries

One 1-pint canning jar, sterilized (see The
  Successful Cannery, page 58–59)

1. In a saucepan over medium-low heat, combine the onion and the pinch of salt. Sweat the onion, stirring, until softened, about 3 minutes.

2. Stir in the sugar, honey, vinegar, ginger, garlic, cardamom, and pepper. Bring to a simmer over medium-high heat and cook until the sugar has completely dissolved, about 2 minutes. Stir in the apricots and cherries and simmer until the apricots are tender but not completely falling apart, 5 to 10 minutes.

3. Using a slotted spoon, remove the fruit, letting any excess juice drip back into the pan. Transfer the fruit to a bowl. Continue to simmer the juice until it is syrupy enough to thickly coat the back of a spoon. Pour the syrup over the apricots, making sure to scrape all of it from the sides and bottom of the pan. Stir in the remaining ¼ teaspoon salt. Transfer the hot mixture to the prepared jar. Seal, if desired (see The Successful Cannery, pages 58–59), or let cool to room temperature before chilling, tightly sealed, for up to 2 weeks.

ASSORTED JAMS & MARMALADE

WHAT IS THE POINT OF FRESHLY MADE CAMP-
FIRE CRUMPETS OR SCONES WITHOUT A GEN-
EROUS SPREADING OF LOVELY HOMEMADE JAM
OR MARMALADE? Why, even a slice of fire-toasted
Crusty Walnut Bread (page 226) seems unnatu-
rally abstemious without a divine dollop of jammy
goodness. Therefore, we propose these remarkably
simple jam and marmalade recipes, which one may
deftly concoct on the stovetop. All yield small batches
of fruity toppings in order to take advantage of any
wild berries one may have found on recent foraging
outings. We think they are simply the tastiest way to
preserve one's fruit, whether it has come from some
happened-upon bramble or berry patch or from the
local organic produce purveyor.

Blackberry Jam

*This almost candylike jam makes an ideal partner for toast
or crackers. We also adore it spread on our pancakes in lieu
of maple syrup.*

PROVIDES 1 ½ CUPS JAM

2 cups blackberries (about 12 ounces)

1½ cups sugar

2 teaspoons freshly squeezed lemon juice

Pinch kosher salt

One 1-pint canning jar, sterilized (see The
Successful Cannery, page 58–59)

1. Put a small plate or saucer in one's refrigerator or icebox.

2. Place the berries in a medium, heavy-bottomed saucepan and smash them with a wooden spoon. Add the sugar, lemon juice, and salt and place the pan over medium-high heat, stirring constantly with a wooden spoon or heatproof spatula. Cook until the mixture bubbles and rises almost to the top of the pan (take care that it doesn't overflow—remove the pan from the heat and stir vigorously if a bubble-over is imminent), 5 minutes. Reduce the heat to medium low and allow the mixture to simmer until slightly thickened, 10 to 15 minutes. Because the jam will have the freshest flavor when it is least cooked, give it a test for doneness around minute 10 by dropping a spoonful onto the chilled plate or saucer. Using one's fingertip, push the edge of the jam puddle inward. If it wrinkles at all, the jam will set and it is time to take the pan off the heat.

3. Pour the hot jam into the prepared jar and seal. When the jam cools to room temperature, place it in the refrigerator for 6 to 8 hours to set.

Strawberry-Champagne Jam

This jam is positively bright and bubbly! We think the presence of a nice, dry Champagne enlivens the breakfast or teatime table and makes the gemlike berries effervescent.

PROVIDES 1 PINT JAM

2 pounds strawberries, rinsed, hulled, and
   roughly chopped

1 cup sugar

½ cup Champagne or other sparkling dry white
   wine

3 tablespoons freshly squeezed lemon juice

Large pinch kosher salt

One 1-pint canning jar, sterilized (see The
   Successful Cannery, page 58–59)

1. Put a small plate or saucer in one's refrigerator or icebox.
2. Place a medium, heavy-bottomed saucepan over medium-high heat. Add the berries, sugar, ¼ cup of the Champagne, lemon juice, and salt. Cook, stirring with a wooden spoon or a heatproof spatula, until the mixture bubbles and rises almost to the top of the pan (take care that it doesn't overflow—remove the pan from the heat and stir vigorously if a bubble-over is imminent), 5 minutes. Reduce the heat to medium low and allow the mixture to simmer until slightly thickened, 8 to 10 minutes. Because the jam will have the freshest flavor when it is least cooked give it a test for doneness around minute 10 by dropping a spoonful of jam onto the chilled plate or saucer. Using one's fingertip, push the edge of the jam puddle inward. If it wrinkles at all, the jam will set and it is time to take the pan off the heat.
3. Pour the remaining ¼ cup Champagne into the jam and stir to combine. Pour the hot jam into the prepared jar and seal. When the jam cools to room temperature, place it in the refrigerator for 6 to 8 hours to set.

Sevillian Orange & Honey Marmalade

Whenever one thinks of orange marmalade, one thinks of Paddington Bear—that darling storybook character would never advocate a journey without a pot of the good stuff for a proper teatime spread. Well, what if Paddington were joined in a cuppa by that other bear of fantasy, Pooh? Surely he would serve this orange-and-honey concoction as a neighborly nod to Pooh's abiding love of all things apiary. It does, however, make one wonder: what is with the imaginary ursine predilection for sweet condiments?

PROVIDES 1 ½ PINTS MARMALADE

5 Seville oranges (about 2½ pounds) or regular
   juice oranges (see Advisement), preferably
   organic, scrubbed and rinsed

1 lemon

½ cup sugar

¼ cup mild, light-colored honey, such as
   wildflower or clover

Pinch kosher salt

Three 1-cup canning jars, sterilized (see The
   Successful Cannery, page 58–59)

1. Put a small plate or saucer in one's refrigerator or icebox.
2. Thinly slice 2 of the oranges, peel and all, and cut the slices into very thin strips. Place the sliced oranges into a medium, heavy-bottomed saucepan. Juice the remaining 3 oranges and the lemon into a measuring cup, and top off the citrus juice with water to obtain 1 cup liquid. Add the liquid to the saucepan and place it over medium-high heat. Stir in the sugar, honey, and salt. Cook, stirring with a wooden spoon or a heatproof spatula, until the mixture bubbles and rises almost to the top of the pan (take care that it doesn't overflow—remove the pan from the heat and stir vigorously if a bubble-over is imminent), 5 minutes. Reduce the heat to medium low and allow the mixture to simmer

until slightly thickened, 15 to 20 minutes. Because the marmalade will have the freshest flavor when it is least cooked, give it a test for doneness around minute 15 by dropping a spoonful of jam onto the chilled plate or saucer. Using one's fingertip, push the edge of the jam puddle inward. If it wrinkles at all, the jam will set and it is time to take the pan off the heat.

3. Pour the hot marmalade into the prepared jar and seal. When it cools to room temperature, place it in the refrigerator for 6 to 8 hours to set.

Advisement: To make marmalade using regular oranges, it is necessary to strain the juice and discard the large and bitter pips, which are not found in oranges native to Seville.

the SUCCESSFUL CANNERY

We fancy ourselves capable of being excellent homesteaders, the sorts who might maintain a chicken coop alongside our wine cellar. But when it comes to canning, we are unapologetically lazy. The likelihood of us filling a hand trolley with crates of tomatoes for furious sauce making is slim. We are far more apt to create on a whim—to, say, simmer up a single jar of Strawberry-Champagne jam as a means of using up the dregs of last night's cru and this morning's basket of market-fresh berries. Our canning is often the result of inspiration, or even the result of whatever odds and ends our icebox tells us must come to a fitting conclusion; it is meant to last us as only as long as the meal at which we intend to serve it. Our kitchens tend toward an infinite, motley rotation of brined, potted, and jellied flavors.

All this is to say that when one is canning in such small batches, preparing a cleanish jar and storing the results for a day or two or even, really, a full week, is often more than sufficient. However, should one aspire to more—to a winter larder crammed with summer's bounty or a gift of bespoke pickles for every acquaintance—then matters are quite different, and precautions must be taken to avoid poisoning oneself or one's friends. It would be grand if the old skull and crossbones magically appeared upon a jar the moment a canned food had gone off, but unfortunately, one cannot always determine these things with a glance or whiff or taste.

We direct those endeavoring to become industrious and versatile canning practitioners to a canning and preserving manual, which will be filled with reams of advice. For those just wishing to avoid a spell of botulism, follow our tips for jar sterilization and sealing, which are suitable for very small batches of high-acid goods (including jams, marmalades, chutneys, tomato sauces, pickles, and relishes):

HOW TO STERILIZE ONE'S CANNING JARS

Method Number One:
Fill a large pot with water. Place clean jars into the water and bring them to a boil; let the water bubble for 10 minutes, remove the jars with tongs, and place them on a clean towel to dry and await filling. Since canning jars are made with glass, and we oppose having shards of glass in cookware, we recommend purchasing wire canning racks to hold the jars in place during boiling. One might use the contraption as a modern-looking fruit bowl during one's canning off-season. Alternatively, one can sterilize jars individually, though this will require some extra time. Simmer the lids separately in hot water, as boiling them might destroy the seal. Leave the bands at room temperature. The jars should still be warm when filled so that the hot preserved item does not shock the glass and break the jar, so time the sterilization process accordingly.

Method Number Two:
This technique is quick and simple, but is limited to those fortunate few who own the newfangled electric device known as a dishwasher. Place the jars and lids in the dishwasher, with or without detergent, and run the machine until it enters the drying cycle. At this point, transfer the jars and lids (which will be surprisingly hot, so don oven mitts or use tongs) to a clean towel, where they can wait to be filled. They should still be warm when filled so that the hot preserved item does not shock the glass and break the jar, so time their removal from the dishwasher accordingly.

HOW TO SEAL ONE'S CANNING JARS

To seal a jar, fill it with one's hot preserved item (be it jam, pickle, marmalade, or chutney), making certain to leave a headspace of about half an inch at the top of the jar. Wipe away any food residue from the top and screw the lid on tightly. Now one must seal the jar. To do so, either (1) process the jars in a canner (a special pot used in preserving) according to the manufacturer's instructions or (2) create a vacuum seal by turning the jar upside down for an hour or so until the center of the metal lid puffs ever so slightly; it should flex when pressed. Once sealed, store the item in a cool, dry, dark pantry or cellar for up to a year.

TRIO OF TART CITRUS CURDS

AS JAMES BEARD, THAT AUDACIOUS PIONEER OF AMERICAN COOKERY, ONCE OPINED, "A GOURMET WHO THINKS OF CALORIES IS LIKE A TART WHO LOOKS AT HER WATCH." We're still not certain of his meaning; perhaps it was an astute commentary on the way time seems to stop when one bites into a fluffy, hot crumpet that's been lavished with any one of these tart citrus curds. Grating a bit of zest into the madly piquant custard makes it all the more toothsome; one need only spread a heaping spoonful onto one's teatime delicacy to enjoy a pleasantly bracing sensation. The butter melted into the curd (maybe a smidge more than other, more commonplace, recipes call for) performs just the trick for a smooth, curd-eating experience.

Classic Lemon Curd

There's no need to improve upon perfection. When one's companions clamor for a tart curd, chances are, this is what they want.

PROVIDES ABOUT 1¼ CUPS CURD

3 large farm-fresh egg yolks
2 large farm-fresh eggs
½ cup sugar
¼ teaspoon kosher salt
Freshly squeezed juice of 4 lemons (about 1 cup)
4 tablespoons (½ stick) unsalted butter, cut into pieces
Finely grated zest of 4 lemons
1 small, clean canning jar

1. In a medium, heavy-bottomed saucepan, whisk together the yolks, eggs, sugar, and salt until thoroughly combined. Whisk in the lemon juice, until combined. Drop in the butter pieces.

2. Place the saucepan over a low heat and cook, stirring constantly with a heatproof spatula or wooden spoon, until the butter melts and the mixture has thickened enough to mound when pushed to one side with a spoon, 10 to 15 minutes. Keep a vigilant watch on the curd as it cooks. If it begins to bubble, take it off the heat and stir even more vigorously to prevent curdling. If the curd takes too long to thicken, raise the heat very slightly and continue to stir unceasingly.

3. When the curd has thickened, push it through a sieve into the bowl containing the lemon zest. Fold the zest into the curd with the spatula or wooden spoon. Place a sheet of plastic wrap directly on the surface of the curd to prevent a skin from forming as it cools. Once the curd cools to room temperature (and it will thicken even more as it does so), scrape it into an attractive jar and chill in the refrigerator for at least 4 hours before serving. If

stored in a tightly closed container, the curd should keep for up to 1 month.

Tangerine Variation: Fresh tangerine juice makes for a slighter sweeter and less tart taste sensation—all in all, a more delicately flavored curd. Substitute 3 tangerines for the lemons and carry on with the recipe.

Grapefruit Variation: Refreshingly tart, with more than a hint of bitterness, this is a curd for more advanced palates. Substitute 1 ruby red grapefruit for the lemons and carry on with the recipe.

various compounds of butter

WE DO NOT UNDERSTAND THOSE WHO ARE BASH-FUL WITH BUTTER. For us, this sweet, creamy nectar of the pasture is among life's surest pleasures. Whipped, creamed, browned, frozen, and scooped into the ice cream dish—there are few ways we've not indulged. If it did not seem profligate, we would no doubt turn to butter as shoe polish, as hand cream, as shaving soap. We once met a Parisian gentleman on a steamer from Dover to Calais who made his living as a professional taster in a butter factory. He was wonderfully bright of eye and pink of cheek, which one can attribute only to the consumption of great quantities of French butter.

Compound butter gives one further reason to partake. Unreasonably simple to produce for something so sublime, it consists of softened butter combined with a pinch of spice, a handful of chopped herbs and garlic, or any savory morsels lying about the kitchen. One can even add a nip of Cognac or a fragrant bit of citrus zest. The butter is then wrapped well and chilled (or even frozen) until called upon to serve as the coup de théâtre on a sizzling filet mignon or dainty tea sandwich (see page 114). Opposite are a few variations we enjoy, though this catalog is by no means exhaustive.

Coriander & Cracked Black Pepper Butter

In addition to using this for our smoked salmon tea sandwiches (page 114), we like to spread this butter under the skin of a whole chicken or goose before cooking, or toss it into a bowl of crisp-steamed haricots verts.

PROVIDES A GENEROUS ½ CUP BUTTER

1 teaspoon coriander seeds

½ cup (1 stick) unsalted butter, softened

2 teaspoons finely grated lemon zest

½ teaspoon freshly cracked black peppercorns

1 pinch kosher salt

1. In a small, dry skillet over medium-high heat, lightly toast the coriander until fragrant (about 30 seconds). If one is preparing this butter at camp, prepare a medium-high-heat fire, with the flames occasionally licking the grill grate.
2. Crush the coriander seeds in a small mortar and pestle. In a bowl, using one's clean hands (or a spoon if fastidious), mash together the butter, coriander, lemon zest, pepper, and salt until well combined.
3. Spoon the butter onto a large piece of plastic wrap or wax paper. Roll it into a log shape and chill or freeze it until ready to use.

Chive Butter

Spread this onto slices of bread for our radish sandwiches (page 117) or serve it with a sumptuous summer meal of boiled lobster and hot grilled potatoes. We also brush it upon our Classic Buttered Cob Corn (page 215)

PROVIDES A GENEROUS ¾ CUP BUTTER

½ cup (1 stick) unsalted butter, softened

6 tablespoons finely chopped chives

1 pinch kosher salt

1. In a bowl, using one's clean hands (or a spoon if fastidious), mash together the butter, chives, and salt until well combined.
2. Spoon the butter onto a large piece of plastic wrap or wax paper. Roll it into a log shape and chill or freeze it until ready to use.

Honey-Pecan Butter

The praline quality of this butter makes it lovely upon Spiced Currant Cream Scones (page 118) or tossed with hot, roasted pumpkin wedges.

PROVIDES A GENEROUS ¾ CUP BUTTER

½ cup (1 stick) unsalted butter, softened

¼ cup very finely chopped pecans

4 teaspoons honey

Pinch kosher salt

1. In a bowl, using one's clean hands (or a spoon if fastidious), mash together the butter, pecans, honey, and salt until well combined.
2. Spoon the butter onto a large piece of plastic wrap or wax paper. Roll it into a log shape and chill or freeze it until ready to use.

MAKE MERRY WITH DAIRY

PREPARE A TANGY YOGURT SAUCE, RICH MAY-
ONNAISE, OR CLOTTED CREAM IN THE STYLE OF
DEVON AT HOME TO BUNDLE UP AND TRANSPORT
WITH ONE'S FROSTILY CHILLED LARDER. When
these saucy treasures are produced upon reaching
one's destination, spirits will rise. And if one should
feel a pang of homesickness, a little dollop from the
dairy is bound to put all to right with a creamy taste
of home right in the midst of the wilderness.

Clotted Cream

*Devonshire, that unassuming county in England's coun-
tryside, has bequeathed a tremendous gift to the culinary
heritage of mankind: the cream tea. The sweetly fortify-
ing meal, taken by all villagers from Tess Durbeyfield to her
D'Urberville relations, consists of a warm scone, split in
twain and slathered with this marvelous thickened cream and
a smidgen of strawberry jam. It takes a bit of effort and rather
a good deal of heavy cream to yield but a partial cup of this
delight. If one intends to serve this freshly made clotted cream
on a daily basis, it is perhaps most practical that one should
become the proprietor of a Hardyesque dairy farm.*

PROVIDES ABOUT ⅓ CUP CLOTTED CREAM

2 cups (1 pint) heavy cream, unpasteurized or
   gently pasteurized

1 small, clean canning jar

1. Pour the cream into the top of a double boiler. Fill
the bottom with an inch or two of water. Alternatively, one can fill a medium pot with about 2
inches of water and place a heatproof bowl over the
water. Just take care that the water does not directly
touch the vessel holding the cream.

2. Place the pot over the lowest heat. Cook, without
disturbing, for 6 to 8 hours, until a thick, golden
crust forms and the cream is reduced by half. Do
not ever let the cream come to a boil. In fact, the
liquid should barely simmer.

3. Let the cream cool at room temperature for 2 hours,
then cover tightly and chill overnight. The next
morning, remove the thick clot. Discard the crusty
surface and spoon the butterlike cream into a bowl
(a thinner liquid will remain in the pan). Beat with
a fork until smooth and spreadable (add a drizzle
of cream from the pan if needed). Scoop the mixture into the jar and chill for up to 5 days. Reserve
any remaining cream (which is slightly thicker than
heavy cream) at the bottom of the pan for another
use (we like to drizzle ours over fresh berries).

MOCK CLOTTED CREAM

We recognize that there are times when one is in need of clotted cream but lacks the time required for its preparation. In sympathy with such a dilemma, we offer this recipe for a tasty sweetened replica of the traditional topping.

PROVIDES 1 ½ CUPS MOCK CLOTTED CREAM

1 cup heavy cream

½ cup mascarpone

1 teaspoon sugar

½ teaspoon vanilla extract

Place the cream, mascarpone, sugar, and vanilla in a bowl and whisk until soft peaks form. Use immediately or refrigerate in a tightly sealed jar for up to 1 week.

Advisement: One is unlikely to find unpasteurized or even gently pasteurized cream in a supermarket. However, it is often available for purchase in farmers' markets or finer shops that specialize in local provisions.

Zestful Yogurt Sauce

Keeping cool in the outdoors is not always simple. A cold compress of ice is liable to compromise one's icebox, and foraging a fan of palm fronds is an awful lot of work when one is already feeling sluggish. Stripping one's garments can quickly become an exercise in immodesty (not that we mind a show of skin, but one must consider the feelings of one's companions). This tangy yogurt sauce, various versions of which are popular throughout hot Middle Eastern climes, is wonderfully cooling and will fill hungry bellies to boot. Because we often serve this atop our Stone-Seared Cornish

Game Hens with Bombay Spice (page 166), we flavor it with complementary lime, but one could easily substitute lemon; we provide a variation to do so below. We also like it with Open-Flame Moroccan Merguez & Red Pepper Brochettes (page 172), Leg of Lamb Lavished with Mint (page 176), or even a simple jumble of grilled vegetables.

PROVIDES A GENEROUS 1 CUP SAUCE

1 cup plain Greek yogurt, or other strained yogurt

½ teaspoon finely grated lime zest

1½ teaspoons freshly squeezed lime juice, plus additional, to taste

1 garlic clove, finely chopped

¼ teaspoon kosher salt

2 tablespoons chopped fresh cilantro, or other favored herb, such as chive, dill, mint, basil, or parsley

In a bowl, whisk together the yogurt, lime zest and juice, garlic, and salt. Adjust the flavorings to taste. Transfer the sauce to an airtight container and chill until ready to use, up to 5 days. Just before serving, whisk in the chopped cilantro or other herb.

Lemon Variation: Substitute ½ teaspoon lemon zest for the lime zest and 1 tablespoon lemon juice for the lime juice, or more, if it pleases one's palate. Carry on with the recipe as directed.

Continental Mayonnaise

We see no reason why those charmed Europeans ought to enjoy all the good mayonnaise, while we across the pond must make do with clunky jars of white supermarket imitations. Homemade mayonnaise is bright, full-flavored, and pretty, with a rich buttery hue. Do not be frightened away by others' silly tales of difficulty or defeat. To avoid a mayonnaise that "breaks" (culinary jargon for the separation of oil and egg), always begin with room-temperature ingredients

MENU PLANNING ADVISEMENT

In the midst of a sunny picnic outing, merriment overtakes attentiveness to food, and after a round or two of competitive badminton, one discovers that the glossy surface of a carefully whisked mayonnaise has dulled to unappetizing congealed peaks. Oh, the trauma! Have we not all considered banishing its presence and that of other perishable foods from our culinary repertoire at times like this?

Such drastic measures need not be taken. One must merely abide by two guiding principles. The first, of course, is that one cannot leave out food on a sunny day to play badminton. Food, especially perishable meat, fish, or egg-based foods, must be consumed immediately or returned, tightly wrapped, to an icebox kept at 41 degrees. If one is going to have a leisurely meal of multiple courses and free-flowing wine, create a dining area sheltered from the sun's direct heat, perhaps in the shade of a tree, an overhanging rock, or a collection of parasols. We also like to keep platters of food loosely covered with a pretty length of lace, which is both attractive and practical.

The second principle regards menu planning. We are great champions of spontaneity, but when it comes to cookery in the outdoors, it must be executed reasonably. Plan to consume one's most perishable foods, such as seafood, meat, and mayonnaise, during the first day or so at camp. Reserve the long-lasting beans, grains, hardy vegetables, and preserved items for the tail end of an adventure. Vegetables and uncracked eggs, properly stored, should last the duration of a short journey. And by all means, limit one's beef tartare and sashimi to urban life—uncooked seafood, meat, or eggs should not be consumed outdoors, unless one happens to be camping in the parking area of an infirmary.

and be sure to whisk in the oil as slowly as possible. Should the mayonnaise break in spite of all efforts, do not hurl the bowl across the room in a frustrated tantrum. Calmly whisk another yolk in a small bowl, then slowly whisk it into the mayonnaise to bring it together. If this does not work, whisking in a teaspoon or two of warm water usually does the trick. This recipe is also the base for the aioli portion of our Bast's Grilled Sardines & Lemon Aioli Tartine (page 110).

PROVIDES A GENEROUS 1 CUP MAYONNAISE

2 large, farm-fresh egg yolks, at room temperature

½ teaspoon kosher salt

2 teaspoons freshly squeezed lemon juice, at room temperature

1 cup olive oil, or grapeseed oil, if one desires a lighter flavor, at room temperature

In a bowl, whisk together the yolks, salt, and lemon juice. Whisking constantly, drizzle in a steady thread of oil. Work slowly and do not let impatience overrun one's sensibilities. To pour in the oil is to ruin one's mayonnaise. Let the oil fall in drizzles or drops until it has been completely incorporated into the egg mixture and the mayonnaise is thick, creamy, and golden. Transfer the mayonnaise to an airtight container and chill for up to 5 days.

VINAIGRETTES

WE HAPPEN TO HAVE A WAY WITH VINAIGRETTES. SOME IN THE WORLD ARE BLESSED WITH A HEAD FOR FIGURES, SOME A KEEN EAR FOR FOREIGN LANGUAGE, OTHERS UNCANNY SUCCESS AT HORSE BETTING. Our forte is the salad bowl, or more precisely, the seasoning of it. Therefore, dear readers, we feel entirely free to insist that a vinaigrette never be an invisible lacquer applied hastily en route to the table. It is the jewel in the crown, *la pièce de résistance*, the hinge upon which the triumph of a salad swings. Treat it as one would any other culinary creation, and strive for a balanced flavor that complements the foods it accompanies.

If one is a novice at vinaigrette creation, begin with the basic formula of three parts oil to one part acid, such as vinegar or lemon juice. From there, one can tweak it, adding more vinegar, chopped nuts, minced shallot, or fresh herbs. If the salad is packed with flavorful ingredients, exercise restraint in the dressing; if the dressing is to be tossed with simple mixed greens, eclecticism might be in order. To start one off in the proper direction, we present a few of our most popular offerings.

Blood Orange & Date Vinaigrette

A sugared vinaigrette sometimes seems a form of vandalism upon the fresh ingredients of a salad, as if one has chosen to scrawl a mustache upon the Mona Lisa. This vinaigrette needs no artificial sweeteners, since the addition of candylike dried dates and tart-sweet blood orange juice enhance it naturally. We use this dressing in our Grilled Radicchio Insalata (page 200) and on Bast's Grilled Sardine & Lemon Aioli Tartine (page 110); season it with salt just before serving, in an amount commensurate with its paired dish.

PROVIDES ABOUT ⅔ CUP VINAIGRETTE

⅓ cup packed dried dates, pitted and finely chopped

Finely grated zest of 1 blood orange (about 1 teaspoon)

1½ tablespoons freshly squeezed blood orange juice

1½ tablespoons red wine vinegar

1 large garlic clove, finely chopped

⅓ cup extra-virgin olive oil

1 small, clean jar

In a bowl, whisk together the dates, orange zest and juice, vinegar, and garlic. Slowly whisk in the oil. Transfer to an airtight jar and chill for up to 1 week.

Moutarde Vinaigrette

A classic French concoction, this mustard vinaigrette is as open to mutation as a Darwinian monkey. Off the top of our heads, we might add fresh chopped herbs, crumbled bacon, minced garlic, or a dollop of mayonnaise, or substitute a bit of balsamic vinegar for the red wine. Toss it with our Orchard Pear & Watercress Salad (page 223) or our Warm Roasted Fingerling Potato Salad (page 213).

PROVIDES ABOUT ½ CUP VINAIGRETTE

2 tablespoons red wine vinegar

CELEBRATING THE NOBLE BEAR

As a matter of practicality, one must successfully avoid the bear whilst in the great outdoors. However, in humanity's collective unconscious, the bear may walk amongst us. The Vikings wore fiercely rough shirts woven from bear fur to prepare for battle. Not only was their burly attire fearsome, but surely the shirt's intense scratchiness propelled the Nordic warriors to theretofore unknown levels of bellicose fervor. The Welsh told epic stories of warriors and magicians who were rumored to be descended from ursine stock (King Arthur and Beowulf are two notable examples), prehistoric French *artistes* created cave paintings depicting bloody battles with the grizzly beasts, whilst Native American tribes paid tribute in dance and song to a gentle, more familial beast, whom they fondly refer to as Brother Bear.

In these modern times, bear worship seems to have fallen out of favor. Perhaps one's outdoor holiday may be an opportune moment to revive the tradition? And rather than celebrating the bear's fighting reputation, we suggest a tribute to his status as culinary tastemaker with a menu carefully chosen in honor of the noble beast. Settle in to a fireside meal of Pine-Smoked and Maple-Glazed Salmon (page 163), Crusty Walnut Bread (page 226) thickly spread with Sevillian Orange and Honey Marmalade (page 57), and a Scatterac cocktail (page 144) with Really Roasted Chestnuts (page 140) as a pre-bedtime snack. Then bundle up in one's bedroll and cozily hibernate, resting as peacefully as a bear in winter. And should one's sleep be disturbed before the appointed hour . . . put on one's scratchiest shirt and go bear-zerk.

1 tablespoon finely chopped shallot
½ teaspoon kosher salt
1 tablespoon the Colonel's Mustard (page 49) or
    Dijon mustard
3 tablespoons extra-virgin olive oil
Freshly milled black pepper, to taste
1 small, clean jar

In a bowl, whisk together the vinegar, shallot, and salt. Whisk in the mustard. Whisking constantly, slowly drizzle in the oil until fully incorporated. Season with black pepper. If the vinaigrette seems too thick, thin it with a teaspoon or so of warm water until it reaches one's ideal consistency. Transfer to an airtight jar and chill for up to 1 week.

Sprightly Lemon Vinaigrette

Lemon and oil is a magical marriage that stumps our companions whenever we serve it. "Sumac?" they guess. "Pickled plum? Verjus?" Beautiful in its simplicity, this vinaigrette is our most-oft served, as it is the one most likely to improve any salad it meets.

PROVIDES ABOUT 1 CUP VINAIGRETTE
2 garlic cloves, finely chopped
3 to 4 tablespoons freshly squeezed lemon
    juice, to taste
Kosher salt, to taste
Freshly milled black pepper, to taste
¾ cup extra-virgin olive oil
1 small, clean jar

In a bowl, whisk together the garlic, lemon juice, salt, and pepper. Whisk in the oil. Transfer to an airtight jar and screw tightly shut. Chill for up to 1 week.

VENI, VIDI, VINO

WE CAME, WE SAW, WE MADE WINE VINEGAR

We deplore waste in our kitchens, and naturally, we especially deplore the wasting of wine and spirits. Yet, invariably, several mornings after some high-spirited dinner party, we stumble upon a half-drunk bottle or two of best-quality Cabernet, abandoned upon the mantel by some absentminded guest (or host). At that point, we'd rather not indulge in a mouth-puckering swallow, but we wouldn't dream of insulting a vintner by allowing the drainpipe to guzzle his labors. The solution is vinegar.

Homemade vinegar has a crisper, more complex flavor than the purchased variety, but can be used just the same, in salad dressings, sauces, and pickles. The most complicated part of vinegar-making is securing the vinegar "mother," or starter, a whitish, leathery-looking slab of healthy bacteria that will transform one's old wine into condiment extraordinaire. Starters are easily procured from beer and winemaking stores, or, if one has the luck to have a vinegar-making friend, one might pinch a layer from their mother instead. Beyond that, the process requires only a large earthenware crock with a spigot (we aim for approximately one gallon in size so that we can make a good deal of vinegar), cheesecloth, wine, and a bit of patience.

To proceed, pour the wine into the crock. We prefer the flavor of young, fruity wines, but really any will do, and frankly, we mix and match with whatever turns up (though we do have the sense to separate white from red). Next, drop in the mother. Top it off with half as much water as there is wine (for example, add 1 cup water to 2 cups wine). Give the whole thing a good stir, cover it with a bound layer of cheesecloth, and place it in a warm spot away from direct sunlight.

After two weeks, begin checking on the vinegar, using one's handy senses of taste and smell. If is to one's liking, the vinegar is ready. If not, continue to let it stand, giving it a gentle shake from time to time, for up to two or three months, by which time one's wine should be thoroughly vinegared.

At this point, we generally transfer the completed vinegar to tightly covered jars, leaving some in the pot so that we can continue to top it off with wine and perpetuate the vinegar cycle ad infinitum. Once one's initial batch is complete, additional vinegar should only take a week or so to ferment.

Potted Spreads

WE HIGHLY ENDORSE MANOR-HOUSE LIVING. The benefits are tremendous: maids to tidy, butlers to answer bells, and cooks to maintain one's larder, which is hopefully stocked with tasty potted spreads.

An age-old English tradition (even British sailors munched on potted peas at sea), potted spreads involve sealing perishable ingredients, like venison or trout, with a layer of butter. Done properly, the technique keeps rot-inclined foods fresh quite a bit longer than the usual several days.

Classic potted spreads entail the use of clarified butter, which has a longer shelf life than regular butter. This fussy step is not necessary if one just wants a small snack a few days into a wilderness adventure, but for those setting off on lengthy treks, we have provided instructions for clarifying one's own butter (page 75). At any rate, clarified butter has a much higher smoke point than regular butter (meaning its oils don't turn into acrid smoke until exposed to greater temperatures), making it a wise choice for sautéing over an open flame.

As with all preserving techniques, it is of the utmost importance that one's equipment and workspace remain pristine in order to avoid food-borne illness, so do make sure one's scullery maid takes extra care on potting days.

Potted Crab with Lemon

When one's crab traps are full to bursting with freshly caught crustaceans, one ought to preserve them by using this potted crab recipe. Do remember to set free any selkies that may be entangled in one's snare, as they simply don't taste very nice—even when dressed with butter and lemon.

PROVIDES ABOUT 1 ½ CUPS SPREAD

8 ounces cooked crabmeat

2 tablespoons chopped fresh chives

1 teaspoon grated zest of lemon (about 2 lemons)

2 teaspoons freshly squeezed lemon juice, plus additional, to taste

¼ teaspoon kosher salt

¼ teaspoon freshly milled black pepper

Pinch cayenne pepper

½ cup melted unsalted butter or Clarified Butter (see box, page 75)

Chive blossoms, for garnish, optional

Crisp Fired Crackers (page 73) or crusty bread, for serving

1. In a bowl, combine the crab, 1½ tablespoons of the chives, lemon zest and juice, salt, black pepper, and cayenne. Pour 3 tablespoons melted butter over the crab and mix well. Transfer the mixture to one medium crock or several individual crocks.

2. Mix the remaining chives into the remaining butter. Pour an even layer of the butter over the crab mixture, like sealing wax. Cover the spread and chill it for at least 1 hours and up to 1 week. Let it come to room temperature before serving, garnished with chive blossoms, if you wish, and accompanied by crackers or bread.

Potted Spiced Pork

This is a favorite of all our fireside companions, most especially when the weather turns blustery. Be sure to serve with strong mustard, piquant cornichons, and a firkin or so of good ale.

PROVIDES ABOUT 3 CUPS SPREAD

1½ pounds boneless pork butt, cut into 1-inch cubes

⅓ cup brandy

1½ teaspoons freshly milled black pepper

1¼ teaspoons kosher salt

¾ teaspoon whole coriander seeds, crushed
   lightly with the back of a knife

¼ teaspoon ground allspice

4 garlic cloves, finely chopped

2 bay leaves

½ pound fatback or lard (easily procured from
   one's butcher), cut into ¼-inch cubes

1 small onion, finely chopped

3 sprigs fresh thyme

Cornichons, for serving

Strong mustard, for serving

Crisp Fired Crackers (page 73) or crusty bread,
   for serving

1. In a large bowl, combine the meat, brandy, pepper, salt, coriander, allspice, garlic, and bay leaves. Cover tightly and chill for at least 1 hour or overnight, then let stand at room temperature for 30 minutes.

2. Meanwhile, preheat one's oven to 300 degrees.

3. Lift the meat and bay leaves from the marinade and transfer them to a Dutch oven. Stir the fatback and onion into the meat; pour ½ cup water over the mixture and drop in the thyme. Cover the pot and let the meat braise slowly until it is meltingly tender and most of the watery liquid has evaporated (with only rendered fat remaining), 3½ to 4 hours. If any liquid remains, simmer gently, uncovered, on the stovetop until evaporated; discard the thyme and bay leaves.

4. Using a slotted spoon, transfer the meat and any bits of partially rendered fatback to the bowl of a mixer fitted with a paddle attachment. Mix on low speed until meat is shredded. (Although we find it a bit unnecessarily tedious, one might also perform this step with a fork.) Slowly beat in all but ¼ cup of the pork fat left behind in the bottom of the Dutch oven.

5. Spoon the potted pork into one medium crock or several individual crocks. Spoon the reserved ¼ cup fat over the pork in an even layer, like sealing wax. Let cool to room temperature, then cover tightly and chill for at least 4 hours and up to a weeks (we have on occasion even frozen this for up to 3 months). Let sit at room temperature for 1 hour before serving with cornichons, mustard, and crackers or crusty bread.

Potted Cheddar Huntsman Spread

The thrill of the hunt lies in its active and all-abiding mystery. One never knows if one's quarry will be won or lost, and is buffeted about by the shifting winds of fortune. If one does not wish to place all one's hopes for filling an empty belly on an elusive stag, pheasant, rabbit (or perhaps snipe?), bring along a jar of this robustly flavored cheese spread. With pervasively aromatic ingredients such as aged cheddar, Stilton, shallot, and mustard, if one's arrow fails to fell its intended target, perhaps one's breath will.

PROVIDES ABOUT 1½ CUPS SPREAD

8 ounces aged Cheddar cheese, cut into ¼-inch
   cubes (about 2 cups), at room temperature

2 tablespoons port

3 tablespoons unsalted butter, at room
   temperature

2 teaspoons Dijon mustard

¼ teaspoon freshly milled black pepper

2 tablespoons chopped shallot

Clarified butter, optional (for longer storage) (page 75)

3 ounces crumbled Stilton cheese, for serving, optional

Fresh chopped parsley, for garnish

Crisp Fired Crackers (below) or crusty bread, for serving

Fresh fruit, such as grapes, sliced apple or pear, or figs, for serving

1. In the bowl of a food processor fitted with the blade attachment, combine the cheese, port, butter, mustard, and pepper. Blend until the mixture is smooth, stopping once or twice to scrape down the sides of the bowl. Add the shallot and pulse until just blended. Transfer the spread to one medium crock or several individual crocks. Chilled as is, it will keep for up to 5 days; alternatively, one can top the spread with an ⅛-inch layer of clarified butter so it will keep for up to 2 weeks.

2. Allow the spread to come to room temperature and serve topped with crumbled Stilton and parsley, surrounded by a ring of crackers or bread and fruit.

Crisp Fired Crackers

It is an established notion that the raison d'être of a cracker is to provide a delicate conveyance for a dip, spread, or other savory morsel—and these crackers certainly accomplish that task with a decisive crunch. But we eschew any idea that presumes only one reason for existence. Such a confining philosophy has echoes of dear Jean-Paul Sartre. How he would go on with all his "one is still what one is going to cease to be and already what one is going to become. One lives one death, dies one's life." His point being, obviously, that a cracker ought to taste good all on its own, regardless of whatever topping fate has dealt it. Its essential crackeriness is not only paramount, it is inescapable. We were only successful at distracting Jean-Paul from his slightly morose philosophizing by stuffing his gob with these delightfully crisp crackers. In addition to their eminently worthy flavor, they are simple to prepare.

MAKES ABOUT 2½ DOZEN CRACKERS

½ cup whole wheat flour

¼ cup plus 2 tablespoons coarse cornmeal

½ teaspoon kosher salt

2 tablespoons extra-virgin olive oil

1. In a large bowl or in the bowl of an electric mixer, whisk together the whole wheat flour, cornmeal, and salt to evenly combine. Pour in the olive oil and ¼ cup water and mix with the hook attachment until the dough comes together in a ball with a tacky consistency—dry, but neither too crumbly nor too stiff. Add 1 to 2 tablespoons more water if necessary to achieve this texture. Alternatively, the dough can be mixed with a spoon, then kneaded by hand on a surface lightly sprinkled with flour. Wrap the dough in plastic and refrigerate for 30 minutes or up to 3 days.

2. Preheat the oven to 450 degrees. Divide the dough into 4 squares. Lightly sprinkle a flat surface with flour and roll each square out to a thickness of about ⅛ inch. Use a knife to cut out crackers into 2-by-1-inch rectangles. Arrange the rectangles on baking sheets (it will be necessary to bake in batches) and bake until the crackers are crisp and the edges are dark brown, 8 to 10 minutes. Store the crackers in an airtight container for up to 2 weeks.

SEASONED SALTS

(INCLUDING SMELLING SALTS FOR THE FAINT OF HEART)

LIKE PROUST'S MADELEINE, A WHIFF OF SEASONED SALT CAN PROVE MOST EVOCATIVE, RECALLING A HAPPY SEASIDE DINNER IN NICE OR A PICNIC LUNCH IN THE CHINESE IMPERIAL GARDENS. (The smelling salts, unfortunately, remind us only of being brought 'round by a kindly British constable after a wretched purse-snatching incident in Covent Gardens. Nevertheless, we include a recipe for it here, as a vial of the stuff does seem useful when traveling with nervous or swoon-inclined companions.)

Although well-meaning physicians advise abstemiousness with regard to salt, we do hope that one will throw caution to the wind and relish the following favorites—we went to great lengths to secure them on our travels. The mixtures are so flavorful that a generous pinch yields excellent results, whether sprinkled upon meat, fish, or grilled vegetables. We even like them tossed into our Spice Market Popcorn (page 137).

French Sel Fou

This recipe, swiped from the apron of a Provençal gardener while he puttered about his shed, is just one of the many "crazy salt" variations encountered in French kitchens. We love it upon roast chicken and fried potatoes.

PROVIDES ABOUT ¾ CUP SALT

2 tablespoons red or black peppercorns

1 tablespoon coriander seeds

6 tablespoons coarse sea salt

1 tablespoon dried thyme

1 teaspoon sweet paprika

Toast the peppercorns and coriander in a dry skillet over a medium-low heat until fragrant, less than 1 minute. Transfer the spices to a bowl with the salt and thyme. Either toss the entire batch into a food processor to blend, or blend it in batches in a spice grinder. Stir in the paprika. Store in an airtight container for up to 1 year.

Italian Salamoia

It took several bottles of Dolcetto, a midnight serenade, and a drunken betrothal to wrench this traditional Italian recipe from the Bolognese chef who introduced it to us, sprinkled over grilled branzino smothered with capers, tomatoes, and olives. We find the results well worth the price paid and believe it would be equally sublime on pork or roasted vegetables.

PROVIDES ABOUT 1 CUP SALT

Finely grated zest of 1 lemon

6 tablespoons fresh rosemary leaves

¼ cup fresh sage leaves, roughly chopped

6 tablespoons coarse sea salt

1 garlic clove, coarsely chopped

Large pinch red pepper flakes

Lay the zest out on a paper towel to dry for 30 minutes or so. Wash the rosemary and sage leaves and pat them completely dry. Transfer the zest, herbs, salt, garlic, and pepper flakes to a food processor and pulse until well blended (the mixture will be slightly moist). Transfer to an airtight container for up to 6 months.

Chinese Wok Salt

Should one ever require a clever and furtive means of spiriting a recipe from an emperor's palace, we cheerfully report that slipping it into a rolled-up scroll will yield great success. This salt is particularly delectable over roast squab or shrimp.

PROVIDES ABOUT ¾ CUP SALT

¼ cup Sichuan peppercorns

1½ tablespoons black peppercorns

⅓ cup coarse sea salt

2 tablespoons sesame seeds, toasted

Combine the peppercorns in a dry wok or heavy skillet. Cook over a medium-low heat, shaking the pan until they are fragrant and lightly colored. Either toss all of the salt and the peppercorns into a food processor to blend, or blend in batches in a spice grinder. Stir in the sesame seeds. Store in an airtight container for up to 6 months.

Smelling Salts

In the past, the production of smelling salts (which curiously contained no salt) involved the distillation of deer horns and hooves into an overpowering solution of ammonia. We're relieved it has since fallen out of favor, for we'd much rather our archer's arrow aim at a bullseye than a beast. Commercial smelling salts still contain ammonia, but it strikes us as an unnecessarily harsh means of rousing the unconscious. We prefer to pack a sachet of our soothing (but sufficiently

sharp) blend of salt and essential oils, certain to settle jangling nerves, ease headaches, and revive the dizzy.

PROVIDES ABOUT 1 CUP SALT

¾ cup Epsom salt

½ cup coarse sea salt

2 to 4 drops eucalyptus essential oil, as desired

2 to 4 drops peppermint essential oil, as desired

2 to 4 drops lemongrass essential oil, as desired

In a large mixing bowl, stir together the salts. Stir in the essential oils, a little at a time, until one reaches an intensity of scent that is certain to awake one from a dead faint. Be sure to stir it enough that the oils sufficiently coat the salts. Divvy the salt among squares of linen or lace and tie tightly with a smart-looking silken ribbon. Keep tucked in a handy place until needed.

CLARIFIED BUTTER

To clarify butter, one heats butter over a flame until the milk solids and water separate from the butterfat, or oils.

Cut 1 cup (2 sticks) unsalted butter into cubes. Heat it in a skillet over a medium-low heat. Skim off any foam that rises to the surface. By the time one is finished skimming, the milk solids will likely have sunk to the bottom of the pan. Check to see that this is so. At this point, all that remains on top is a clear, straw-colored layer of butterfat. Carefully pour this off into a clean jar, leaving the milk solids clinging to the pan's bottom. If stored tightly covered and chilled, the butter will keep for approximately 1 month. This batch yields 1½ cups clarified butter.

CONFECTIONERY SYRUPS FOR TEAS & TIPPLES

ON OUR TRAVELS WE HAVE HAD AMPLE OPPORTU-NITY TO MAKE THE ACQUAINTANCE OF A BARMAN OR TWO. And we were pleased to be indoctrinated into some of the privileged secrets of their potable profession. Through careful study of the beverage arts, we have come away with an avid appreciation of confectionery syrup. The syrup (lightly cooked sugar water with an infusion of enticing flavor) is easy to prepare and lends sundry drinks a lightness of flavor that is close to unbearable.

Meyer Lemon Limoncello

Unfortunately, one cannot always pop off to the Amalfi coast anytime a craving strikes for a bit of sea and sun, or a jaunt upon a vintage motorbike. This sunnily sweet, citrus-infused liqueur will warm one through and give entirely new meaning to the phrase la dolce vita. For extreme thrill seekers, we recommend the mandarin and ginger variations.

PROVIDES 1 BOTTLE TO SERVE VARIED NUMBERS,
DEPENDING ON TOLERANCE LEVELS
10 Meyer lemons (approximately 2½ pounds),
    preferably organic
One 750-milliliter bottle vodka
2½ cups sugar
One 2-quart canning jar, sterilized (see The
    Successful Cannery, page 58–59)

1. Using a vegetable peeler or paring knife, peel the zest from the lemons in long strips, leaving as much of the bitter white pith behind as possible. One should ultimately aim for no pith at all, as it will embitter one's spirits (the alcohol, although we imagine one would also be left emotionally bereft by a failed batch). With this in mind, use a paring knife to trim away any remainder of pith from the zest.

2. Drop the zest into the jar; pour the vodka over them. Screw lids upon the jars and let stand at room temperature for 1 week or longer—if one can bear it. Some wait for up to a full month; the longer the mixture sits, the more infused the alcohol becomes. Shake the jar every couple of days or so.

3. Strain the vodka into a bowl, then pour it back through the zest-filled strainer, pressing it down upon the solids with the back of a spoon to release any additional flavor. Discard the zest and return the vodka to the jar.

4. In a small saucepan, combine the sugar with 2½ cups water. Simmer over a medium heat until the sugar dissolves. Let the syrup cool completely, then

stir it into the vodka. Screw the lid tightly upon the jar and chill overnight. At this point it can be consumed, but will probably taste immature, much like a young wine. We try to age our limoncello for at least a fortnight before drinking it, though if one pilfers a glass or two beforehand, we say no harm done. It can be aged and stored in the freezer or refrigerator and will last for 1 year or more. Serve in cold, frosty aperitif glasses.

Mandarino Variation: Substitute the zest of 10 organic mandarin oranges (approximately 2 pounds) for the lemon zest.

Zenzerino Variation: Substitute the zest of 6 organic navel oranges (approximately 3 pounds) and ½ pound peeled and finely grated fresh ginger for the lemon zest.

Lemon Confectionery Syrup

Making a confectionery syrup out of one's tree-ripened lemons is the most expedient way to capture their tart sweetness just at the pinnacle of their glory.

PROVIDES ABOUT 1¼ CUPS SYRUP

2 lemons

1 cup sugar

Use a Microplane to finely grate the zest from both lemons into a medium, heavy-bottomed saucepan. Extract the juice from the lemons. Place a sieve over the pan and pour the lemon juice through it. Add the sugar and 1 cup water to the pan and place it over a medium heat. Cook, stirring occasionally, until the sugar dissolves and bubbles appear (there is no need to bring the liquid to a full boil). Store the liquid refrigerated or at room temperature in a jar with a tightly fitting lid for up to 3 months.

Mint Confectionery Syrup

This syrup makes an elegantly clear mint concoction, suitable for flavoring a variety of beverages from lemonade to juleps.

PROVIDES ABOUT 1¼ CUPS SYRUP

1 cup sugar

¼ cup fresh mint leaves

Place the sugar and 1 cup water in a medium, heavy-bottomed saucepan over a medium heat. Cook, stirring occasionally, until the sugar dissolves and bubbles appear (there is no need to bring the liquid to a full boil). Stir in the mint leaves and cover the pan. Let it sit at room temperature for at least 1 hour and up to 3 hours, depending on the desired mintiness. Strain the syrup into a jar with a tightly fitting lid and store refrigerated or at room temperature for up to 3 months.

Basil Syrup Variation: Basil is so happily abundant in the days of summer. Preserve it in this fashion to make beverages of sophistication throughout the calendar year. Substitute basil leaves for the mint and carry on with the recipe.

Chamomile Syrup Variation: Find this pleasant plant (there are those who call it a weed, the silly things) on one's nature walk or in the stalls of the neighborhood farmers' market. Some may brew it into a tea, but we find this confectionery so much more festive. Substitute 2 bunches fresh chamomile, roots trimmed and rinsed well, for the mint and carry on with the recipe.

Ginger Syrup Variation: Ginger-infused syrup makes an ideal flavoring for any tea, tonic, or spirit that wants a soupçon of island flavor. Substitute one 4-inch piece fresh ginger, peeled and chopped, for the mint and carry on with the recipe.

A MODICUM OF STRATEGY MAY BE SO SWEET

EVERY SPECTACULAR CAMPFIRE DESERVES A SPECTACULAR FINISH—AND SOMETIMES THAT REQUIRES TAKING A LITTLE TIME IN ONE'S HOME KITCHEN TO PROVISION THE OUTDOOR DESSERT MENU. The custard base for ice cream is easily prepared before expedition's onset and quickly churned at the campsite. The same holds true for flaky, buttery piecrust, which can be used for sweet or savory dishes baked in the blaze. And at the apex of outdoor gustatory achievement, s'mores can be crafted from homemade graham crackers and marshmallows. Campfire guests are sure to be dazzled by one's clever stratagem. It is simply astounding what a teensy bit of forethought and a smidgeon of effort may accomplish.

Melissa Clark's Pie Crust Unparalleled

It is a truism that bons vivants are not born but made. We did not begin as the two adventurous ambassadors of campfire cookery who penned these pages. We were fortunate to be guided (however unwittingly) to this novel niche by our friend and mentor, the culinary chronicler nonpareil, Melissa Clark.

Melissa has graciously allowed us to use her recipe for flaky pie crust, which we happen to think has no equal anywhere pie is served. When made correctly (and by that we mean with a gentle touch, both whilst mixing the dough and rolling it out), it is as light and buttery a pastry as ever one might wish to experience. A crust that all other crusts will undoubtedly be compared to—although they will fall short. This, dear readers, is the sole flaky pie crust recipe one will ever need.

PROVIDES ONE 10-INCH PIE CRUST

1¼ cups all-purpose flour

¼ teaspoon kosher salt

10 tablespoons (1¼ sticks) unsalted butter, chilled and cut into pieces

2 to 5 tablespoons ice water

1. In a food processor or large mixing bowl, combine the flour and salt. If using a food processor, drop in the butter pieces and pulse until the mixture forms chickpea-size crumbs. If mixing by hand, cut the butter into the flour using a pastry cutter or fork until the desired texture is reached. Mix the ice water into the dough 1 tablespoon at a time, until the dough is just moist enough to hold together. Wrap the dough in plastic wrap and refrigerate it for at least 1 hour and up to 2 days.

2. Place the dough between 2 large sheets of plastic wrap and set it on a hard surface. Roll it into a 10-inch circle about ¼ inch thick. Gently fold the still-wrapped dough into a half-circle and freeze until needed for up to 6 months.

Sylvester Graham's Crackers

This style of biscuity-sweet cracker was invented by the nineteenth-century Presbyterian minister Sylvester Graham. In addition to cracker-inventing, the good minister is notable for inspiring a utopian community where members eschewed all alcohol, white flour, red meat, and spices. Sorry, did we say utopian community? We meant ghastly dystopian hellscape.

In any event, his crackers are simply lovely. Naturally, they are nothing short of divine when making s'mores (page 247) around the campfire, they are equally glorious when spread with Strawberry-Champagne Jam (page 57) or tart Classic Lemon Curd (page 60), and store-bought grahams really can't hold a candle to the crackers one can make at home. But Mr. Graham's acolytes beware: We do include a bit of cinnamon spice in this recipe. And we recommend a beverage pairing of Tree Toddy (page 289), Gent's Rosemary Gin Fizz (page 146), or, at the minimum, a proper cup of tea (page 127). Sylvester would not be amused.

MAKES ABOUT 2½ DOZEN CRACKERS

1 cup (2 sticks) unsalted butter

¼ cup firmly packed dark brown sugar

¼ cup granulated sugar

¼ cup mild, light-colored honey, such as clover
  or wildflower

1½ cup graham or whole wheat flour

1 cup all-purpose flour

1 teaspoon kosher salt

½ teaspoon ground cinnamon

1. In the bowl of an electric mixer, cream the butter, sugars, and honey until smooth. In a medium bowl, combine the flours, salt, and cinnamon. Add the dry ingredients to the mixer bowl and beat until the dough just comes together.

2. Wrap the dough in plastic wrap and pat it into a disk. Chill the dough in the refrigerator for at least 1 hour and up to 2 days.

3. Preheat the oven to 325 degrees. Lightly grease 2 baking sheets or line them with parchment paper.

4. Turn the dough out onto a lightly floured surface, and roll it into a 12-inch square. Use a knife to cut the dough into 2-inch squares. Carefully transfer the squares to the prepared baking sheets, spacing them evenly apart, and prick them all over with a fork. Bake until golden brown, 15 to 18 minutes. Store in an airtight container at room temperature for up to 1 week.

Honeyed Marshmallows

A long time ago, in a land not so very far away, the marshmallow was made from the sap of the marshmallow plant, a natural marvel with an astounding medicinal appeal (see box page 83), but a flavor rather similar to a pot of glue. Small wonder that apothecaries began to sweeten it for the sake of palatability. As is usually the case with Progress, the squishy confection soon became mass-produced, and today's interpretations rely heavily on icky sweeteners like corn syrup and other ingredients with chemical designations too rife to name. The ultimate cost of improving this beloved candy's flavor has been, to put it bluntly, the rotting of one's innards.

Considering that the marshmallow is a key component of outdoor merrymaking, vital to the preparation of s'mores (page 246) and Minty Chocolat Chaud (page 125), not to mention that it is perfectly delectable on its own, we endeavored to create a better one—slightly more wholesome and of a more mouth-pleasingly chewy texture. After careful consideration, we hit upon the idea of employing honey to flavor these poufy dainties. It adds just the sort of old-fashioned sweetness that marshmallows of the jet-puffed variety lack.

MAKES ABOUT 2 DOZEN MARSHMALLOWS

½ cup confectioners' sugar, plus additional for
  sprinkling if desired

3 envelopes unflavored gelatin (about 3
  tablespoons)

Orienteering
OR HOW TO MAKE ONE'S VERY OWN COMPASS

Losing oneself is not always such a terrible thing. We heartily approve of getting lost in a fanciful reverie, or the collected works of Lord Byron, or in the eyes of a handsome companion. Even losing one's temper can be a productive activity under proper circumstances. Losing oneself in the outdoors, however, is not recommended. For although one might think getting lost is the spirited way of a good adventurer, once turned about in a thicket or tangled in jungle vines, one wishes to be armed with more than wits to guide the way home.

The compass is a most handy orienteering tool and has a long, complicated history, and to understand how it works requires more than a cursory comprehension of physics and nautical navigation, both of which we lack. Suffice it to say that it has been serving civilization since at least the second century, when the clever Chinese developed a rudimentary model to help dynastic decorators organize rooms and cities in the feng shui way. Between then and now, it has been taken up by Medieval mariners, astronomers, miners, spelunkers, Ernest Shackleton, and, with less cheerful results, Amelia Earhart. Many sorts of compasses exist, but all operate upon the same principle: A needle is magnetized (traditionally upon a lodestone, a naturally magnetic rock) and then placed upon a nearly frictionless surface so that it can spin dizzily about until properly aligned with the earth's magnetic field, which runs along a north-south axis.

Making one's own compass in the wild is easy—and while we adore the look of a shiny, well-crafted brass compass, one needn't go to such expense when a pop into a haberdashery for a basic sewing needle will serve the same purpose.* So should one look up one day from an innocent hike to find unfamiliar surroundings, the howling of hungry coyotes, and the toasty fire of camp a long way off, proceed as follows:

1. Remove the trusty needle from one's pocket.

2. Rub the needle fifteen to twenty times in one direction across a small magnet, lodestone, or even the fabric of one's own clothing. Silk works particularly well for this; we have even used our stockings upon occasion, to great success.

3. Plunge the needle's eye into the cork from an emptied wine bottle, emptying the wine into one's gullet if necessary. Alternatively, pluck a smooth, glossy leaf from a tree and place the needle upon it.

4. Pour out an inch or so of water from one's canteen into an empty coconut shell or other bowl-shaped vessel. Gently lay the corked needle or leaf bearing the needle upon the surface of the water.

5. Wait a moment while the needle flounders to orient and then settle itself. Regard the needle. The sharp, slender tip will be pointing south if one is in the northern hemisphere and north if one is below the Equator. Proceed in the direction of camp.

---

* We must note that the homemade compass will not work nearly as well for the Arctic explorers among us. The pull of the magnetic field is most reliable nearest the earth's equator; once one reaches the poles, a more sophisticated instrument is required. We also do not recommend using a homemade compass in a moving vehicle, as the needle will become disoriented, which is the precise opposite of the desired effect.

2 cups granulated sugar

¼ cup mild, light-colored honey such as orange
  blossom or clover

2 large farm-fresh egg whites

¼ teaspoon kosher salt

1 tablespoon vanilla extract

1. Line a 9-by-13-inch baking dish with foil, smoothing the foil into the dish so there are no wrinkles to leave an unsightly pattern on the marshmallows. Sift ¼ cup of confectioners' sugar into the bottom of the dish.

2. Place the gelatin in 1 cup cold water to bloom. Place a candy thermometer in a saucepan over a medium heat; cook the granulated sugar, honey, and ½ cup water, stirring until the sugar dissolves, until the mixture reaches 240 degrees.

3. In the bowl of an electric mixer, whisk the egg whites and salt until soft peaks form. When the sugar mixture has come up to temperature, carefully pour it into the egg whites while whisking. Continue whisking until the mixture has cooled slightly, about 1 minute, then add the gelatin mixture and the vanilla. Continue whisking until the mixture begins to thicken and quadruples in volume, 5 to 7 minutes. Scrape the marshmallow into the prepared pan and smooth the top with a spatula. Sift the remaining ¼ cup confectioners' sugar on top. Allow the marshmallows to set for 4 hours or overnight. Cut them into 2-inch squares and store in an airtight container in the refrigerator or at room temperature. The marshmallows will keep for 2 to 3 days at room temperature, and up to 1 week if chilled.

4. Sprinkle with additional confectioners' sugar before serving, if desired.

Madagascarian Bean Ice Cream

The gentle shores of Madagascar are famous for more than baobab trees and pirate havens; they are the primary producer of vanilla beans in all the world. How fortunate that these fragrant pods are not locked up in some buried treasure chest, but are shipped out to markets and bazaars in every port of call! We celebrate these heady island pods in this traditional French recipe. It produces a reliably creamy custard-style vanilla ice cream that makes an exemplary complement to any dessert, or indeed, an oasis of enjoyment on its own.

PROVIDES ABOUT 1 ½ PINTS ICE CREAM

2 cups whole milk

½ cup heavy cream

⅔ cup granulated sugar

4 large farm-fresh egg yolks

1 vanilla bean

1 pinch kosher salt

1. In a large saucepan over a medium heat, bring the milk, cream and ⅓ cup of the sugar just to a simmer, stirring until the sugar is dissolved. Whisk until the mixture is smooth, but not frothy.

2. Meanwhile, have ready a large bowl of ice and water. In the bowl of an electric mixer using the whisk attachment, combine the egg yolks and the remaining ⅓ cup sugar until thick and pale. Add the milk mixture in a slow stream while whisking. Use a sharp knife to split the vanilla bean lengthwise. Scrape out the seeds and whisk them into the custard mixture. Pour the custard back into the saucepan and place it over a medium-low heat, stirring constantly, until a candy thermometer set inside the saucepan reads 170 degrees. Pour the custard through a sieve into a metal bowl set in the larger bowl of ice water and let cool.

3. When the custard reaches room temperature, pour it into an ice cream maker and freeze according to the manufacturer's directions. Transfer the ice

HOME-AWAY-FROM-HOME SPUN ICE CREAM

When it comes to divvying up the labor involved in a fireside feast, we are sometimes reminded of this nugget from a certain Prussian economic philosopher: "From each according to his ability, to each according to his need." Is it possible Mr. Marx was ruminating on the internal struggle of our campsite companions who yearn to contribute to an elaborate outdoor meal yet lack the skills (or at least the confidence) for campfire cookery? Fortunately, there is a way for the less able amongst us to perform a need for the greater good. And that is to transform one's premade ice cream base into a gloriously soft-serve frozen confection—an elite creation from valiant workers' toil. One will need:

Madagascarian Bean Ice Cream, not yet
  frozen (page 81)
One small (1-pound) coffee can, rinsed and dried
One large (3-pound) coffee can, rinsed and dried
Crushed ice
1 beach towel
2 valiant workers

1. Place the ice cream base inside the 1-pound coffee can and ensure that the lid is fastened securely. Drop the sealed coffee can into the 3-pound coffee can and pack the space between the cans with crushed ice. Place the lid firmly on the larger can.
2. Lay the towel flat between two valiant workers. Allow the workers to roll the can back and forth until the ice cream is frozen and churned to the desired consistency (the longer one rolls it, the firmer the ice cream will become), 10 to 15 minutes.

cream to an airtight container and store in the freezer.
4. Alternatively, one might make the custard up to 4 days ahead and transport the chilled-but-unfrozen ice cream base to one's campsite. There one may transform it into frozen ice cream using a hand-crank ice cream contraption or the Home-Away-from-Home Spun Ice Cream method (see left).

Advisement: Sometimes vanilla ice cream begs for adornment. So allow us to suggest a few of our most beloved, effortless toppings: freshly foraged berries, a splash of Grand Marnier, shaved chocolate curls, shards of toffee, and thinly sliced fresh herbs, such as lemon balm or mint.

Stalking the Great Marshmallow
(ALTHAEA OFFICINALIS)

We are so accustomed to encountering the marshmallow in its confectionery form—molten upon the roasting stick, pastel-colored and peanut-shaped at the circus, purchased for a penny at one's general store—that the mallow's botanical origins have become unjustly obscured. In fact, today's sweet and fluffy marshmallow does not bear even a hint of its ancestral roots, but rather gets its gooey texture from the addition of gelatin. Naturally, the contemporary marshmallow is a far more convenient alternative to mallow foraging; however we do enjoy a challenge and thus encourage our dear readers to also embark upon the hunt, if only for the novelty of the thing.

The true marshmallow happens to be a lovely plant that thrives in salt marshes and other damp, spongy earth. Rather itinerant in nature, it has traveled the globe; one might encounter it in the fields of Africa, Europe, and the North American continent. To distinguish it from other greenery flourishing in the muck, look for a plant that is three to four feet high, with a thick, hoary stalk and downy, lobed leaves that boast a gentle serration. In late summer, one will easily spot its pinkish whitish flowers.

Once one has harvested the mallow (taking care also to dig up the thick white root, which contains much of its gooey sap), there are a number of things that might be done with it. The blossoms nicely offset a blushing cheek or rosy lip when slipped behind one's ear, while the leaves can be sliced—very finely to make the down most palatable—and thrown into one's salad bowl. Reserve the stems and roots for the special task of supplying the sticky sap. To extract it, simmer the two together in water until a thick mixture is obtained. One might use this sap as the ancient Egyptians did, sweetened with honey and nuts, or as the French preferred, whipped with egg whites and sugar to make a meringuelike candy that predates modern marshmallow by a century or two.

Herbalists also tell us that the marshmallow possesses many health benefits, including emollient properties that might soothe wounds, irritated skin, and sore throats. Should a member of one's camping party develop a hacking cough from inhaling too much fire smoke or lounging about in rain-soaked pajamas, we suggest the following remedy, provided in *Cassell's Dictionary of Cookery* (1875):

CUT THE ROOTS INTO THIN SLICES, AND POUR OVER THEM BOILING WATER (ABOUT A PINT TO AN OUNCE OF THE ROOT), CLEANSING AND PEELING OFF THE OUTER SKIN BEFORE INFUSION. THE WATER MAY BE FLAVOURED WITH THE SQUEEZED JUICE AND GRATED RIND OF AN ORANGE, AND SWEETENED WITH HONEY OR BROWN SUGAR-CANDY. . . . TIME, TWO HOURS TO INFUSE.

"Why, sometimes I've believed as many as six impossible things before breakfast."

—THE WHITE QUEEN, IN **THROUGH THE LOOKING GLASS**, LEWIS CARROLL

CHAPTER THREE

Campfire Breakfast

WHILE IT'S QUITE NATURAL TO THINK OF THE DINNER HOUR AS THE OCCASION TO EMPLOY ALL THE BELLS AND WHISTLES OF SOCIAL GRACES AND CULINARY EXTRAVAGANCES, IN FACT, BREAKFAST SETS THE TONE FOR THE DAY AND THEREFORE SHOULD BE LAVISHED WITH LOVING ATTENTION. This is particularly true when the day promises to be an everlasting culinary adventure, which our days (and especially our holiday getaways) always are.

One can burrow quite cozily into a tent for the night, but truth be told, come sunrise, it's difficult to think of reemerging into the chill morning light before the crack of noon without some sort of inducement. Fortunately for us, the sound of a growling belly is inducement enough—without it, we'd never witness the luxurious sparkle of the morning dew. Let the day's cookery begin!

Lest one think it a chore to build the morning fire, we confess we always look forward to tending the flames and adore the poetry of greeting the day with a cooking technique from the dawn of time. Besides, our bedrolls are warm, but the fire is warmer. As the coffee brews, the bread bakes, and the sausages begin to sizzle, one by one, our companions emerge from their makeshift abodes to take their places by the crackling fire. If, for some reason or another, one's companions refuse to budge, chances are that sending a whiff of strong coffee (Irish, if one must) wafting through the tent flap will do the trick.

Believing as we do that breakfast deserves just as much oohing and aahing as every other meal, in this chapter we present recipes that deliver theatrical punch and joie de vivre with minimal fuss. These dishes are as comforting and familiar as one's best silk kimono, yet somehow extraordinary. A delight to prepare, each is its own miniature adventure nestled inside a greater expedition, served sunny-side up.

Bon Vivant Breakfast Tartine with Chocolate Hazelnut Spread

WE SIMPLY ADORE AN ELABORATE MEAL TO BREAK OUR MORNING FAST AND DON'T MIND WAITING FOR IT TO BE PREPARED. Dawn in the wilderness is so still and peaceful; it's an ideal time and place to meditate on the beauty that surrounds. However, we do find the grumbles and growls emanating from our companions' midsections distract us from our gathering thoughts if we don't supply a bite of loveliness to tide our friends over as they wait for the bounty of the day's first meal. These wee toasted baguettes topped with everyone's favorite spread are just the thing to maintain a happy morning reverie.

One 12-ounce baguette, split horizontally and cut crosswise into 6 pieces

¾ cup chocolate-hazelnut spread, purchased

1. *Prepare a high-heat fire, with the flames licking the grill grate.*

2. *Place the bread, cut side facing the flame, upon the grill. Stand by until the bread is lightly charred, a feat that should take only a dozen seconds or so.*

3. *Smooth the chocolate hazelnut spread thickly upon the toasts. Serve piping hot.*

BRûLéeD BROWN SUGAR GRAPEFRUIT BROCHETTES

AN UNADORNED GRAPEFRUIT MIGHT BE A FINE MEAL FOR SOME, BUT WE PREFER TO DRESS OURS UP WITH A GENEROUS SHOWER OF SUGAR AND SPICE. We find this refreshing citrus dish an ideal means of whetting one's appetite for a heartier breakfast to follow, though it also makes a light and lovely meal on its own.

1. Prepare a medium-high-heat fire, with the flames occasionally licking the grill grate. Let it burn steadily for 30 minutes. Sprinkle the sugar and ginger evenly over a large platter.

2. On a clean, flat surface, using a sharp knife, slice off the top and bottom of each grapefruit. Stand the grapefruit on its flat end and slice off the rind, removing as much of the bitter white pith as possible (see Advisement). Cut the fruit into 1½-inch chunks.

3. Thread the grapefruit onto the skewers. Place each skewer on the platter and turn it to coat the fruit with the spiced sugar.

4. Hold each skewer over the flame and cook to one's desired level of char. For a deeper brûlée, hold the skewer over the high flame (or indeed, directly in it). To lightly caramelize the fruit, hold it over a lower flame.

5. Slide the grapefruit from each skewer onto the platter. Sprinkle the mint over the fruit and serve.

Advisement: We practice the meditative arts when peeling our grapefruits: taking slow, easy breaths and calming the spirit, ready the knife. First, place the fruit on a clean, flat surface. With one hand on the top of the fruit, gently pull the fruit away from the knife, while slicing in a downward motion, always following the curve of the fruit. By creating this tension between fruit and knife, one can remove the pith without sacrificing more fruit than necessary. This technique is useful for many round fruits, including oranges, pineapples, and melons.

¾ cup firmly packed light brown sugar

1 teaspoon ground ginger

4 large pink grapefruits

Chopped fresh mint, for garnish

4 metal skewers

Arabian Mornings

OR, WHAT ONE CAN LEARN FROM THE OTTOMAN EMPIRE

Although one may be inclined to cart an espresso machine on a woodland holiday, we promote a celebration of the bean by preparing it the Turkish way, which is ideally suited to the outdoors, as it requires nothing more than a pot and the open flame. Indeed, coffee's roots are in Constantinople (or is it Istanbul?), where the first coffeehouse opened in the mid-sixteenth century. A famous old Turkish proverb states that "coffee should be black as hell, strong as death, and sweet as love," a recipe that is open to such interpretation that we adjust the proportions according to our morning mood. The details of Turkish *kahve* ceremony are numerous. We've whittled them down to the basics:

1. Begin with a darkly roasted bean for the strongest aroma and flavor. The truly dedicated brewer will bring a mortar and pestle to grind the beans; however, a coffee mill is adequate, so long as the grind is powder- fine. Don't fret if one's mill or mortar is not up to the task—Turkish ground coffee is available for purchase at many specialty stores, and one can always substitute ground espresso.

* The key to authentic Turkish coffee is to brew it slowly over a low heat. Light the coals for the daily fire; the coffee will brew as the coals come to life.

2. Measure a quart of cold water into the basin of a Dutch oven to allow for four portions, then spoon in ¼ cup of ground coffee and sugar to one's preference. Turks like to add a pinch of cardamom, and so do we. Stir until the sugar dissolves before placing the pot over the coals. This is the last chance for stirring, as agitating the brew will dissipate the froth and unsettle the grounds.

3. Just as the coffee begins to boil, take the pot off the heat and ladle it into the serving vessels. Typically, Turkish coffee is consumed from a demitasse. We use a bowl. Either way, it's important to remember not to scrape one's ladle against the bottom of the pot unless one wishes to serve up a cupful of grounds.

4. Reserve one's grounds for fortune-telling (page 94).

OTHER FAVORED FOREIGN BREWS

The basic Turkish coffee recipe is surprisingly versatile and can be augmented to suit the tastes of one's party. If hot chocolate is more one's cup of tea, turn to the Campfire Teatime chapter (page 109) where, incidentally, one will also find plenty of information about tea.

Vietnamese: Add sweetened condensed milk to the bottom of each drinking vessel and top it with coffee. Try using a chicory blend, the traditional choice for Southeast Asian coffee, and serving it over ice in the sultry summer months.

NAPOLEON'S COFFEE: NATURAL CHICORY TO BREW A REVOLUTION

The diminutive Corsican general who presided over a Gallic empire and wrecked havoc upon the land and seas of Europe was certainly an infamous bon vivant. Whatever else one may say about the man—and one assumes he was not exiled to the isle of Elba for nothing—it bears mention that no matter how far flung his military campaigns, he always traveled with a retinue of chefs. An army, Napoleon is known to have said, marches on its stomach. We feel the same way about our nature walks.

As so often our hikes commence in the ante meridian (as did, presumably, the marches of French soldiers), it is simply imperative that we partake of a rousing mug of hot coffee before we pull on our boots. Shocking to think that prior to Waterloo, Boney's men had to do without such motivational brew: The necessary coffee beans were being sunk by British ships long before they reached the infantry's percolators. *Quelle horreur!* The French catering staff had to come up with some other morning beverage to serve the troops (it is never wise to disappoint men with loaded muskets) and that is how Napoleon's Coffee was born.

The chicory used for this ingenious coffee substitute is a particularly long-rooted species of endive (roots may grow up to two-and-a half feet, so one must really put one's back into it whilst digging them up), one that, unfortunately for foraging devotees, does not grow in the wild. But if one has a taste for a non-caffeinated cuppa, one may certainly cultivate a patch of chicory in one's own garden. Simply shred the roots and roast in a low temperature oven or atop a metal sheet in the afternoon sun. When the roots are coffee-colored and very, very dry, they are ready to be ground up and brewed.

Use a higher ratio of ground chicory to water than you would normally use with ground coffee beans. Chicory coffee is best brewed in a French press, as the roots have a tendency to grind very fine and this lovely contraption will prevent any grit from flowing into one's mug. The malty, earthy flavor of chicory coffee is most tastefully set off with a swirl of blackstrap molasses and a good dram of steaming hot milk to counteract chicory's vaguely astringent bite, instead of the usual sugar and cream. Drain at least a cup before marching off to expand one's empire.

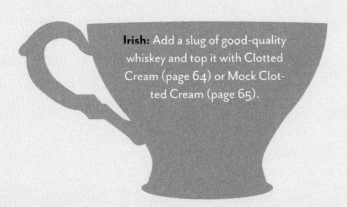

Irish: Add a slug of good-quality whiskey and top it with Clotted Cream (page 64) or Mock Clotted Cream (page 65).

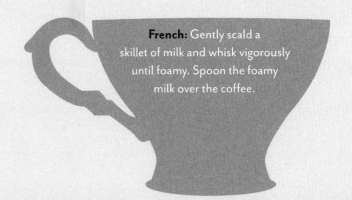

French: Gently scald a skillet of milk and whisk vigorously until foamy. Spoon the foamy milk over the coffee.

MEYER LEMON DUTCH BABY WITH WILD STRAWBERRY SAUCE

LIKE TOAD-IN-THE-HOLE (PAGE 102), THE DUTCH BABY IS A PLAY ON YORKSHIRE PUDDING, ONLY SWEETER. We're rarely timid with the use of lemon in cookery, and this is no exception—here we've worked the fragrant zest into the batter for lemony goodness in every bite. We often prepare this on our inaugural camping excursion each spring, taking full advantage of the season's bounty of sprightly Meyer lemons and delicate *fraises des bois*. We confess we have been known to sneak in a splash of our limoncello to make the strawberry sauce extra saucy. Consider it an ode to spring.

Dutch Baby:

4 tablespoons (½ stick) unsalted butter, plus additional for coating sides of pot

4 large farm-fresh eggs

¾ cup whole milk

¾ cup all-purpose flour

¼ teaspoon vanilla extract

Finely grated zest of 1 Meyer lemon

1 pinch kosher salt

Strawberry Sauce:

1 pound wild strawberries, hulled and coarsely chopped

5 tablespoons wildflower honey

Freshly squeezed juice of 1 Meyer lemon

Splash Meyer Lemon Limoncello (page 76), optional

1. Prepare a medium-high-heat fire, with the flames occasionally licking the grill grate. Let it burn steadily until it forms glowing ash-covered coals and embers, about 45 minutes. Meanwhile, nestle the skillet lid into the flames to heat.

2. Coat the interior of a cast-iron skillet with the butter, taking care that the sides are not neglected. Use a coal shovel or like implement to scrape a bed of embers off to the side of the fire pit. Place the skillet on the embers. Warm the butter until it is melted and bubbly, 5 to 7 minutes.

3. Meanwhile, in a medium bowl, whisk together the eggs, milk, flour, vanilla, zest, and salt until few lumps remain.

4. Remove the skillet and the lid from the fire. Carefully pour in the batter. Put the lid on the skillet and return it to the ember bed.

5. Use the shovel to heap embers onto the lid of the skillet and cook 15 to 18 minutes. By this time, one's pudding will have puffed marvelously, and the edges will be a crisp golden brown.

6. While the Dutch baby is in the fire, prepare the sauce. Combine the strawberries, honey, and lemon juice in a Dutch oven and give the mixture a good stir. Place the Dutch oven upon the grill grate and simmer gently, stirring occasionally, until the strawberries soften and the juices reduce and become syrupy, about 15 minutes. Remove the skillet from the fire, and stir in the limoncello, if desired.

7. Divvy up the Dutch baby and top it with sumptuous spoonfuls of sauce.

MORNING DRINKY-POOS

The hallmark of any holiday is the carefree lack of obligation. In one's workaday existence, a morning might commence with any number of tedious errands, but out in the wild, there are no such mundane responsibilities. One may swill at leisure. Should traditional brunch cocktail offerings pall, we provide our own twist on some favorites here, with and without alcohol:

Wawosa: Push several large chunks of watermelon through a medium-mesh sieve into a pitcher. Top off with French Champagne of any vintage.

Spiced Apricot Lassi: Using a cocktail shaker, combine two parts plain yogurt with two parts apricot nectar and one part whole milk. Shake. Decant into a serving glass and garnish with freshly grated nutmeg and a pinch of cinnamon.

Mosquito Bite: Stir together tomato juice, fresh horseradish, a dash of Tabasco, and the appropriate amount of tequila (appropriate levels may vary). Swizzle with a cucumber stick.

Rosy Dawn: Add a cube of ice to one's serving glass and drizzle in 1 tablespoon grenadine syrup. Top off with freshly squeezed blood orange, peach, or pineapple juice. Sprinkle with pomegranate seeds or drop in a maraschino cherry or two.

Super Fuzzy Sparklin' Sasquatch: Peel and dice several ripe kiwis and peaches. Place the fruit in the bottom of a pitcher and muddle away. Pour in Prosecco and garnish with additional fruit.

❧ *Variations: Those who are inclined to, might switch out the limoncello for its Mandarino or Zenzerino variations (page 77), both of which also partner well with strawberries.*

Bananas Foster Pancakes

Pancakes:

¾ cup all-purpose flour

1 tablespoon sugar

1 teaspoon baking powder

1 teaspoon kosher salt

½ teaspoon ground cinnamon

½ teaspoon freshly grated nutmeg

⅓ cup whole milk

¼ cup sour cream

1 large farm-fresh egg

½ teaspoon vanilla extract

2 tablespoons unsalted butter, plus more if necessary

Sauce:

4 tablespoons (½ stick) unsalted butter

3 bananas, peeled and sliced into rounds

½ cup chopped walnuts

½ cup grade-B maple syrup, preferably freshly tapped

1 tablespoon dark rum

AS THE BEWHISKERED SWISS PHILOSOPHER HENRI-FRÉDÉRIC AMIEL WROTE, "EACH NEW DAWN SIGNS A CONTRACT WITH EXISTENCE." Although we prefer our male companions to be clean-shaven, we cannot help but agree with this sentiment. For our part, we often choose to celebrate the dawn's new contracts as we do any successfully completed paperwork—by serving something sweet. These pancakes, fragrant with spice, are brilliant on their own, or with toppings more austere than our concoction of bananas, walnuts, maple, and rum. Any version makes for the start of a smashing new day.

1. *Prepare a medium-high-heat fire, with the flames occasionally licking the grill grate. Let the fire burn steadily for 30 minutes. Place the skillet upon the grill to preheat.*

2. *In a large bowl, mix together the flour, sugar, baking powder, salt, cinnamon, and nutmeg. In a separate bowl, whisk together the milk, sour cream, egg, and vanilla. Make a well in the dry ingredients and pour in the wet. Fold the batter together with a spatula or wooden spoon until few lumps remain.*

3. *Drop 1 tablespoon of the butter into the skillet and let it melt. Carefully pick up the skillet and swirl it about, coating the bottom. Cooking 3 pancakes at a time, drop 3 heaping tablespoons of batter into the skillet. Allow the pancakes to cook until*
bubbles form on the surface, 2 to 3 min-utes. Use a heatproof spatula to flip the pancakes and cook for 1 minute longer. Transfer the pancakes to a plate and cover with foil to keep warm while one prepares the remaining pancakes, adding more butter to the skillet as necessary.

4. *After the pancakes are made, prepare the sauce in the skillet. Drop in the butter, and once melted, add the bananas, walnuts, and maple syrup. Stirring occasionally with a long-handled spoon, allow the fruit to brown and the syrup to thoroughly warm, about 5 minutes. Transfer the skillet to a resting place to cool slightly, then stir in the rum.*

5. *Top the pancakes with the sauce and serve them hot.*

Les Matins Pain d'épices

WHILST TOURING THE GREAT CATHEDRALS OF FRANCE, WE BECAME ACCUSTOMED TO WAKING JUST BEFORE THE DAWN TO THE SOUND OF BELLS CALLING THE DEVOUT TO MORNING PRAYER. *Les matins,* as the chimes were known, were a signal to the Gallic faithful that the hour was at hand to kneel in reverence, but to us they were a blessed snooze alarm, which told us we had about thirty remaining minutes to rest before we must hustle to the shops in search of warm slices of *pain d'épices.* This breakfast treat was something between a bread and a cake, made just a little bit differently in each rustic French village. Our version couples our favorite aspects of the spiced *pain*—not too sweet, and flecked with the added crunch of hazelnuts. *Mon Dieu,* but it is worth the clang of church bells!

1. Prepare a high-heat fire, with the flames licking the grill grate. Let it burn steadily until it forms glowing, ash-covered coals and embers, about 45 minutes. Drop the butter into a metal bowl and place the bowl directly upon the grill grate until the butter melts, 1 to 2 minutes. Transfer the bowl to a resting place to cool slightly.

2. In a separate bowl, combine the flours, baking soda, anise, cinnamon, ginger, salt, nutmeg, cloves, and pepper. When the butter is no longer hot, whisk in the honey, milk, and egg. Fold the dry ingredients into the wet until just combined. Fold in the hazelnuts. Scrape the batter into the prepared metal bowl.

3. Using a coal shovel or like implement, scrape a bed of embers off to the side of the fire pit, where the flames cannot touch them. Place the baking stones or folded tea towel in the bottom of a Dutch oven. Rest the batter-filled bowl on top of the stones or towel. Pour enough water into the Dutch oven to reach halfway up the side of the bowl. Cover the pot and rest it on the pile of glowing embers. Shovel additional glowing embers on top of the lid. Steam the cake for 40 to 50 minutes, or until it is firm to the touch and a wooden skewer inserted in the center comes out clean. Allow the cake to rest in the pot, uncovered, for 15 minutes before turning it out onto a platter. Cut the cake into slices and serve.

4 tablespoons (½ stick) unsalted butter, plus additional for baking bowl

3 cups all-purpose flour

1 cup whole wheat flour

2½ teaspoons baking soda

1½ teaspoons whole anise seeds

1½ teaspoons ground cinnamon

1½ teaspoons ground ginger

½ teaspoon kosher salt

½ teaspoon freshly grated nutmeg

¼ teaspoon ground cloves

¼ teaspoon freshly milled black pepper

1 cup mild, light-colored honey, such as wildflower or orange flower

¾ cup whole milk

1 large farm-fresh egg

1 cup chopped hazelnuts, lightly fire-toasted (see Advisement, page 206)

4 smooth stones or a folded tea towel, for lining the pot

The Art of Tasseography

It does seem that our favorite type of person is one who is a bit of a dreamer, attuned to intuition and gut instinct, yet a tad impatient. Above all, we esteem the sort who is perfectly bubbling over with curiosity. A person who, though content to enjoy a meditative moment sipping a cup of tea, may become quietly agitated mulling over the question: What does the coming day hold? Perhaps the answer may be divined at the bottom of one's morning brew by practicing the ancient art of tasseography.

This reading of tea leaves or coffee grounds (according to one's preference), is best undertaken with a light heart and an open mind. Just because one may become fidgety with nervous glee at the prospect of learning what's around the bend doesn't mean one will necessarily fulfill the fortune that has been foreseen. In other words, do not become too attached to the outcome of this imperfect science. Rather, let the mind wander whilst gazing into the cup. One may be surprised at the configurations one sees—for the future is oft stranger than fiction, and it takes a carefree heart to discern its many twists and turns.

We have no doubt that, with a little practice following our step-by-step guide to tasseography, the dreamers amongst us will be a little better prepared for their day, armed with foreknowledge of the misty march of time. And for the more practical-minded, we have this advice: when one spots one's airier friends staring into a tea cup then decisively reaching for an umbrella, it would be wise to follow suit, even if there's not a cloud in the sky.

Acorn: felicity in matters of money and health

Ax: the means of overcoming adversity

Bouquet: imminent romance

Bear: trouble from a grouchy or difficult person

Bee: a busy time at work

Bell: unexpected joyful news in love or business

Boat: one's ship coming in

Book: a question soon to be answered (if open); the need for further investigation (if closed)

Bottle: a caution against overindulgence

Butterfly: overdue happiness

Cake: a wish to be fulfilled, or possibly overdue happiness

Cat: deceit, trouble from an untrustworthy friend

Clock: a warning against procrastination

Clover: well-deserved good luck

Coin: a good financial omen

Dashes or dots: many short trips causing wasted time

Deer: a shy, timid person taking a role in one's life

Diamond: surprise gifts

Duck: a devoted lover

Feather: the need for concentration

Flower: imminent praise and compliments

Frog: love in disguise

Hammer: forceful persuasion

Heart: love and romance

Horseshoe: very positive omen of good luck

Kettle: friendship, not romantic love

Leaf: inevitable change

Lightning: startling events or insights

Mountain: a difficult, but not impossible challenge

Mushroom: rapid growth, success, possibly children

Parasol: protection from harm, also sustained youthfulness

Rake: standing at a crossroads, also destiny determined by hard work

Star: success, recognition, praise

Sword: the need to cut off an unhappy relationship

Umbrella: the approach of inclement weather

"Curiosity is one of the permanent and certain characteristics of a vigorous mind."
—SAMUEL JOHNSON

STEP ONE:

Brew the tea or coffee. If following our recipe for Turkish coffee (page 88), one is assured of a wealth of grounds to read when the coffee is drunk. If tea is one's beverage of choice, do be sure to brew it using loose tea leaves, *sans* strainer. Yes, one could simply open up a tea bag and use its contents for divination. However, the quality of the tea leaves will be markedly poorer than loose leaves; one's reading is sure to say something along the lines of "stop being such a spend-thrift" or "pinched pennies will not grow." Or "seriously, buy some better tea, tightwad." But we digress.

STEP TWO:

Pour the beverage into a white or light-colored cup. Whilst it steeps, take a moment to quiet one's thoughts. Try to avoid distractions and to make a blank slate of the mind. If one is practiced at meditation, put those skills to use now. If one is not, just endeavor to sit still and be quiet. Steeping times will vary according to one's preference for a light- or dark-brewed drink—the style will not affect the reading.

STEP THREE:

Drink the tea or coffee. Continue in meditative silence, but now, if one has a particular question for the reading to address, hold it in the mind. Instead of asking a yes or no question (the answers given by tasseography are rarely so straightforward), phrase it as if one were consulting a trusted and wise mentor. For example, think not "Does X really love me?" but rather "What role will X play in my life's journey?" Think not "Should I take this job?" but rather "What pursuit will yield the most happiness?" Or, one can simply hold a thought such as "tomorrow," to yield a more general reading. Drink all the liquid in the cup, using one's lips as a sort of strainer to keep from swallowing the dregs. Whilst taking the final sip, throw one's head back with some abandon and rotate the cup to give the leaves one last jostle. Yes, one may look a bit vulgar, but that is the way the future gets told.

STEP FOUR:

Identify the symbols in the cup. Tasseography is a highly personal and subjective technique; one reader may see a butterfly, while another sees a wasp, even when gazing at the same blob of leaves. Symbol recognition is a key to unlocking our own inner path; therefore, one will always get the most attuned reading when analyzing one's own cup.

Hold the handle of the cup in the twelve-o'clock position. Read the symbols in a clockwise direction, spiraling downward from the uppermost parts of the sides to the bottom center of the cup. The symbols that lie further down in the cup represent the most distant future, while those toward the top are more immediate. If one likes, one may keep a little notebook to jot down the symbols found.

STEP FIVE:

Discern meaning from the symbols. Like the images in dreams, tasseography's symbols ought to be translated according to each reader's experience and intuition. The adjacent list of traditional symbols and their meanings will no doubt be helpful, but one should always follow the gut instinct in response to anything seen in one's cup. For example, the traditional meaning of "cat" might be "deceit," but if one has positive associations with felines, then a cat symbol may actually be a good omen, portending friendship, or at least good grooming. Once more, read one's cup with a lighthearted sense of fun, record what one sees, and enjoy the excitement of knowing the future is never set in stone.

Sweet Cinnamon Beignets

WE CONFESS THAT WHEN ONE OF OUR FIRESIDE COMPANIONS REQUESTED DOUGHNUTS FOR BREAKFAST, WE WRINKLED OUR NOSES INTO THE MEREST MOUE OF DISTASTE. Fried dough dripping with waxy fondant glaze is to be found at 'round-the-clock doughnut shops, the sort that have garish lighting and grease-slicked counters, not in the pristine (albeit somewhat smoky) wilderness.

But then we recalled the ethereal beignets we enjoyed in the stately city of New Orleans, those Creole doughnut incarnations made famous by the French Quarter's bustling Café du Monde. No waxy pallor dressed this crisply fried dough, just a light dusting of sugar. We quickly agreed to our friend's request and set about perfecting a recipe anyone could reproduce over the fire. One reminder, dear campers: do be careful around the bubbling oil. This is a good time to make use of those handy heatproof tongs. Though one needn't fear deep-frying, it is wise to maintain a healthy respect for hot oil.

2¼ teaspoons active dry yeast

¼ cup evaporated milk

1 large, farm-fresh egg, lightly beaten

2 cups bread flour

1 tablespoon unsalted butter, softened and at air temperature

2 tablespoons sugar

¼ teaspoon kosher salt

3 cups vegetable oil, such as canola or safflower (see Advisement, page 98)

Cinnamon sugar (see Advisement, page 98)

1. *Prepare the beignet dough at least 3 hours before service. Alternatively, one may prepare it up to 8 hours ahead of time if it is covered and kept chilled in an ice cooler or refrigerator.*

2. *Heat ½ cup water until it is lukewarm. In a medium bowl, gently whisk together the water and yeast until the yeast dissolves. Stir in the milk and beaten egg until just combined. Add the flour, butter, sugar, and salt and stir vigorously with a wooden spoon or spatula until a wet and sticky dough comes together. Cover the dough loosely with a tea towel or plastic wrap and leave it to rise in warm, dark place, away from direct sunlight for 3 hours, or in a cold place overnight.*

3. *Prepare a medium-heat fire, with the flames just below the grill grate. Let it burn steadily for 30 minutes.*

4. *Pour the oil into the Dutch oven and attach a candy thermometer to the side of the pan. Place the Dutch oven upon the grate over the heat. In the interests of prudent fire safety, do not permit the fire to lick the sides of the pot. Wait for the temperature of the oil to reach 350 degrees, this may take up to 20 minutes over the medium flame, but once the temperature is reached, it should remain steady.*

5. *Whilst the oil heats to the proper degree, use a sharp knife to cut off 1-inch squares of the beignet dough. Place the squares on a plate and keep them covered with*

TIME-TESTED CURES FOR MORNING MALAISE

They say an ounce of prevention is worth a pound of cure. Naturally, the preferred preventive measure is to limit one's overindulgence . . . to the highest quality of wines and spirits. Anecdotal evidence (and a bit of personal experience) tells us that top-shelf tipples offer the smoothest transition from an evening of imbibement to a day of activity. Unfortunately, this prevention is not always sufficient. Following are some age-old remedies to soothe even the most unsavory morning lethargy.

Honey: Two spoonfuls of apiarian nectar consumed après drink (avant sleep) will expedite the digestion of alcohol during slumber so that one awakens fresh as the morning dew.

Sparkling Water with Lime and Bitters: Bitters is an herb-infused, mildly alcoholic elixir once used by the British Royal Navy to combat nausea. If it's good enough for the squaddies, it's good enough for the landlubbers, we say.

Acupressure: A firm pinch of the nerve junction between the thumb and forefinger on the left hand is just the cure for a pounding head. Applied pressure for thirty seconds every five minutes for half an hour or so ought to do the trick.

Pickles: Although it can't unpickle one's liver, a briny bite of a classic sour dill (or Pickled Ramps, page 51) will restore the body's natural salt equilibrium, an essential step on the road to rehydration.

Full and Hearty Breakfast: When all else fails, a rich morning meal, such as the Queen's English Fry-Up (page 104) or Duck Eggs with Rosemary Salted Potatoes (page 107) will set one right again in short order.

the tea towel or plastic wrap until ready to cook. Have ready a large bowl of cinnamon sugar and the platter upon which one wishes to serve the beignets.

6. *Using one's long-handled tongs (no other piece of equipment will suffice for this endeavor), gently lower 3 squares of dough at a time into the bubbling pot, taking good care not to splash hot oil into the fire. Allow the beignets to cook for 2 minutes, then use the tongs to turn them in the oil and cook for 2 to 3 minutes longer. The beignets are ready when they are a uniform dark brown color, with no light patches. They will feel light when one takes them out of the oil.*

7. *Use the tongs to transfer the cooked beignets to the bowl of cinnamon sugar. Roll them in the sugar briefly to coat, then arrange them on the platter. Allow one's guests to help themselves while one continues cooking the remaining squares of dough. Beignets are best eaten whilst hot.*

∽ ***Advisement:*** *Allow the cooking oil to cool after use, then use a funnel to pour it back into its bottle. Cooking oil should never be discarded in the great outdoors.*

∽ ***Advisement:*** *Cinnamon sugar is wonderful to have around at breakfast or teatime, when one's toast, scone, or beignet would profit from a bit of spiced sweetener. Simply whip up a batch of 2 cups sugar to 4 teaspoons ground cinnamon to keep handy in a sealed jar or shaker.*

STEAK & OEUFS EN MEURETTE

THIS DISH IS JUST WHAT ONE MIGHT FIND IN THE SIDEWALK CAFÉS OF GAY PAREE, FROM THE BELLE ÉPOQUE TO THE PRESENT DAY. We serve this moderately elaborate creation to our Gallic guests when we suspect they may be suffering from a touch of homesickness (even whilst enjoying the forest hospitality). This dish, a marvelous way to use up the previous evening's red wine remnants, is a fitting souvenir of the City of Lights and instantly perks up even the most morose Frenchman. And if we don't see happy faces as fast as one can say Marcel Marceau, we simply trap them in an invisible shrinking box whilst we devour the *oeufs* ourselves.

1. *Prepare a high-heat fire, with the flames licking the grill grate. Let it burn steadily for 30 minutes.*

2. *Place a skillet upon the grill grate and let it become very hot, practically smoking. Coat the steak with 1 tablespoon of the oil and season with salt and pepper. Transfer the steak to the skillet and cook, without moving it, until the meat forms a gorgeous golden crust, 5 to 7 minutes per side for medium rare. Let the steak rest on a plate, covered loosely with foil, while one moves along to the eggs.*

3. *Return the skillet to the cooking grate. Add the remaining oil to the skillet. Add the shallot and garlic and cook until fragrant, about 30 seconds. Remove the skillet from the heat. Pour in the wine, stock, and thyme (please do this away from the fire so that one does not splash alcohol into the flame, causing an eyebrow-singeing flare-up). Return the skillet to the cooking grate. Simmer vigorously until the liquid has reduced by half, about 5 minutes. Adjust the heat*

to medium-high should it begin to boil outrageously.*

4. *While the sauce simmers, mash together the butter and flour in a small bowl: this is one's beurre manié. Whisk this mixture into the skillet, a small piece at a time, until the liquid has thickened slightly, 2 to 3 minutes.*

5. *Crack the eggs into a large bowl (do not beat them). Pour them carefully into the skillet and sprinkle the tops with salt and pepper. Cook gently until the bottom edges of the eggs are lightly set, about 3 minutes. Place the lid upon the skillet and cook until the tops are lightly set, about 2 minutes longer. Do not be alarmed that one's eggs have been stained mauve by the wine. This is as it should be.*

6. *Thinly slice the steak against the grain. Divvy the eggs amongst 4 plates and top each portion with some meat. Drizzle sauce over the whole thing. Sprinkle with thyme leaves and tuck in.*

1 pound flank steak

3 tablespoons extra-virgin olive oil

Kosher salt, to taste

Freshly milled black pepper, to taste

1 shallot, finely chopped

2 garlic cloves, crushed

2 cups fruity red wine, such as Pinot Noir

1 cup chicken stock

2 sprigs fresh thyme, plus additional thyme leaves, for garnish

1 tablespoon unsalted butter

1 tablespoon all-purpose flour

8 large, farm-fresh eggs

Off-to-the Races Irish Porridge with Chestnut Honey

AS THE QUINTESSENTIAL IRISH ROGUE, OSCAR WILDE, ONCE SAID, "ONLY DULL PEOPLE ARE BRILLIANT AT BREAKFAST." FOR THAT REASON, WE LIKE TO SOAK OUR SULTANAS (ALSO KNOWN AS GOLDEN RAISINS) IN A NIP OF WHISKEY BEFORE ADDING THEM TO OUR MORNING PORRIDGE. We find it loosens the tongue and unclouds the minds of our companions and ourselves—we all shine so brightly at night that we do tend toward dullness at daybreak. This steadying bowl of oats is just the thing to fortify one for the day to come.

¼ cup sultanas, black raisins, or other dried chopped fruit

3 tablespoons good-quality Irish whiskey, plus additional if desired

1 cup steel-cut oats

½ cup diced Bramley apple or other tart apple, such as Macoun or Cortland (about ½ apple)

¼ cup heavy cream

¼ cup full-flavored honey such as chestnut

¼ cup chopped walnuts, fire-toasted (see Advisement)

1. *In a small bowl, combine the sultanas and the whiskey. Allow to stand while the fire is built.*

2. *Prepare a medium-heat fire, with the flames just below the grill grate. Let it burn steadily for 30 minutes. Pour 4 cups of water into a medium skillet and place it on the hottest part of the grill.*

3. *Bring the liquid just to a boil and slowly stir in the oats. When the mixture is smooth and beginning to thicken, move the skillet to the moderate or low heat level. The essential thing here is to keep the oats at a steady simmer so as to avoid scorching them. Simmer the porridge, stirring occasionally, for 20 minutes.*

4. *Stir in the apple. Continue to simmer, stirring occasionally, for another 10 minutes. The best way to know when the porridge is ready is to taste it. The oats should be tender and creamy. If they are not to one's liking, add more water, continue to cook, and taste again in 5 minutes' time.*

5. *Swirl in the cream and honey. Sprinkle in the nuts and raisins and swish in additional whiskey, if tempted. Serve piping hot to the first pony out of the gate.*

Advisement: *Although nuts can certainly be pretoasted before leaving home, we prefer the smoky flavor afforded by toasting them over the open flame. Simply place the nuts in a small skillet in a single layer. Set the skillet over a moderate heat and toast, tossing occasionally, until they are fragrant and golden, 5 to 8 minutes, depending on the nut variety.*

TRUFFLED TOAD-IN-THE-HOLE

LONG A STAPLE AMONG BRITISH NURSERY FOODS, THIS YORKSHIRE PUDDING VARIATION WAS CREATED TO USE UP MEAT FROM THE LARDER, FROM CHICKEN LIVERS TO LAMB CHOPS TO BITS AND PIECES OF SCRAP. But we feel this dish is too divine to restrict it to leftovers and love to slip delicacies like fresh truffles and toasted hazelnuts into its billowing golden pockets. Always use top-quality sausage—one can even experiment with lamb, duck, or venison varieties. Particularly intrepid cooks may be tempted to try the eighteenth-century pigeon version, by clever cook Elizabeth Raffald, which we've tucked alongside our own.

Extra-virgin olive oil, for coating

1 pound good-quality pork sausage (about 5 links), cut in half crosswise

3 large farm-fresh eggs

1 cup whole milk

¾ cup all-purpose flour

1 generous pinch kosher salt

4 sprigs fresh thyme

Foil-Roasted Wild Mushrooms with Hazelnuts and Chives (page 206), piping hot

Freshly shaved truffle or drizzle of truffle oil, for garnish

1. Prepare a medium-heat fire, with the flames just under the grill grate. Let it burn steadily until it forms glowing, ash-covered coals and embers, about 45 minutes. While it's heating, nestle the skillet lid into the flames to heat. Then use a coal shovel or like implement to scrape a bed of embers off to the side of the fire pit.

2. Coat the interior of a cast-iron skillet with the oil, taking care that the sides are not neglected. Place the skillet upon the grill grate to heat. Warm the oil until it shimmers like a mirage in the Sahara, then set the sausages in the skillet. Brown them well on all sides, about 7 minutes. Meanwhile, in a medium bowl, whisk together the eggs, milk, flour, and salt until few lumps remain.

3. Remove the skillet and the lid from the fire. Scatter the thyme sprigs over the sausages and carefully pour the batter on top. Put the lid on securely and place the skillet on the bed of glowing embers.

4. Using the coal shovel, scatter additional glowing embers onto the lid and cook for about 20 minutes. By this time, one's pudding will have puffed marvelously and the edges will be crisp and golden brown.

5. Spoon the mushroom mixture onto the pudding and shave fresh truffle over the top. Truffle can be quite a strong flavor, so use a light touch; start slowly, more can always be added to suit one's personal taste.

> "Pick, draw, and wash four young pigeons, stick their legs into their belly as you do boiled pigeons. Season them with pepper, salt, and beaten mace, put into the belly of every pigeon a lump of butter the size of a walnut. Lay your pigeons in a pie dish, pour over them a batter. . . . Bake in a moderate oven and serve them to table in the same dish."
>
> —"PIGEONS IN A HOLE," FROM THE EXPERIENCED ENGLISH HOUSEKEEPER (1769)

THE QUEEN'S ENGLISH FRY-UP

IT IS SAID THAT THE ENGLISH AUTHOR W. SOMERSET MAUGHAM ONCE REMARKED "TO EAT WELL IN ENGLAND IS TO HAVE BREAKFAST THREE TIMES A DAY." As he survived to the quite dignified old age of ninety-one, one must presume he had the thrice-daily privilege of the Great British Breakfast, or "fry-up" to thank for his longevity. The fry consists of an impressive catalog of deliciously savory fried items, including (but not limited to) eggs, bacon, black pudding, sausages, tomatoes, bread, and baked beans. Though we avoid tinned foods when possible, in this dish tinned baked beans are simply nonnegotiable.

Although commonly found in England's public houses at any time of day, one ought not to consider it lowly pub food—we have it on good authority (though to reveal whose would be vulgar) that the dear queen herself is devoted to this national dish. It inspires just that sort of universal devotion.

Two 15-ounce tins baked beans

8 strips bacon

4 pork sausages, pricked with a fork

4 thick slices black pudding (see Advisement)

8 large farm-fresh eggs

Unsalted butter, as needed

Kosher salt, to taste

Freshly milled black pepper, to taste

2 firm, but ripe tomatoes, halved crosswise

4 slices, good-quality bread, sliced ½ inch thick

1. Prepare a medium-high-heat fire, with the flames occasionally licking the grill grate. Let it burn steadily for 30 minutes. Pour the baked beans into the Dutch oven and warm them gently in the embers.

2. Place a skillet upon the grill grate and get it very hot. Add the bacon and fry until crisp. Transfer the bacon to a large paper towel–lined plate. Add the sausages to the hot skillet and cook them, turning, until they are no longer pink, 10 to 15 minutes. Transfer to the plate of bacon. Add the black pudding to the skillet and cook it until golden, 1 to 2 minutes per side. Transfer it to the meat platter. Now, take the entire platter of meat and tip it into a large sheet of foil. Wrap the edges of the foil to seal, and situate the packet near the embers of the fire to keep warm (not too close to the flame or the meat will burn).

3. Crack the eggs into a large bowl. If the skillet looks dry, drop in a knob of butter. Pour the bowlful of eggs into the skillet; sprinkle them with salt and pepper. Cook until the eggs' edges are browned, about 5 minutes. Cover the skillet and cook until set, 3 to 5 minutes longer. Carefully slide the eggs, in one large mass, onto a big china platter.

4. Season the tomato slices with salt and pepper and then lay them in the skillet and cook until soft and golden, 2 to 3 minutes per side. Transfer them to the platter alongside the eggs. Toast the bread upon the grill grate until lightly golden (this will take only about a dozen seconds, so remain vigilant). Arrange the toast next to the tomatoes. Unwrap the sausages, bacon, and black pudding and arrange the pieces neatly upon the platter

wherever one finds space. Serve immediately with warm baked beans, letting
one's companions help themselves from
the platter.

↝ **Advisement:** Black pudding (also
known as boudin in France, buristo in
Italy, morcillo in Spain, and blutwurst
in Germany) is a sausage prepared from
pork and fillers of rice, apple, onion, and
various seasonings. And did we mention it contains a dab of pork blood as
well? Quite common throughout Europe
and even parts of Asia, some variety or
another is usually available at specialty
markets. We love some black pudding
upon our breakfast plates, but should
one feel squeamish, substitute Canadian
bacon or pork sausage patties. They are
not the same in flavor or texture but will
do nicely.

A BEVY OF BIRD APPELLATIONS

All creatures, even those on one's dinner table, ought to be called
by their proper names. Ornithological nomenclature is an essential
part of a bon vivant's vocabulary. Commit these to memory and
one will never run afoul of nature's law.

Band of Jays	Exaltation of Larks
Bevy of Quail	Fall of Woodcocks
Bouquet of Pheasants	Flight of Cormorants
Brood of Hens	Flush of Mallards
Cast of Falcons	Gaggle of Geese
Clamor of Rooks	Kettle of Nighthawks
Charm of Finches	Knob of Widgeons
Cauldron of Raptors	Murder of Crows
Chattering of Starlings	Mustering of Storks
Company of Parrots	Ostentation of Peacocks
Congregation of Plovers	Paddling of Ducks
Convocation of Eagles	Parliament of Owls
Covey of Ptarmigans	Pitying of Turtledoves
Deceit of Lapwings	Siege of Herons
Descent of Woodpeckers	Unkindness of Ravens

THE FLYING DUTCHMAN'S ASPARAGUS & AGED GOUDA OMELETTE

CAMPING NEAR THE SEA POSSESSES AMPLE BENEFITS, CHIEF AMONG THEM PLENTIFUL OPPORTUNITIES FOR SWIMMING AND DAMP, SALTY AIR THAT DOES WONDERS FOR OUR COMPLEXIONS. That said, when the early morning mist envelops our camp, we sometimes peer into the foggy, distant waters and shudder. We are reminded, naturally, of the *Flying Dutchman*, that ghostly seventeenth-century ship doomed to drift the oceans forever, warning sailors of impending doom. Since the only way to dispel such chilly gloom is a warming breakfast, we turn to this hearty asparagus omelette. And though we scarcely consider ourselves superstitious, it never hurts to add some good, briny Dutch cheese—a whiff of home is sure to appease any portentous apparitions.

6 ounces pencil-thin wild asparagus, ends trimmed

1½ teaspoons extra-virgin olive oil

½ teaspoon kosher salt

Freshly milled black pepper

8 large farm-fresh eggs

2 tablespoons unsalted butter

2½ ounces aged Gouda cheese, grated (about ⅔ cup)

1. Prepare a medium-high-heat fire, with the flames occasionally licking the grill grate. Let it burn steadily for 30 minutes.

2. Toss the asparagus with the oil, salt, and ¼ teaspoon pepper. Carefully lay the asparagus across the grill grate. Place the stalks perpendicular to the grate vents, lest they drop into the flame. Grill the asparagus, turning it occasionally, until tender and lightly charred, 4 to 5 minutes. Transfer it to a plate.

3. In a bowl, whisk together the eggs and pepper to taste. Place a skillet over the grill grate. Drop in 1 tablespoon butter and let it melt. Pour in half of the eggs and sprinkle them with half of the cheese.

Cook until the sides and bottom of the omelette are lightly set, about 2 minutes. Arrange half of the asparagus on top of the omelette.

4. Use a long-handled spatula to gently release the eggs from the skillet. Fold the omelette over the asparagus and cook 1 minute longer.

5. Don one's heatproof gloves and remove the skillet from the flame. Divide the omelette in half, then tip each onto a plate and top with additional pepper, if desired. Return the skillet to the flame and repeat to make the remaining portions.

DUCK EGGS WITH ROSEMARY SALTED POTATOES

ONE MORNING, AFTER AWAKENING TO A PARTICULARLY BREATHTAKING LAKESIDE VISTA THAT INCLUDED A PADDLING OF DUCKS, WE CREATED THIS DISH. Duck eggs are a bit larger than chicken eggs and have an outsized flavor to match—the yolk is rich and vibrant, and the whites have the most luscious, silky texture imaginable. We adore them paired with these crisp potatoes pan-roasted in duck fat. We don't advocate snatching the young from migrating mallards; rather, hunt for them at local farmers' markets.

1. *Prepare a medium-high-heat fire, with the flames occasionally licking the grill grate. Let it burn steadily for 30 minutes.*

2. *Melt 2 tablespoons of the duck fat in a large skillet upon the grill grate. Drop in the potatoes, giving them a brief stir until they glisten with fat. Cook, stirring occasionally, until they are crisp, golden and almost tender, 12 to 15 minutes. Sprinkle in the rosemary and season generously with the salt and pepper. Push the potatoes to one side of the skillet.*

3. *Add the remaining duck fat to the skillet. Crack in the eggs and season them with salt and pepper. Fry them sunny-side up, until the whites are opaque and the yolk is set, 3 minutes or so.*

4. *Gently nudge the potatoes onto the plates and tip in the eggs. Devour lakeside.*

3 tablespoons duck fat or extra-virgin olive oil

1 pound French fingerling potatoes, cut into ½-inch chunks

2 teaspoons chopped fresh rosemary

Kosher salt, to taste

Freshly cracked black peppercorns, to taste

4 farm-fresh duck eggs

"I am so fond of tea that I could write a whole dissertation on its virtues. It comforts and enlivens without the risks attendant on spirituous liquors. Gentle herb! Let the florid grape yield to thee. Thy soft influence is a more safe inspirer of social joy."

—FROM JAMES BOSWELL'S LONDON JOURNAL

CHAPTER FOUR

CAMPFIRE TEATIME

TEA MAY WELL APPEAR THE MOST COMMON-PLACE OF BEVERAGES, NO LESS ORDINARY THAN A HANDKERCHIEF, OR A HAT PIN, OR THE BUTTONS ON ONE'S WAISTCOAT. But let us pause a moment to consider its import to society, for world history is steeped with the influence of the brew—from the ancient dynasties of the Orient to the tsars and tsarinas of Russia to the parlors of England and all her unruly colonies. One might hit upon no better communion with the great arc of civilization than a proper cup of tea.

In the bohemian wild, we celebrate this jumbled pedigree. Once beyond earshot of polished society, we are at liberty to snub any rigid formality so often associated with taking tea, and can appreciate teatime for the fanciful event it truly is. According to dreary British authorities on tea, three strict classes of teatime exist: *afternoon tea*, a fussily ceremonial, late-in-the-day affair filled with tiered stands of pastries, cake, and crustless sandwiches; *high tea*, an early evening tea break and light supper, consisting of eggs, chilled meats, fish, sandwiches, and cakes; and *cream tea*, that unequaled hour of warm scones, clotted cream, fresh jam, and hot milky brew.

But, really, why must one choose? A life unbound from convention means a teatime where one may nosh on a quotidian sardine toast alongside a tray of elegant petits fours or a crumpet laden with cream. It is the sort of afternoon when one may choose to thoughtfully sip tea from bone china, minty hot chocolate from an espresso cup, or cooking sherry from a canteen. The sort of teatime that might, at various intervals, involve the usual dignified conversation, a swing in a hammock, a forest amble in search of wild herbs, a meditative whittle, or a dabble in Asian arts and crafts.

Not that this should be a higgledy-piggledy occasion—far from it. We encourage the cultivation of an organized and handsome teatime—after all, *un petit homage* to history is in order. Set out one's finest doilies and linens, the heirloom silver service, the samovar, and the creamer. Venture into the nearest pasture for a spray of violets or sweet clover to grace the fireside. Inquire whether one's companions prefer one lump or two. Our standards of refinement and grace are never to be lowered; only our pretentious pinkie fingers.

FUN & FANCY TARTINES

THERE MIGHT BE NO END TO THE GASTRONOMIC INGENUITY OF THE FRENCH. What other nation dazzles with the audacity of their *béchamels* and *pots de crème* and then turns about to soothe with simple, honest fare like the glorious *tartine*?

A whimsical appellation for what some might call an open-faced sandwich, the tartine is a slice of crusty bread slathered with goodness, perhaps a dollop of freshly churned butter, a glossy layer of sticky sweet jam, or a rich slab of foie gras. The topping possibilities are as infinite as one's imagination, so do not feel hemmed in by traditional French conventions. We never do. Consider the recipes provided—delectable though they are—as merely the starting points of culinary creation.

To quiet one's cantankerous belly in the peckish hours before the evening meal, one can do no better than these nibbles; we also find that children flock, as if following the Pied Piper, to the tartine table.

Bast's Grilled Sardines & Lemon Aioli Tartine

This recipe ranks quite high in our repertoire of campfire dishes. If this revelation elicits a raised eyebrow or two among our readers, we are not surprised. After all, ever since some well-meaning fisherman opened the first sardine cannery, this small saltwater fish has become associated with tightly packed tins and claustrophobic crowds. Terrible shame, really, since fresh sardines are exceedingly delicious. Plumper, sweeter, and flakier than their tinned siblings, we find the less one fiddles with them, the better—a quick grill and dollop of lemony mayonnaise is all one really needs.

In spite of our firm preference for fresh sardines, one might still enjoy this dish using tinned. As they are already cooked, grill the drained fillets for just a moment on each side to give them a touch of char.

PROVIDES 6 PORTIONS

1 garlic clove, chopped

Kosher salt, to taste

½ teaspoon finely grated lemon zest (from approximately ½ lemon)

½ batch Continental Mayonnaise (page 65)

6 fresh sardines (about 1¼ to 1½ pounds), gutted and scaled (ask one's fishmonger to perform this service)

2 tablespoons extra-virgin olive oil

Freshly milled black pepper, to taste

One 12-ounce baguette, split horizontally and cut crosswise into 6 pieces

Chopped fresh dill, for garnish

1. Prepare a high-heat fire, with the flames licking the grill grate. Let it burn steadily for 30 minutes.
2. Using a mortar and pestle (or the back of a knife), pound the garlic and a pinch of salt until it forms a paste. Whisk the garlic paste and lemon zest into the mayonnaise; voilà! We now consider this aioli. Cover it well and return it to one's icebox.
3. Rinse the fish under cold water and pat them dry.

Slick them with the oil, then season generously with salt and pepper.

4. Transfer the fish to the grill grate. Cook for 2 to 3 minutes, until the undersides are golden, then use the tongs or one's own gloved hand to flip the fish and grill for an additional 2 to 3 minutes. When the fish flake easily with a fork, they are ready; transfer them to a plate. Lift each sardine by the tail and pull up the bone. The flesh should separate with ease from the vertebrae.

5. Place the bread, cut side facing the flame, upon the grill. Stand by until lightly charred, a feat that should take only a dozen seconds or so.

6. Spread the aioli thickly upon the toast. Lay a fish across each toast and scatter dill on top as garnishment.

Lavender Honey & Fresh Ricotta Tartine

One of our most treasured travel memories remains a train journey across Bulgaria undertaken one sultry August. Just as we began to consider unbuttoning our chemises for fear of fainting dead away from heat exhaustion, the train suffered a mechanical mishap and screeched to a halt—in the middle of a lavender field. All the passengers spent that afternoon deliriously lolling about in the fragrant fields, eventually wandering back to our seats with purple flowers clinging romantically to our mussed hair. This light and creamy toast recalls that happy hour.

PROVIDES 6 PORTIONS

One 12-ounce baguette, split horizontally and cut crosswise into 6 pieces

¾ cup freshest, creamiest ricotta

2 tablespoons lavender honey, or other fine, floral honey

Lavender flowers, for garnish, optional

1. Prepare a high-heat fire, with the flames licking the grill grate. Let it burn steadily for 30 minutes.

2. Place the bread, cut side facing the flame, upon the grill. Stand by until it is lightly charred, a feat that should take only a dozen seconds or so.

3. Spread the ricotta thickly upon the toasts. Drizzle with honey. Should one be in proximity to a field of fresh English lavender, gather a pinch of blossoms and sprinkle lightly upon the toasts.

Charred Fennel & Finocchiona Tartine

Fennel is a most useful plant. In this era of nose-to-tail eating, fennel prevails, bearing edible seeds, stems, leaves, and rootstalk. Here we've grilled the succulent bulbs and gilded them with a layer of Florentine finocchiona sausage. After a long day amongst the Boticellis at the Uffizi, nothing pleases like a stroll to the nearest piazza for a goblet of Chianti and a platter of this revelatory sausage laced with wild fennel seed harvested from the wooded hills and uninhabited fields of Tuscany. Our blood orange and date vinaigrette provides the perfect finish, though we suggest chewing on feathery fennel fronds post-consumption to sweeten one's garlicky breath.

PROVIDES 6 PORTIONS

2 medium fennel bulbs, fronds chopped and reserved; fibrous outer leaves removed

6 ounces thinly sliced finocchiona salami, or other good-quality dried sausage

1½ tablespoons extra-virgin olive oil

Kosher salt, to taste

Freshly milled black pepper, to taste

One 12-ounce baguette, split in half horizontally and cut crosswise into 6 pieces

3 anchovies, finely chopped

½ batch Blood Orange & Date Vinaigrette (page 67), for drizzling

1. Prepare a high-heat fire, with the flames licking the grill grate. Let it burn steadily for 30 minutes.

2. Slice the fennel lengthwise into ¼-inch-thick

slabs. Toss the fennel slices with the oil and season lightly with salt and pepper.

3. Transfer the fennel to a grill basket. Should one not possess a basket, proceed using a well-heated, cast-iron skillet placed upon the grill grate.) Cook the fennel until lightly charred and tender, approximately 7 minutes altogether. Turn once halfway through using tongs or a long-handled fork. Remove the fennel from the heat and roughly chop it into bite-size pieces.

4. Place the bread, cut side facing the flame, upon the grill. Stand by until lightly charred, a feat that should take only a dozen seconds or so.

5. Whisk the anchovies into the vinaigrette; season with salt and pepper, then drizzle the toast with the mixture. Spoon the fennel over the dressing. Pause a moment to envision a stroll across the Ponte Vecchio; fold sausage slices prettily over the fennel, garnish with fennel fronds, and serve.

Grilled Tomato, Marinated Artichoke & Fresh Gruyère Tartine

Should one be in a wooing state of mind, we believe this tartine might be just the thing—the humble artichoke joins the ranks of oysters, chocolates, truffles, and Spanish fly in its supposed possession of aphrodisiacal powers. We've even heard murmurs that King Henry VIII nurtured an extreme fondness for them, and are we not all familiar with his insatiable, er, appetite?

Although there is simply no comparison to the clean, grassy flavor of fresh artichokes (which are abundant in spring and fall), if one does not wish to fritter away time removing the prickly purple chokes, then do substitute a tin of drained and marinated artichokes.

PROVIDES 6 PORTIONS

8 ounces baby artichokes (about 4), peeled and cut into eighths (see Advisement)

1½ tablespoons extra-virgin olive oil

Kosher salt, to taste

Freshly milled black pepper, to taste

2 cups ripe grape tomatoes

One 12-ounce baguette, split horizontally and cut crosswise into 6 pieces

1 garlic clove, cut in half

12 ounces Gruyère cheese, thinly sliced

Metal skewers

1. Prepare a medium-high-heat fire, with the flames licking the grill grate. Let it burn steadily for 30 minutes.

2. Toss the artichokes with ½ tablespoon of the oil and sprinkle with salt and pepper. Wrap the artichokes tightly in a square of foil. Place the artichoke packet on top of the grill grate or nestle it into the coals. Cook until a knife pierced through the artichokes proves them tender, 15 to 20 minutes.

3. Thread the tomatoes onto several metal skewers. Coat them with the remaining oil, sprinkle them with salt and pepper, and grill them, turning them occasionally with one's own gloved hand, until blistered and soft (the tomatoes, not the hand), 2 to 3 minutes.

4. Place the bread, cut side facing the flame, upon the grill. Stand by until lightly charred, a feat that should take only a dozen seconds or so.

5. Remove the bread from the heat and rub the cut surfaces with the garlic cloves. Top them with the roasted tomatoes, grilled artichokes, and cheese slices. Wrap each toast loosely in lightly oiled foil. Grill until the cheese is melted, 4 to 5 minutes.

Advisement: To make quick work of preparing the artichokes for the fire, begin by slicing away the top third of the artichoke. Next, remove any particularly fibrous and stiff outer leaves, one at a time, as if descaling a dragon. Use a spoon to carve out the bristly core.

COOL & CRISP TEA SANDWICHES

WHEN THE SWELTERING SUMMER HEAT MAKES THE POMP AND CEREMONY OF WORKING OVER A BLAZING MIDDAY FIRE AS APPEALING AS A TÊTE-À-TÊTE WITH THE MARQUIS DE SADE, CONSIDER THESE SANDWICHES ONE'S SAVIOR. Filled entirely with ingredients that require not a lick of flame, cooling tea sandwiches gently stave off hunger until evening, but are light enough so as not to spoil one's appetite.

Here we offer our favorite interpretations of the quintessential tea sandwiches: salmon, cucumber, chicken salad, and radish. Select one or two that appeal or create a platter of all four. Note that while tea sandwiches can be assembled up to one hour in advance, they are susceptible to drying out in the air, so we recommend covering the finished platter with faintly moistened paper towels. Overlapping the sandwiches on the tea tray will also prevent drying, as less of the bread's surface will be exposed to the elements.

Cracked Pepper–Coriander Smoked Salmon Sandwich

Ah, coriander. We would be happy to fill our stocking drawer with a sachet of this sweet, woodsy-floral spice. The mellow seed of the pungent and sometimes divisive herb cilantro, coriander makes a lovely mate for delicate seafood. If one seeks more bracing flavor, strew the salmon with the leaves.

PROVIDES 2 DOZEN TEA SANDWICHES

24 slices pumpernickel, about ¼ inch thick, or
  48 slices party pumpernickel
¼ cup Coriander & Cracked Black Pepper Butter
  (page 63)
6 ounces smoked salmon, thinly sliced

Spread one side of each bread slice with a thin layer of butter. Top with smoked salmon. Slice off the crusts (don't bother if using party pumpernickel). Cut the sandwiches in half diagonally (once more, pass over this step if using party pumpernickel).

Cucumber & Garden-Herb Goat Cheese Sandwich

Occasionally we elect to fill a flask with some warming brew, pack a pannier of sandwiches, and venture from camp in search of a tucked-away knoll where we might enjoy a teatime of tranquility. This sandwich, filled with crunchy cucumbers and a sturdy spread of tangy cheese, stands up well to the jostle of travel. Seedless English cucumbers are preferred over the squat and seedy varieties (which tend to dampen the bread); we love that one needn't bother to peel the thin, edible skin.

PROVIDES 2 DOZEN SANDWICHES

4 ounces fresh creamy goat cheese
  (approximately 1 cup)
2 teaspoons chopped fresh dill
2 teaspoons chopped fresh parsley
1 teaspoon chopped fresh chervil

How to Whittle Away

AN HOUR OF LEISURE

We have heard it said that whittling is a tedious pastime of the idle, a quaint and archaic misuse of one's fine motor skills. Please banish such thoughts from the head. Does one regard the alluring curves of the *Venus de Milo* as quaint? We think not. Let's not presume that because the artistic medium is a chip of wood and not a block of marble that one's sculpture is any less a masterpiece.

And as for the former accusation, we retort, as Sir John Lubbock once did, "Rest is not idleness, and to lie sometimes in the grass under the trees on a summer's day, listening to the murmur of water or watching the clouds float across the sky, is by no means a waste of time." In addition to championing restful activities, Lubbock was a lover of nature and archaeological artifacts. We suspect that among his surviving ephemera lies a miniature bust of his chum Charles Darwin, carved from a twig. Our point: hold one's whittling tool with pride, and let us begin.

INSTRUCTIONS:

1. Above all else, one needs a small, lightweight knife that feels good in the hand; one will be holding it for the stretch of time that leisure permits. A pocketknife is simple to use and easy to procure, although for those feeling particularly dedicated to the craft, a special whittling knife makes a prudent investment. Its short, plump handle allows for greatest control and safety, and we don't want anything sharp flying about the campsite unless it is the wit of one's companions.

2. Next, hone said knife. Professional whittling knives often arrive unsharpened, as many whittlers prefer to determine their own blade angles. This is a fairly demanding process; for detailed instructions, we direct our readers to a specialized whittling guide. That said, we can provide the following advice: a sharpening block and strop (a flexible length of canvas or leather used to remove the burr; the leather surface of a work boot serves this purpose well) work nicely to sharpen one's blade. A diamond pocket file will also serve in a pinch. Do not be tempted to use this file upon the nails; it will wreck one's manicure.

3. Which brings us to the next item of business: gloved hands. We recommend the wearing of carver's gloves not only to ward off nasty blisters and calluses, but also to protect from the occasional slip of the knife. Should one be too proud to heed this advice, then do take care to cut away from the direction of one's hand, fingers, and general person.

4. Choose a piece of wood small enough to hold with ease but large enough to whittle down. Softwood, naturally, will be more malleable.

5. Take a moment now to ascertain one's spirit. Locate a place of calm within, and consider the wood. Folklore suggests that one's work of art is captive inside the wood; imagine what that might be and prepare to release it. A novice might perhaps sense only a marshmallow skewer within the raw wood. This is no cause for shame.

6. Pin the elbows close to the sides and lock the wrists. In measured fashion, shave away at the wood. Stop occasionally for a bite of toast, spot of tea, or swallow of port. Whistle while working, retire whenever it pleases, and remember that rest is not idleness.

1 teaspoon chopped fresh thyme

1 teaspoon chopped fresh mint

½ teaspoon chopped fresh tarragon

½ English cucumber, thinly sliced

24 slices white Pullman bread, ¼ inch thick

Kosher salt, for sprinkling

1. In a small bowl, mash together the cheese with the herbs.
2. Spread one side of each slice of bread with the goat cheese mixture. Top each with a layer of cucumber slices. Sprinkle with salt. Slice off the crusts; cut the sandwiches in half diagonally.

The Raj's Curried Chicken & Pear Salad Sandwich

Some years ago, when Queen Victoria's head hung heavy with the crown, England (amongst others) was involved in a wicked little business called imperialism. While we do not condone the misguided dealings of the British Raj, we remain grateful for at least one effect—the subsequent availability of Indian curry powder in every Western corner shop.

In lieu of roast chicken, we heartily endorse the substitution of leftover Stone-Seared Cornish Game Hens with Bombay Spice (page 166).

PROVIDES 2 DOZEN TEA SANDWICHES

1¼ cups finely chopped roast chicken

2 tablespoons mayonnaise

1½ teaspoons Dijon mustard

1 small celery stalk, finely chopped

1 scallion, finely chopped

¾ teaspoon curry powder

⅛ teaspoon kosher salt

⅛ teaspoon freshly milled black pepper

¼ cup finely chopped ripe pear

1½ tablespoons finely chopped pistachio nuts, fire-toasted (see Advisement, page 206)

24 slices whole grain bread, ¼ inch thick

Watercress, for garnish

1. In a small bowl, stir together the chicken, mayonnaise, mustard, celery, scallion, curry, salt, and pepper. Gently fold in the pear and nuts.
2. Sandwich a heaping spoonful or two of the salad between 2 slices of bread. Cut off the crusts; cut the sandwiches in half diagonally.

Radish & Chive Butter Sandwich with Salt of the Sea

Whenever we clap eyes on a tower of sad, untouched radishes languishing along the perimeter of a crudité platter, our souls weep. So severely judged, yet so worth the effort of acquaintance! Here we've mellowed the radish's peppery bite with a sweep of butter and a light rain of sea salt. We are especially fond of using the delicately sweet and prettily bicolored French Breakfast radish.

PROVIDES 2 DOZEN TEA SANDWICHES

24 slices white Pullman bread, ¼ inch thick

6 tablespoons Chive Butter (page 63)

6 large radishes, very thinly sliced (about 1½ cups)

Fleur de sel, for sprinkling

Spread one side of each bread slice with a thin layer of butter. Top with radishes and sprinkle with fleur de sel. Slice off the crusts; cut the sandwiches in half diagonally.

SPICED CURRANT CREAM SCONES

Scones, originally cooked upon a griddle over a hot fire, make a natural embellishment to one's camp cookery repertoire. These days, resourceful cooks find reason to add any number of elaborations to scone dough, from pumpkin puree to butterscotch nibs to candied ginger. We admire such gumption and have been known to partake greedily of the results, but tend to favor the classic marriage of currants, spices, and cream.

Split and steaming, topped with a dab of good butter and a drizzle of treacle, golden syrup, or honey, these scones reign supreme at tea or as breakfast victuals. But do make certain the fire is hot enough for baking so that they achieve their characteristic crisp crust and moist, buttery interior.

2 cups all-purpose flour

¼ cup sugar

2 teaspoons baking powder

1 teaspoon ground cardamom

¼ teaspoon freshly grated nutmeg

¼ teaspoon ground cinnamon

¼ teaspoon kosher salt

5 tablespoons cold unsalted butter, cut into pieces

½ cup heavy cream, plus additional, if necessary

1 large farm-fresh egg, lightly whisked

½ cup dried currants (see Advisement)

Demerara sugar, for sprinkling

Clotted Cream (page 64), Honey-Pecan Butter (page 63), jam, treacle, or honey, for serving

4 smooth stones, for lining the pot

1. Use a fork or pastry cutter to combine the flour, sugar, baking powder, cardamom, nutmeg, cinnamon, and salt in a mixing bowl. Mash in the cold butter pieces until pea-size crumbs form.

2. In a separate bowl, mix the cream and egg together. Make a well in the dry ingredients and pour in the cream mixture. Fold it all together using a spatula or wooden spoon. The dough should be quite dry, but if it's just not holding together, add 1 to 2 tablespoons more cream. Gently fold in the currants until the mixture is just combined.

3. Turn the dough out onto a lightly floured surface and gently pat it out and fold it over, as one would a puff pastry dough, making 4 to 6 turns. Divide the dough into halves and pat each lump into a circle about 1½ inches thick. Cut each piece of dough into quarters, to make 8 fat triangles. Wrap the triangles in foil, making 2 packages, and place them in the cooler or refrigerator while one readies the fire.

4. Prepare a medium-high-heat fire, with the flames occasionally licking the grill grate. Let it burn steadily until glowing, ash-covered embers begin to form, about 45 minutes. Then use a coal shovel or other like implement to scrape a bed of embers to the side of the fire.

5. Rest the Dutch oven for 5 to 10 minutes upon the bed of glowing embers and place the lid near the flames. Place the baking stones inside the Dutch oven and cover them with a sheet of foil. Place the scones in a single layer on the foil and sprinkle each with a generous pinch of Demerara sugar. Carefully place the lid on the Dutch oven and nestle it into the embers; shovel glowing embers on top and mound them around the sides.

CRACKERS & POTTED SPREADS PLATTER

In our chapter Preparing for the Feast, we assured our readers that these dishes would make an ideal and effortless teatime feast if brought along on one's camping journey. That time has come. Now one need only muster the energy to tip the ingredients onto a platter and the strength to endure incessant flattery from one's companions. Feel free to serve one, two, or all three of the spreads.

- Potted Cheddar Huntsman Spread (page 72)
- Potted Spiced Pork (page 72)
- Potted Crab with Lemon (page 70)
- Crisp Fired Crackers (page 73)
- Several bunches of grapes
- Sliced apples and pears

Arrange the spreads on a large platter and surround them with crackers and fruits in the most attractive way. Consume.

6. *After 10 minutes, rotate the Dutch oven 180 degrees.*

7. *Let the scones bake for another 10 minutes, then use the coal shovel to scrape the embers and ash off the lid. Check the scones. If they are golden brown, take the Dutch oven out of the fire and replace the lid, allowing the radiant heat to bake the scones for a further 5 minutes. If the scones are still pale, re-cover the Dutch Oven, return it, covered, to the embers, and let the scones bake for another 5 to 10 minutes. The scones are done when they are firm to the touch, and they should feel light when one lifts them (heavy-feeling scones may have raw dough in the center).*

8. *Remove the scones from the oven and place them on a dainty plate to serve with one's desired accompaniment.*

∾ ***Advisement:*** *We have observed a swirling befuddlement surrounding the question of dried versus fresh currants. They are, in fact, not related. The sweet-tart red and musky black currants that one finds fresh and jewel-like in country brambles are berries. The dried Zante currants relied upon for baking and adding a sweet touch to salads, stews, and other savories are tiny black grapes that flourish in the Ionian Islands of Greece.*

CaST-iRON CRUMPETS & CLOTTED CReaM

1½ cups milk

2¼ teaspoons (1 envelope) active dry yeast

2 tablespoons sugar

2½ cups bread flour

1 teaspoon kosher salt

½ teaspoon baking soda

2 tablespoons unsalted butter

Clotted Cream (page 64) and jam, or scrambled eggs and speck, for serving

Four 3-inch metal crumpet rings, greased (see Advisement)

To paraphrase Ralph Waldo Emerson, the hush of nature doth permit us to hear the whispers of the gods. However, truth be told, when the tea hour strikes at camp, we yearn only to hear the tinkling bell of the muffin man hawking hot crumpets in the city streets. If one has never indulged, freshly baked crumpets (not to be confused with those foul packets of rubbery, peculiar-smelling "English muffins") are soul-shattering—chewy, buttery, and begging for a healthy slather of fruit curd and cream, or, if one inclines toward the savory, a pile of scrambled egg and sprinkling of speck.

Admittedly, preparations must be made. One need arrive armed with yeast to ensure the proper loft and small metal baking rings (which resemble open cookie cutters and are easily procured at a baking supply shop or the local smithy) to contain the oozing batter. But such inconveniences are fleeting; they will dissolve like sugar upon the tongue when one stands before a warm stack of crumpets.

Ordinarily, one cooks a crumpet's underside to a crisp, golden color, while the face retains its pallid, honeycomb appearance. This is because at home, one is apt to cook the crumpet a second time by toasting it just before serving. Here, we've omitted that step and cook the crumpet on both sides from the start.

1. Begin preparing the crumpet batter a minimum of 30 minutes (and a maximum of 8 hours) before the crumpets are to be served. Heat ½ cup water until it is tepid. In a medium bowl, gently mix the milk and yeast with the water. When the yeast has dissolved into the liquid, stir in the sugar and let the mixture rest until it swells and froths, about 5 minutes.

2. Fold in the bread flour, salt, and baking soda with a wooden spoon or spatula until a sticky dough forms. Cover the bowl with plastic wrap or a clean tea towel and allow the batter to rest at air temperature, away from direct light, for 30 minutes. If one wishes to serve the crumpets in a few hours' time, place the batter in a cooler or refrigerator until needed.

3. To cook the crumpets, prepare a medium-high-heat blaze, with flames that occasionally lick the grill grate. Let it burn steadily for 30 minutes until hot.

4. Place 1 tablespoon of butter in a cast-iron skillet set upon the grill grate and allow it to melt, about 30 seconds. Place the crumpet rings in the skillet. Drop 2 tablespoons of batter into each crumpet ring, patting it down with the back of the spoon, if necessary, to fill the entire ring.

5. Let the crumpet cook until it puffs up and bubbles appear on top, 1 to 2 minutes. (If the telltale multitude of holes fails to appear, the batter may be too thick; add a drizzle of milk to the batter, which should improve one's luck on the next go-round.) Using the tongs, or one's gloved fingers, ease off the rings (setting them at a ready distance for the next batch) and flip the crumpets on the skillet. Allow the crumpets to cook for an additional 1 to 2 minutes, until both sides are golden brown. Repeat with the remaining batter to make 8 crumpets. Place the crumpets on a plate, and serve with clotted cream and jam, or scrambled eggs and speck.

∾ **Advisement:** *Although metal baking rings are to be had at most kitchen supply shops, should one have difficulty securing them, we suggest imitating the inestimable cookery author Elizabeth David, who sometimes relied on well-scrubbed seafood tins (about 7 ounces), with the top and bottom lids smoothly cut away.*

DELICATE CRUSHED ALMOND MACAROONS

SOMETIMES ONE EMBARKS ON AN ADVENTURE WITH SWEET IMAGININGS OF SEV-ERAL DAYS SPENT SUNNING ONESELF ON A WARM ROCK, REFRESHED BY A PINE-SCENTED BREEZE. And then, to one's chagrin, the weekend brings little more than a slate-colored sky and a brisk Northern gale that leaves the group huddling beneath a woolly Pendleton. At times like these, we turn to the macaroon, a beguiling coconut confection that instantly transports us to a sun-drenched terrace atop Montmartre, or even to the chic and swaying coconut palms of tropical Bora-Bora. Devour them at teatime and, if possible, save enough to serve later as a *friandise,* that tiny sweet served with coffee or tea following a meal.

1 cup sweetened shredded coconut

3 large farm-fresh egg whites, lightly whisked

¼ cup sugar

¼ cup chopped whole almonds

1 pinch kosher salt

4 smooth stones, for lining the pot

1. Prepare a medium-high-heat fire, with the flames occasionally licking the grill grate. Let it burn steadily until glowing, ash-covered embers begin to form, about 45 minutes. Then use a coal shovel or other like implement to scrape a bed of embers to the side of the fire pit.

2. Rest the Dutch oven for 5 to 10 minutes atop the bed of glowing embers and place the lid near the flames. Place the baking stones inside the Dutch oven and cover them with a sheet of foil.

3. While the Dutch oven is preheating, prepare the macaroon batter. In a mixing bowl, use a spatula or wooden spoon to combine the coconut, egg whites, sugar, almonds, and salt until a sticky dough forms. Using one's fingers or a spoon, drop tablespoon-sized lumps of macaroon dough onto a plate; one should have about one dozen lumps.

4. Gently arrange the macaroons on the foil in the Dutch oven, allowing at least a ¼-inch space between them. Carefully cover with the lid and shovel glowing embers on top. Use the shovel to mound more embers around the sides of the Dutch oven.

5. After 10 minutes, rotate the Dutch oven 180 degrees.

6. Let the macaroons bake another 10 minutes, then scrape the embers and ash from the lid. Check the macaroons. If they are a toasty shade of golden brown, remove the Dutch oven from the embers and pop the macaroons onto a serving plate. If they are still pale, continue baking, covered, for an additional 5 minutes.

PATRICK'S CAMPFIRE COOKIES

IT ISN'T THAT WE MIND SO-CALLED "TRAIL MIX," THAT DRYISH JUMBLE OF NUTS, PRETZELS, CHOCOLATES, AND UNIDENTIFIABLE CHEWY BITS SO DOGGEDLY POPULAR ON NATURE ADVENTURES. After all, it bestows much-needed energy upon one's lagging chi. But given the choice, we'd prefer something that offers the same spiritual boost in a more compact package, free from the competition of tangled fingers diving into a sack for the same peanut (excepting of course, those instances in which tangling fingers is precisely the point). This tasty sweetmeat, first introduced to us by our friend and fire god, Patrick J. Wessel, fits the bill and requires no baking—an unusual feat for a cookie. We also promise that they will melt decadently in the mouth the way a soggy pretzel never could.

1. *Prepare a low- to medium-heat fire, with the flames occasionally licking the grill grate. Let it burn for 30 minutes.*

2. *Place the sugar, butter, milk, and cocoa powder in the Dutch oven and set it upon the grill grate. Stir the mixture occasionally with a heatproof spatula or wooden spoon until the butter melts and the sugar completely dissolves, about 5 minutes. Transfer the Dutch oven to a resting place to cool slightly.*

3. *Drop in the oats, peanut butter, and vanilla and stir vigorously with the spatula or wooden spoon until the dough is thoroughly combined. Use a spoon to scoop out portions of the dough. Roll the portions into balls and let them rest on a plate until completely cool. Arrange the cookies on a platter, or store in an airtight container for up to 1 week. Dust ever so lightly with confectioners' sugar before serving, if desired, and allow one's guests to help themselves before or after taking a hike.*

1 cup sugar

4 tablespoons (½ stick) unsalted butter, cut into pieces

2 tablespoons whole milk

2 tablespoons cocoa powder

1½ cups old-fashioned rolled oats

5 tablespoons smooth, all-natural peanut butter

1 teaspoon vanilla extract

Confectioners' sugar, for dusting, optional

Teatime beverages

FAIRYCAKES, PETITS FOURS, BISCUITS, AND SANDWICHES ADD IMMEASURABLE HAPPINESS TO THE TEA HOUR. Like the frills upon a petticoat, one might easily become distracted by the sweet array of goodies spilling over the tea tray.

But do remember that the tea hour without its beverages would be no tea indeed. If times grew leaner, or days grew shorter, or tastes grew humbler, one could easily swap the sponge cake for a slice of toast, or even dispense with edibles entirely. But without a piping hot tea, steaming *chocolat chaud*, or icy, tart-sweet lemonade to sip upon, one might as well skip ahead to supper. Necessity begetting invention as it does, we include here some of our favorite outdoor tea incarnations, tailored especially to those who take a bit of adventure in their brew.

Forest Forager's Kettle of Tea

After an autumn morning spent cavorting among the trees and bellowing to companions across wide meadows, one will probably suffer from chilled bones, aching limbs, and a scratchy throat. This soothing tisane of freshly foraged herbs provides a marvelous remedy. (It also restores those suffering a bout of lassitude caused by gobbling too many teacakes while waiting for the kettle to boil.)

A cursory glance at the ingredient list might lead one to think we've gone a bit far, boldly combining in one teapot multiple strong-tasting herbs, such as oregano, rosemary, and sage. Have faith—the overall effect is subtle. On humid days, one might even serve this tea iced, with a drizzle of Ginger, Lemon, or Chamomile Confectionery Syrup (page 77).

PROVIDES 4 PORTIONS

A small handful of several or all of the following, well rinsed:

Lemon balm or lemon verbena

Wild thyme

Oregano

Wild mint

Lavender

Rosemary

Wild sage

1. Prepare a high-heat fire, with the flames licking the grill grate. Fill a kettle or large pot with 1 generous quart of water and transfer to the grate. Bring to a boil.

2. Remove the kettle from the heat and drop in herbs. Cover and let steep 10 minutes before pouring the tea out into one's waiting teacup. Drop in Hand-Crafted Sugar Cubes (page 126), if desired.

Gingered Sun Tea

One might even presume that the great ball of fire hanging in the noontime sky burns only to warm one's skin. This would not only be an inaccurate assumption, it would be short-sighted, for the sun does so many things for one: it banishes darkness from one's day, dries one's foraged berries, and—to our keen happiness—makes this iced tea possible.

Why waste one's wood supply boiling water in a kettle, when the heat of a summer day can brew tea just as well? One needs only a favorite tea, a clean jar, fresh water, ice, and a splash of spicy ginger syrup. And, of course, a cloudless day (see Advisement).

PROVIDES 4 PORTIONS

4 teaspoons loose tea
Ginger Confectionery Syrup (page 77), to taste
Ice cubes, for serving
1 clean 1-quart jar, with lid

1. Fill the jar with 4 cups of clean, cold water and stir in one's tea leaves. Screw the lid on tightly and place the tea in the brightest patch of sunlight available.
2. Revisit the tea in about 1 hour. Regard its color and sip a small spoonful. If the strength of the tea is to the party's liking, strain it into ice-filled glasses and add ginger syrup to taste. If one desires a stronger brew, return it to its place in the sun until it reaches the ideal strength.

Advisement: While a cloudless day will hasten one's tea-making, an overcast day will yield the same results; one must just exercise a bit more patience in the process.

Muddled Mixed Berry Lemonade

Mixing lemonade always compels us to don our natty white linens and straw boater hats, string up a hammock between two poplars, and lounge languidly with a tall glass of this classic summer beverage in hand. Of course, should one follow our lead, do exercise caution when muddling the berries—although a gratifying activity, bursting berries are wont to splatter, and the mauve-hued stains upon one's crisp clothing are impervious to laundering.

Just-plucked and plump blackberries, raspberries, blueberries, or strawberries are our favorite fruits to use here, though one can hardly go astray with more fanciful options such as currants or elderberries. We also enjoy a garnish of chopped fresh mint, basil, or lemon thyme.

PROVIDES 4 TO 6 PORTIONS

1 cup mixed berries, freshly foraged if possible
¾ cup Lemon Confectionery Syrup (page 77),
    plus additional to taste
Freshly squeezed juice of 2 lemons (about ⅔
    cup), strained
Chopped fresh mint, basil, or lemon thyme, for
    garnish
Ice cubes, for serving

Drop the berries into a large pitcher and drizzle in about half of the lemon syrup. Use a muddler or wooden spoon to crush the berries, pressing them against the bottom of the pitcher. Add the remaining syrup and pour in the lemon juice and 4 cups cold water, stirring vigorously to combine. Sip the beverage and add more syrup, if one seeks a sweeter refreshment. Serve in chilled glasses, garnished with herbs. Allow one's guests to select their own ice cubes, as one's desire for chill varies.

Minty Chocolat Chaud

Occasionally, eager to reach the Great Outdoors without delay, we plum forget to pop into our local chocolatier for a box of bonbons to nibble 'round the fire. While some might find this cause for alarm, or indeed, even cause for motoring back into town, we do not. We simply turn out our pockets in search of a few stumps of chocolate bars. They prove perfect

HAND-CRAFTED SUGAR CUBES

We might consider feeding store-bought sugar cubes to the horses, but certainly not to our tea-time companions. Hand-crafted sugar cubes are a snap to make and sweeten the appearance of the outdoor tea tray. One advisement: do resist the impulse to use fancy candy molds for these dainty cubes. They really work best in a simple mold. If one requires a bit more drama, we suggest adding a modicum of food coloring for a vibrant look.

1 cup sugar
1 scant drop food coloring, if desired
1 sugar cube mold, such as novelty ice
    cube tray, preferably silicone

1. Place the sugar in a bowl. If colored cubes are desired, mix the coloring into 1½ tablespoons water. Add the liquid to the sugar and stir until the sugar resembles wet sand. Drizzle in a touch more, if needed, to achieve the proper consistency. Pack the wet sugar into the molds. It is not necessary to fill the molds all the way to the top. Keep in mind that each cube (or other novelty shape) need only sweeten a cup of tea—use no more than 2 teaspoons per mold.
2. Allow the sugar to set for a minimum of 15 minutes and up to 1 hour. Gently pop the cubes out of the mold and store in a jar or other airtight container.

for whipping up this lavish drink, which has the creamy opulence of a melted chocolate truffle.

The secret to this confection is the use of whole chocolate rather than cocoa powder. Since the ideal richness of chocolate is a subjective thing, we advocate tinkering here. Thicker? Substitute cream for the milk. More bitter? Increase the dark chocolate. And though we adore the lift and balance offered by the mint and salt, even these elements can be adapted (or omitted), according to one's inclinations. We do hope, however, that one will not abstain from marshmallows.

PROVIDES 4 TO 6 PORTIONS
4 cups whole milk
8 ounces bittersweet chocolate, finely chopped
2 ounces milk chocolate, finely chopped
2 ounces mint chocolate, finely chopped
Generous pinch coarse sea salt
Honeyed Marshmallows (page 79), for serving

1. Prepare a medium-heat fire, with the flames just under the grill grate. Let it burn steadily for 30 minutes.
2. Pour 2 cups of the milk into the Dutch oven and drop in all the chopped chocolate and the salt. Transfer the pot to the cooking grate. Stir occasionally, keeping a vigilant watch on the mixture so that the chocolate doesn't burn. Once the milk begins to bubble, transfer the Dutch oven to a resting place off the heat and whisk the mixture vigorously until the chocolate is completely melted. Continue whisking with one hand whilst pouring in the remaining 2 cup milk with the other. If necessary, place the Dutch oven over the fire briefly to reheat the beverage. Serve in mugs, or even diminutive espresso cups, and plop in a marshmallow or two.

The Proper Cup of Tea

What makes a proper cup of tea is a subject of much-heated debate, and one upon which many a soul fears to tread. For our part, we might have marched through the remainder of our earthly years entirely oblivious to the controversy had we not unexpectedly received a tea-making tutorial some years ago from our friend Ronan's mother, visiting from Galway. After brewing the tea in our standard fashion, we popped out of the kitchen for a flash only to return to an empty pot, whereupon Mrs. Killeen informed us that she had found our technique riddled with egregious errors. In her estimation, she continued kindly, she had no choice but to discard our work.

Should one not enjoy the advantage of having an Irishwoman voyage across the Atlantic to bin one's breakfast cuppa, we've set to paper her subsequent advice, along with further instructions collected along the way.

INSTRUCTIONS:

One should not underestimate how much difference the quality of water makes to the final infusion. If one is able, draw from the purest stream possible. And always begin with fresh, cold water, which is cleaner-tasting and boasts a fuller flavor.

Overcooked water tastes unpleasantly flat. While bringing the water to a boil is essential for black tea (see Advisement for green tea), take care to fetch the kettle the moment it bubbles—or whistles, as the case may be.

If one's water source allows for generosity, swirl a splash of pure boiling water into the teapot; a hot pot brews better tea.

Always use loose leaves, as there is nothing more unappetizing than a bloated, soggy tea bag bobbing in one's pretty pot. Lest one accuse us of pure snobbery, an explanation: whole leaves contain flavorful essential oils that evaporate quickly if cut, as the leaves are for bagged tea. What's more, the aromatic leaves need room to unfurl, a luxury not permitted in a cramped bag. Tea bags may be fine for the lazy, but a superior cup begins with whole leaves.

Allow one teaspoon of leaves for each cup, and place the leaves directly in the pot. Cover and steep; brewing time will vary. The longer the steep, the darker and more bitter the brew. Whether one prefers a cup on the lighter or the darker side, we find 3 to 5 minutes' steeping suffices for the refined palate.

Adding milk and sugar to tea is such a personal decision, we feel it the height of impropriety to force our prejudices here. However, we prefer a soupçon of milk to lighten our brew and a sprinkling of sugar stirred in, just as one would finish a savory dish with coarse sea salt just before serving.

Advisement: Black sheep abide in every family; in the tea family, green and white leaves are those dark little lambs. Rather than pour boiling water over these delicate varieties, allow the water to cool for a minute first. By preventing the scalding of these leaves, one preserves the flavor and dodges the letdown of a too-bitter brew (please turn to our section on coffee, Arabian Mornings, page 88, if bitter is what one craves).

Foraging for Forest Herbs

One need never travel far to find a profusion of herbs. We encounter them in the herbalist's healing apothecary jars and find them hung—dried and systematically classified—in the botanist's herbarium. They crown the heads of conquerors and festoon our holiday mantles. In our kitchen potager we always grow a collection of cuttings, and herbs are always ready at hand, if for sometimes too dear a price, at the greengrocer.

And yet, as great a society as we may be, too often we wander down the country lane blind to the herbaceous bounty gracing the emerald floor.

In his 1699 compendium *Acetaria: A Discourse of Sallets*, John Evelyn presented seventy-three salad herbs. Here we discuss a more manageable seven. We wish we could wax on unfettered by a consideration for space, but alas, it cannot be; instead we encourage serious foragers to purchase a comprehensive botanical guide.

Fortunately, space does allow a few tidbits of advice: When trampling through the grass, adhere to the forager's oath—pick only a few stems from each discovered plot and only from patches of herbs that are plentiful (so that other campers and other forest creatures might eat too); never pluck from private land; and only consume those plants which are positively identifiable (primarily to avoid death by poison). The best time to forage is late morning on dry, sunny days—the dew will have dried on the leaves, but the brutish heat of the sun has yet to wilt them. Collect herbs in an open-weave basket to allow for proper air circulation, using a small, sharp knife for snipping the delicate stems. And finally, segregate the herbs in one's basket, both for ease of identification and to avoid having delicate lemon balm take on the potent scent of rosemary.

We hope that this modest tutorial will inspire our readers to pick up a pair of garden shears, put on their walking shoes, and roam the meadows in search of their favorites.

Yarrow (*Achillea millefolium*). Full of medicinal properties, yarrow was christened *Herbal militaris* in days of yore; it is said that Achilles himself used the herb to stanch wounds upon the battlefield of Troy. If one forgets to pack Band-Aids, lay a bit of yarrow leaf upon the cut. It is a feathery looking plant—strew the feathery leaves into soups and salads (they boast a strong, sagelike flavor), and place the feathery, pink-tinged flowers in a pitcher for a pretty campside bouquet. Look for it in grasslands and open forests.

Lovage (*Levisticum officinale*). Tasting of celery, this mountain-loving herb has large, dark-green leaves with a toothy appearance, much like flat-leafed parsley. Its tiny, citrine flower clusters are pretty but inedible. With its natural antiseptic and deodorizing properties, one might do well to tuck a few leaves into weary hikers' shoes for a pick-me-up. One can also muddle it into cordials and liqueurs.

Meadowsweet (*Filipendula ulmaria*). One might find this aromatic herb swaying in the damp meadows where it flourishes. Nicknamed "bridewort," it was once scattered at the feet of newlyweds, though that seems long out of fashion, replaced, it seems, by the ubiquitous Gerber daisy. Meadowsweet's jagged, lobed leaves are green on top and silvery beneath, and the fragile, snowy flowers dance, fairylike, upon slender, purple stems. Stir the leaves into soups and steep the blossoms in beer, mead, wine, or jam.

Rosemary (*Rosmarinus officinalis*). To our minds, rosemary seems most at ease in the wild, smelling as it does of towering pines. Even its leaves, tightly packed green spears upon a wooden twig, echo branches of evergreen. Surprisingly, this astringent-tasting herb is native not to North American forests, but to the Mediterranean region, where it is often found growing near the sea. Should one's outdoor adventures not include travel abroad, rosemary is easily cultivated on one's windowsill at home. It is also available at most greengrocers. Rub the leaves onto meat before grilling, or scatter them over a dish of potatoes before roasting.

Wild Sage (*Salvia verbenaca*). The downy, verdigris leaves of this meadow herb boast an intoxicating, balsamic scent to which butterflies flutter. Something of a diva, sage does not always get on well with other herbs, but used alone, it flatters rich game, poultry, beef, and cheese. We tuck it amongst our linens to ward off forest insects.

Wild Thyme (*Thymus serpyllum*). Kipling famously enthused about "close-bit thyme that smells like dawn in Paradise." And while our personal imaginings of paradise carry a whiff of wood smoke, we do grasp the sentiment. It is a lovely scented plant. Many varieties exist, but most resemble each other in appearance, bearing minute green leaves on creeping woody stems and crimson, mauve, or lilac blossoms. Wild thyme tends to appear a bit straggly, as it does not receive the stimulatory benefits of regular pruning. It prefers solitude, proliferating in barren heaths and moorlands. Drop it into soups, salads, wine-based sauces, and hangover tonics.

Lemon balm (*Melissa officinalis*). Ah, lemon balm. The heart-shaped, ridged leaves look to us like mint, aside from the faintly yellow-tinged perimeter and white blossoms. Its fragrance is tantalizingly citrusy, and complements fresh fruit, salads, and ice creams. Because the scent repels insects, we sometimes pin a nosegay of lemon balm to our lapels to discourage bloodthirsty mosquitoes. In keeping with its bright flavor, it thrives in sun-drenched fields.

chinese tea eggs

SINOPHILES THAT WE ARE, WE COULD NOT RESIST INCLUSION OF THIS ELEGANT SNACK WE DISCOVERED DURING AN AFTERNOON RAMBLE IN THE MIST-SHROUDED MOUNTAIN PEAKS OF RURAL CHINA. One moment a person is enjoying a contemplative pause among the crumbling ruins of the Great Wall; the next, a band of raucous Buddhist monks approaches bearing a beautiful luncheon of slow-simmered eggs.

Considering that China is a nation flush with tea leaves, it is hardly surprising that the populace felt hard put to find uses for the brew beyond the drinking of it. These petite eggs (we used quail eggs because they are prettier than cumbersome, albeit traditional, chicken eggs) make an eye-catching supplement to the tea tray, or can be tucked into the rucksack for easy and attractive sustenance along the hiking trail. One can also substitute six regular eggs: simply double all the other ingredients and proceed as directed.

This also happens to be a jolly project. Anyone, from the pint-sized to the full-grown will derive inexplicable pleasure from spoon-tapping the shell to form the *cracquelure* that gives the egg its marbleized appearance. One can prepare the eggs before departing for the wild or cook them over a flame, *en pleine air*.

6 quail eggs

1 tablespoon Pu'erh tea (see Advisement)

3 tablespoons soy sauce

1 teaspoon kosher salt

1 teaspoon sugar

2 pieces star anise

½ cinnamon stick

¾ teaspoon black peppercorns

2 strips mandarin zest

1. Build a high-heat fire, with the flames licking the grill grate. Let it burn for 30 minutes.

2. Place the eggs in a Dutch oven or a medium pot with water to cover. Bring the pot to a boil over the fire, then adjust the heat to medium-low and simmer for 3 minutes. Remove the eggs with a slotted spoon (do not discard the water) and let them cool until one can handle them without scorching one's fingers. Tap the eggs with the back of a spoon to crack the shells evenly all over.

3. Return the eggs to the pot and add the remaining ingredients. Bring the water to a boil, reduce the heat, and simmer for 1½ hours. Add water to cover the eggs if they become exposed to the air. Remove the pot from the heat and let the eggs cool completely in the water.

4. Carefully peel away the shells, slice them in half lengthwise, and arrange them on a platter. Serve with more tea, preferably Chinese in origin.

> **Advisement:** Pu'erh tea is an earthy, tannic tea, which the Chinese turn to most frequently for tea egging. If one cannot find it, any dark tea (such as Earl Gray or Darjeeling) will do; green tea and herbal tisanes are not appropriate.

On the Art of Water Divination:

ENTHUSIASM, PRECAUTIONS, TECHNIQUE

Our companions sometimes express astonishment at the thought of ever feeling desperate for water. Preposterous! they scoff. Why, this great globe is three-quarters covered with the stuff! Touché. And yet, logic must prevail. One might stumble unexpectedly into desert lands or have the ill-fortune to choose an improvident companion who wastes a party's drinking supply. Perhaps one has set up camp on ocean sands; salt water, sadly, is not potable, despite its enticing plenitude. One may even land at an old, familiar spot only to discover a dusty riverbed, bereft of the bathing water that babbled past the summer before.

Our point: The art of water divination—also known as dowsing or, rather intimidatingly, as water witching—might well rescue one from extreme, life-threatening thirst and an abominable dearth of hygiene when least expected. Divination consists of using a Y-shaped stick, preferably made of hazel wood, to locate sources of underground water. One might also use this technique to search for pirate treasure or black gold (oil), though personally we find abuse of the technique for vulgar material gain rather off-putting.

Do reserve divination for the direst circumstances only—not only will one have to dig quite a long way to unearth the water that may be below (perhaps not all the way to China, but nearly), we also do not suggest the pock-marking of unspoiled land in the name of pure sport.

INSTRUCTIONS:

1. Find a suitable place to begin. Steer clear of mountaintops. One is far more likely to succeed in the geological dips of valleys and ravines. In a drought-struck locale, look for a glimpse of green vegetation, which may be a sign of water nearby. One can also track furred and feathered critters at daybreak and twilight, the hours at which they are inclined to seek out water themselves.

2. Holding a Y-shaped stick, or "doodlebug," by the pronged ends, slowly pace the land. The stick should be 12 to 24 inches long and point upward at an angle of approximately 45 degrees. Lower the eyelids and focus. Focus intently. More intently. Envision cascades of water, bountiful and sweet. When one feels the stick tilting downward towards the ground or waving side to side with a violent shuddering, presume success.

3. If thoroughly dehydrated, begin digging. If only modestly parched, clap oneself on the back and head back to camp for a snifter of brandy, which can quench one's thirst quite nicely, thank you.

"ALWAYS DO SOBER

WHAT YOU SAID

YOU'D DO DRUNK."

—ERNEST HEMINGWAY

CHAPTER FIVE

CAMPFIRE COCKTAILS

LIKE TEATIME, THE COCKTAIL HOUR IS HELD AT A PRESCRIBED TIME OF THE DAY. Certainly one can partake of these snacks and beverages at any moment that suits one's fancy, but it is during the twilight (known in some poetic circles as the *gloaming*) when the magic of the cocktail hour is most potent. Truly, during the tick-tock of those sixty minutes, one can perform a kind of alchemy whereby a fastidiously concocted elixir and a simple handful of nibbles transform one's companions from drab, worker drones wrapped up in the mundane concerns of the world into sparkling creatures of the night, senses attuned to the possibility of every thing. It is no mere happenstance, surely, that this transformation of the soul is accomplished whilst our planet transitions from the brilliant clarity of day to the muted ambiguity of night. There are no coincidences in nature.

The cocktail hour is also the time for avant-dinner socializing. A quick bite of something appetizing will whet one's desire for the meal to come, and a slowly sipped drink will temper one's hunger in case one has to wait a bit for satiety. Cooking over the open fire is not necessarily a timely endeavor, after all. (Perish the thought!) When enjoying a feast prepared in this fashion, there is always time for a chilled beverage and a witty chat with one's companions.

And because we have this novel luxury of the open fire, we can serve our guests delicacies such as squash seeds toasted on the fire, chestnuts roasted on the fire, and popped corn fragrant with fire-warmed spice. Decadent offerings such as potatoes topped with caviar or escargot with buttery garlic sauce are made all the more pleasurable when cooked with that wily element, fire. We love the smoke and flame because they add a little bit more flavor to the drama, a little bit more sparkle to the dusky hour. And we simply cannot resist extra sparkle.

And if one is inspired to forage for snails, or make a termite tapenade, or simply to tell the correct hour of the night by gazing at the stars, we shall give direction on such matters in the pages of this chapter. Because we believe that while one's mind may be besotted with spirits, one's spirit ought to strive for acuity.

Nibbles for the Gloaming

WE TAKE A COOKERY LESSON FROM SHERLOCK HOLMES, WHO SAID, "IT HAS LONG BEEN AN AXIOM OF MINE THAT THE LITTLE THINGS ARE INFINITELY THE MOST IMPORTANT." He might have been speaking of these marvelous wee nibbles with which we welcome the twilight hour. They are a scrumptious way to prepare the digestion for the spirits one is about to consume. When confronted by a cocktail companion who is unaware of this, we can only tut-tut and say, "Oh, my dear, these nibbles are elementary!"

Potatoes with Caviar, Crème Fraîche & Red Onion

We consider this dish the apex of gracious entertaining. A soupçon of caviar and hard-cooked egg on toast make a lovely, light refreshment at a ball when one needs refueling and sits out a quadrille or minuet. Our guests naturally expect a similar treat when they attend our firelight soirees. Indeed, we improve upon the preparation by eschewing the dry toast and serving the prized fish roe on red potato rounds, still warm from the grill. It is just the thing to get everyone in the right frame of mind for this ballroom under the stars. Though the music is supplied by ukulele and harmonica rather than the harpsichord, there will still be caviar to set one's feet to dancing.

PROVIDES 10 TO 12 PORTIONS

1¾ pounds red baby potatoes

2 tablespoons coarse sea salt

3 large, farm-fresh eggs

Olive oil, for brushing

½ red onion, peeled and finely chopped

2 tablespoons finely chopped chives, optional

Crème fraîche, for serving

2 ounces caviar, for serving

1. Prepare a medium-high-heat fire, with the flames occasionally licking the grill grate. Let it burn steadily until it forms glowing, ash-covered coals and embers, about 45 minutes. Using a coal shovel or like implement, scrape a bed of embers off to the side of the fire pit.

2. Drop the potatoes and salt into a Dutch oven and fill it with enough fresh water to cover the potatoes. Place the pot upon the embers; cover it and allow the water to come to a boil, removing and adding coals as necessary to maintain a steady heat. Uncover and continue to boil the potatoes until they are almost tender, about 20 minutes. Using a slotted spoon, transfer them to a bowl to cool.

3. Use the slotted spoon to gently lower the eggs, one by one, into the boiling water. Boil for 7 minutes. Remove them with the spoon and let them cool completely; peel and finely chop.

4. Cut each potato in half lengthwise and slice a sliver from the bottom of each piece so that it will sit firmly upon its derriere. Arrange the slices on a large platter. Brush the tops and bottoms of the potatoes lightly with olive oil. Maintaining a high heat over the fire, transfer the potatoes to the grill grate and cook them until lightly charred, 2 to 3 minutes per side.

5. In a small bowl, toss together the onion and chives.

6. Spoon a dainty dollop of crème fraîche onto each potato, followed by an even daintier scoop of caviar, a smattering of chopped egg and a light sprinkle of the onion-herb mixture. Serve, to much applause.

Garlic Buttered Escargots

Who does sauce better than the French? Scads of butter, garlic, parsley, and, of course, Pernod with plenty of hot and crusty bread for dipping—really, the escargots are beside the point. But if snails provide the excuse for this magnificent sauce, then we say three cheers for gastropods! And as we check between our teeth for stray bits of chopped parsley, we can't help but give a thought to poor, misunderstood Napoleon Bonaparte. Clearly he was trying to bring the sublime joy of escargots in butter sauce to all the people of Europe. Yes, perhaps he was a bit too aggressive about it. We can only hope the garlic butter-loving little general was able to forage some snails on the Isle of Elba—and that someone thought to send him there with a few bottles of Pernod. Vive les escargots!

PROVIDES 6 PORTIONS

1 cup (2 sticks) unsalted butter

3 garlic cloves, peeled and finely chopped

1 shallot, finely chopped

One 14-ounce can snails

¼ cup chopped fresh parsley

3 tablespoons Pernod, or dry white wine

1. Prepare a medium-heat fire, with the flames just below the grill grate. Let it burn steadily for 30 minutes.

2. Plunk the butter into the skillet and set it upon the grill grate to melt, 3 to 5 minutes. As soon as the butter melts, add the garlic and shallot and sauté briefly, stirring with a long-handled, heatproof spoon, about 1 minute. When the butter begins to bubble, carefully add the snails. Cook, turning the gastropods occasionally until they are browned all over, 8 to 10 minutes. Stir in the parsley and Pernod during the last minute of cooking.

3. Transfer the skillet to a resting place to cool slightly. Sprinkle on sea salt and freshly milled black pepper to taste. Serve the escargots with their glorious butter sauce on a communal platter with plenty of good, crusty bread.

Spice Market Popcorn

In preparation for our society debut, we were privileged to journey along the Silk Road in search of materials for our coming-out frocks. Little did we know we would find the route's exotic markets brimming with spices as well as silks. These aromatic additions need something simple to convey them to the mouth—and what could be better than a bowl of freshly popped corn? We give two modes of preparation here: for savory and for sweet. We love the flavor imparted by a few crushed garlic cloves, and we heat them in the oil to really bring out the garlic fragrance; we add sugar and spice after popping, to keep the sugar from burning and overwhelming the subtle cinnamon or garam masala. Though the conventions of fashion have required retiring those ball gowns of yore, this popcorn will be in our party repertoire for all time.

PROVIDES 4 TO 6 PORTIONS

3 tablespoons oil (such as canola, soy, or peanut)

¾ cup popcorn kernels

For Savory Popcorn:

2 cloves garlic, smashed

One of the following:

   2 sprigs fresh rosemary

   2 teaspoons herbes de Provence

   2 teaspoons ground Aleppo pepper

   2 teaspoons ground sumac

   2 teaspoons ground caraway

Foraging for Snails

(*HELIX ASPERSA*)

The art of snail foraging is different from other sorts of foraging activities. For starters, unlike one's immobile, passive mushrooms, greens, or berries, snails can see, which is to say they are slightly more living and breathing than plant life. In order to eat a snail for supper, one is obligated to do more than snip it with a set of garden shears and plop it into one's foraging basket. On the other hand, hunting snail is nothing like ordinary mammal hunting, either. It requires no furtively laid traps, no silent squatting in the trees awaiting approach, no bloodshed; one has no fear of startling snails because, let us be frank, this gastropod's reputation is hardly one of fleet-footedness. All things considered, snail-foraging is in a category of its own, one in which a biological underdog turns out to be the darling of the culinary world, the escargot. Is Nature not marvelous?

To begin that slow crawl from ordinary land snail to French delicacy, one must first reserve a week in the wild, as the entire process of preparing snails for consumption takes approximately that long. Next, the creatures must be captured. They are nocturnal, so we advise setting out on a hunt while the world is darkish, perhaps during the wee hours before dawn, or during the waning light of dusk. Next, one must be sure to have along a large bucket with a tightly fitting lid into which one has poked numerous breathing holes. The lid is terribly important, because although snails have only that one muscular foot, it is a very robust foot, and they will find their way out of the bucket with a strength that makes one's jaw drop.

Snails inhabit many different sorts of climates, from the deep ocean to the desert to one's back garden lettuce patch. In the wild, one is likely to find them skulking upon the undersides of stones and leaves. One can also cast about the ground with one's lantern for the glistening trail of slime left in a snail's wake. Once one snail is discovered, dozens more are at hand. To make the effort worthwhile, we suggest aiming to collect two to three dozen snails.

Once the snails have been brought back to camp, it is necessary to begin the process of purging them, which is simultaneously a means to rid the critters of any toxins lurking in the intestinal tract and a way to fatten them up for the feast. Into the bottom of one's bucket, place some tasty edible leaves, like dandelion, watercress, or herbs. Consider the snails miniature grass-fed cattle—the more flavor consumed, the better one's end result. Make sure to also place a shallow dish of water in the bucket (one's tea cup saucer makes a perfectly low trough for the snails). Let this feasting continue for a week or so; clean out the cage and change the water every other day.

At this point, some experts in heliciculture—that's snail farming—will say it is time to begin the starvation period, which is meant as the final intestinal cleanse. We pass over this process, as it seems a bit cruel. We are quite certain one's karma will be entirely improved by allowing them to leave the world with a full belly. So instead, blanch the snails in a pot of boiling water for a minute or two to loosen them from their coiled shells (this also serves as the snail's coup de grâce). Then dig up an escargot fork, or an ordinary fork, and pull each snail from its home. Give them a good rinse under cold water.

Next, fill a clean pot with water, white wine, some crushed garlic cloves and a handful of fresh thyme and bring the whole thing to a boil (do not worry about proper quantities, just aim for about one-third wine to two-thirds water. Let the snails simmer in the mixture until they are very tender, about an hour or so. Drain them well; they are now ready to be used in any escargot dish one pleases (we are partial to the classic butter-garlic concoction on page 137).

1 teaspoon ground cumin with a pinch of cayenne

1 teaspoon ground turmeric with a pinch of freshly milled black pepper

Coarse sea salt, to taste

For Sweet Popcorn:

1 tablespoon granulated sugar

Coarse sea salt, to taste

2 teaspoons garam masala (see Advisement, page 168) or ground cinnamon

1. Prepare a medium-heat fire, with the flames just below the grill grate. Let the fire burn steadily for 30 minutes.
2. Place the oil in the Dutch oven. If one desires savory popcorn, add the garlic cloves to the oil (we find garlic goes wonderfully well with any additional spice), then choose another herb or spice and add that in as well. If one will be serving sweet popcorn, do not add garlic to the oil. It will not taste good.
3. Scatter the popcorn kernels into the Dutch oven in an even layer and cover the pot. Place it upon the grill grate and wait for the popcorn to pop. The popping noise will be audible in about 5 minutes, and in about 10 minutes, most of the kernels will have popped. Carefully take the Dutch oven off the fire and decant the corn into a large bowl.
4. If serving savory popcorn, simply toss in salt to taste. For sweet popcorn, immediately add the sugar, salt, and spice; toss well to combine.

Fire-Toasted Squash Seeds

As some know-it-all once said, "Waste not, want not." And while the advice of those advocating sensibility ought to be taken with a grain of salt, we can't help but concede this point. In that spirit, we propose fire-toasting the seeds reserved from the making of the White Bean Stew with Pancetta & Pumpkin (page 192). They are a just-right spicy, salty snack to enjoy along with an aperitif to celebrate the close of another glorious day.

PROVIDES 4 TO 6 MODEST PORTIONS

1 cup pumpkin or other squash seeds, rinsed and air-dried

1 tablespoon extra-virgin olive oil

¾ teaspoon kosher salt, plus additional, to taste

¼ teaspoon smoked paprika, plus additional, to taste

1. Prepare a medium-high-heat fire, with the flames occasionally licking the grill grate. Let it burn steadily for 30 minutes. Place a cast-iron skillet over the flame to warm.
2. Toss the squash seeds with the oil, salt, and paprika. Carefully scrape them into the skillet and cook, stirring frequently, until golden and dry to the touch, about 15 minutes. Transfer to a bowl. Taste, and adjust seasonings, as desired.

Flame-Licked Marinated Olives

These are wonderful to serve just as guests arrive for a meal. The olives cook very quickly over a high-heat fire, and the jumping flames are sure to impress the early arrivals. Be sure to have the cocktails mixed when the olives are put out—they have a less-than-subtle spiciness not at all conducive to patiently waiting for one's beverage.

PROVIDES 4 TO 6 PORTIONS

1 cup mixed, pitted, unmarinated olives

2 tablespoons extra-virgin olive oil

Two 3-inch strips orange peel, white pith removed

2 small sprigs fresh rosemary

1 cinnamon stick

1 garlic clove, peeled and crushed

1 bay leaf

Pinch red pepper flakes

Metal skewers

1. Gently combine all the ingredients in a bowl. Cover

and let stand at air temperature for 1 hour.

2. While the olives are marinating, prepare a high-heat fire, with the flames licking the grill grate. Let it burn steadily for 30 minutes.

3. Thread the olives onto long metal skewers. Place the skewers upon the grill grate and cook, turning once, until they are lightly charred, about 1 minute per side. Slide the olives into a bowl and serve.

Really Roasted Chestnuts

If one is going to go about roasting things on an open fire, what better way to start than with a pound of chestnuts? Apart from being featured in that charming yuletide carol, chestnuts are celebrated by important ancient chroniclers like Homer and Pliny, who would have gobbled up the toasty, breadlike nuts as part of their healthful Mediterranean diets. According to those two, Mount Olympus, the home of the gods, was absolutely awash in chestnut groves. Zeus, Hera, Hestia & Co. must have been roasting them every evening as part of their cocktail-hour ritual. Perhaps it was the chestnut-scented smoke wafting down to Earth that emboldened Prometheus to steal that fateful bit of fire? In any event, roasted chestnuts are a welcome treat in any season, whether they put one in mind of Jack Frost or of the hierarchical struggles of Greek gods.

PROVIDES 6 TO 8 PORTIONS

1 pound chestnuts

1. Use a paring knife to cut a small *X* into the flat bottom end of each chestnut. Place the chestnuts in a large bowl and cover with cold water for 30 minutes to 1 hour. (The cutting and soaking will facilitate removal of the shells later on.)

2. While the chestnuts soak, prepare a medium-high-heat fire, with the flames occasionally licking the grill grate. Let it burn steadily for 30 minutes.

3. Drain the chestnuts. Arrange them in a single layer on a large sheet of foil. Tightly wrap the edges to seal and nestle the package into the fire's embers. Try to keep the packet as close to the fire as possible without allowing it to be licked by the flames.

4. Continue roasting until the chestnuts are tender when pierced with a knife and the edges of the *X* whittled into the shell peels back attractively, 20 to 25 minutes. Serve the chestnuts hot, allowing guests to peel the nuts themselves (be aware that the chestnuts will become increasingly difficult to peel as they cool).

Alpinist's Fondue

It is lovely to go for an outdoor holiday in the Alps. The mountain air is crisp and clean, and affords an unparalleled view, without all that oxygen to get in the way. . . . Truthfully, the heights can be more than a bit dizzying and it may be desirable to steady oneself with a solid foundation of hot, melted cheese (especially if a bibulous evening is planned). A diet of fondue is what gives intrepid explorers the gumption necessary to scale the Matterhorn or Mont Blanc. Of course, one might enjoy this dairy-laden appetizer with a glass of Riesling or hard cider, whether or not one has plans to mountaineer. One will find it eminently satisfying, even when consumed preparatory to sedentary plans.

A word to those who wish, like the Swiss, to express neutrality: German Kirschwasser (a subtle cherry brandy) is added to traditionally prepared Swiss fondue. If one desires an Italian Piedmontese-style dish, add shaved white truffles or a drop or two of truffle oil to the cheese.

PROVIDES 6 TO 8 SERVINGS

1 small garlic clove, peeled and halved

1 bottle dry white wine

¾ pound Gruyère cheese, grated (3 cups)

¾ pound Emmanthaler or raclette cheese, grated (3 cups)

1½ tablespoons cornstarch

Freshly milled black pepper, to taste

Splash kirsch, optional

Crusty bread, chunks of crisp apple and pear, blanched asparagus or broccoli, for dipping

1. Prepare a medium-high-heat fire, with the flames occasionally licking the grill grate. Let it burn steadily for 30 minutes.

2. Rub the inside of a large Dutch oven or heavy-bottomed saucepan with the garlic; discard the garlic (tossing it into the flame is a pleasantly fragrant way to do this). Place the pot upon the grill grate. Pour 1 cup of the wine into the pot; divvy the remainder among one's party (or keep for oneself). Bring the wine in the pot to a simmer.

3. Meanwhile, in a large bowl, toss the cheeses with the cornstarch. Add the cheese to the simmering wine; reduce the heat to medium and stir constantly until the cheese is completely melted. Heat until bubbling, about 5 minutes. Season with pepper and kirsch. Transfer the Dutch oven to the resting place to cool slightly, then serve it with crusty bread, chunks of crisp apple and pear, or a platter of blanched asparagus or broccoli for dipping.

Advisement: Although in life it is often necessary to choose between two evils, in the world of fondue, this is fortunately not the case. Having reached the bottom of the fondue pot, one has two blessed choices: One can allow the remaining cheese to bake onto the bottom of the pan until it forms *la religeuse,* a delicious, savory, crackerlike crust. Or, if one wishes to stretch the cheesy remains just a bit further, one can adopt the French custom of scrambling an egg or two into the bottom of the pot when the cheese dwindles. Consume as one would any cheesy scrambled egg.

Aperitifs

We consider a campfire cocktail party, complete with mixed drinks, passed hors d'oeuvres, and little black neckerchiefs, an event unto itself. When guests gather specifically to dine, it is aperitifs that are in order. A small-but-strong drink just before dinner is a charming custom for which we may thank the French, the Italians, and the Spanish. The word itself comes from the Latin aperire, which means "to open." An aperitif is intended to declare, "The season of the dinner party is open!" Or perhaps, "Time to open the gullet and enjoy a magnificent feast!" Or maybe (just maybe), "Keep an open mind, people. We are preparing this entire meal over an open fire, so please try to be open to the idea of eating at two in the morning!" Whatever the message, a glass or two of Sherry, Campari, or Lillet whets the appetite and softens the mind in preparation for the meal to come. It is a light and refreshing signal that the repast will be one to linger over. When yours is an al fresco gathering, there is all the more reason to settle in, sip an aperitif, and wish upon the first twinkling star. So merci, little aperitif! Or grazie! Or gracias! Oh, let's just all have another!

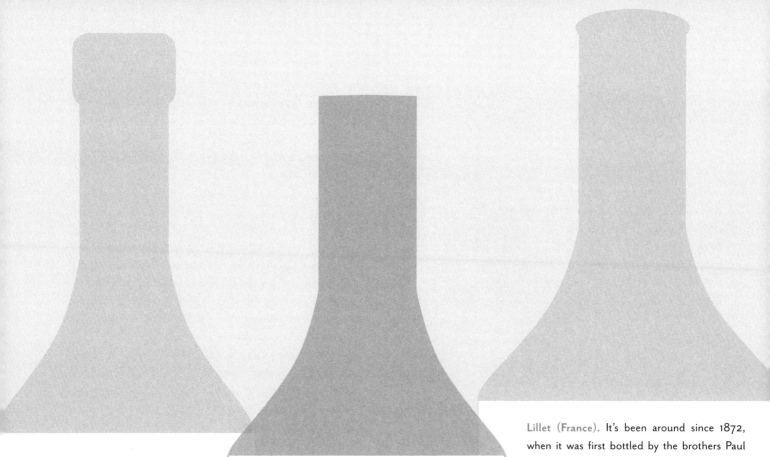

Campari (Italy). First distilled in Milan in 1860 by Gaspare Campari, this distinctive liqueur is thought to be a blend of quinine, rhubarb, ginseng, and aromatic herbs—but nobody really knows for sure, as the recipe is a secret as well concealed as the seam of a Pucci print. Serve Campari in a chilled glass (keep the glasses tucked away in an icy cooler until just before they're needed) with a splash of soda water to release the flavor. The flavor of Campari is an acquired one. While some are devoted to its bitterly nuanced sophistication, others swear it tastes like poison. Either way, this aperitif is a sure-fire conversation starter.

Sherry (Spain). Produced in the Jerez region on the southern tip of Spain, sherry has been enjoyed since the thirteenth century. It is a fortified wine, meaning it is a wine to which distilled alcohol has been added. Vineyards growing the sherry's Palomino grape survived the Moorish occupation of the Dark Ages by claiming to supply Holy War forces with raisins. Maybe there were some dried-up grapes making their way to Jerusalem, but chances are, some were fermented and aged in oak barrels. And ever since Sir Francis Drake made off with three thousand casks of the stuff during on raid on Cadiz, aperitif lovers first in England and then all over the world have been enamored with the amber-hued wine. Depending on whether one's palate is tempted by bitter or sweet, choose Manzanilla or Oloroso to serve before dinner. Manzanilla, more traditionally used as an aperitif, is light and crisp—some drinkers swear they taste the flavor of the sea air trapped in the liquid. Oloroso is darker, and rich with the flavors of burnt sugar and dried fruits.

Lillet (France). It's been around since 1872, when it was first bottled by the brothers Paul and Raymond Lillet, using wine from the Bordeaux region of France. It was aged in barrels with a secret combination of ingredients. The swanky beverage comes in two varieties—blanc or rouge—and has a delicately balanced flavor profile fragrant with herbs, roots, and fruit. Lillet is generally served in a chilled glass with a citrus garnish, a twist of orange, a thinly sliced lemon, or even a chunk of pink grapefruit rubbed around the rim. It's simply adored by the modern-leaning jet set. Wallis Simpson (the American divorcee for whom the Duke of Windsor abdicated the crown and glory of his birthright) famously kept a bottle of Lillet tucked away in her luggage. And as she seems to have done all right for herself, at least insofar as climbing the social ladder is concerned, we feel that this an excellent stamp of approval. Serve Lillet at any function where there is an opportunity for the classes to mix.

COCKTAILS

THESE ARE BUT A FEW OF THE WHIMSICAL MIXED DRINKS THAT HAVE FOUND SUCCESS AROUND OUR CAMPFIRE. We encourage all readers of this tome to let their imaginations take flight and to come up with their own signature concoction. Do use our humble offerings as a starting point. We ask only that one drink a toast to us, as we certainly will to thee.

Witch in the Woods

The Italian liqueur known as Strega (which means "witch") is a sweetish beverage with hints of springlike fennel and mint. It's a cheery yellow color, not at all what one might associate with a witchy old crone. Perhaps it is the favored drink of those misunderstood, magical ladies who populate the woodlands of fairy tales? Perhaps they quite need a cocktail after oven-roasting those misbehaving urchins who seem unable to resist nibbling at houses? Well, if that is the case, we say these frustrated women are welcome to alight from their brooms and have a drink with us. So long as they leave their poisonous apples (or tangerines, as the case may be) at home.

PROVIDES 1 COCKTAIL

½ lime

Freshly squeezed juice of 3 tangerines (about ⅓ cup)

2 ounces (¼ cup) Strega

1 sprig fresh mint, for garnish

Shave a strip of zest (avoiding any white pith) from the lime and set aside. Squeeze the juice into a highball glass filled with ice. Stir in the tangerine juice and Strega. Rub the rim of the glass with the lime peel, and drop the twist into the drink. Garnish with a fresh mint sprig.

Firefly

One evening whilst enjoying a sparkling Cava around the fire, our friend and fire consultant, Patrick J. Wessel, was moved to compose a melancholy little rhyme to the fireflies blinking in the distance. "Firefly, firefly why do you try to shine, when the moon's light is so much brighter than thine?" young Patrick sang. Well, perhaps the poem is more touching when one has already consumed a cocktail or two. We suggest trying a Firefly, in which the Cava acquires a bit more spark through the addition of vodka. The pomegranate juice is really just there for looks, which are so important when one is in a poetical mood.

PROVIDES 1 COCKTAIL

3 ounces Cava, or other top-quality sparkling wine

1 ounce vodka

Pomegranate juice, for color

Pour the Cava and vodka into a Champagne flute. Add just enough pomegranate juice to give the drink a nice rosy color.

Scatterac

Dear reader, we hesitate to be indelicate. Yet one lives in the world and cannot always turn a blind eye to the indelicacies one may encounter on, say, a walk in the woods. So do forgive our frankness, for the moment has arrived to recognize a reality of forest adventure: bear poo. From time to time, one will come across this natural phenomenon—one hopes one

will see it before it is too late, for, truly, it seems large enough to have a gravitational pull all its own. After an encounter with this evidence of ferocious animal life, we concocted this steadying drink, a riff on the traditional Sazerac Cocktail. We added a splash of amaro to make it a bit woodsier and garnished it with wild berries because, well, if one should ever see this beverage's inspiration, the reason will be readily apparent.

PROVIDES 1 COCKTAIL

1½ ounces rye whiskey such as Sazerac

¼ ounce absinthe

Splash amaro

1 sugar cube (page 126)

Wild berries, for garnishing

Place the rye, absinthe, amaro, and sugar cube in a cocktail shaker. Make sure the lid is closed securely, then shake vigorously until the sugar has dissolved, about 1 minute. Pour the drink into a chilled cocktail glass and garnish with berries.

Gauguin's Tahitian Punch

From time to time, a thoughtful guest turns up bearing a bottle of wine of an inferior vintage. What is a gracious outdoor host to do? In our younger days, a few bridges were burnt after we poured out the offending oenological offering. We've since decided it is more hospitable to devise a cocktail that gives swill the potability that it previously lacked. The combination of triple sec and pineapple is evocative of the French equatorial islands, and after knocking back a few glasses of this punch, one envisions all the vivid colors employed by that rascally impressionist Gauguin, who brought the vibrancy of Tahiti to the Paris art scene. We provide punch enough for all one's guests to join in the tropical bonhomie.

PROVIDES 4 TO 6 PORTIONS

One 750-milliliter bottle white wine, any variety

½ cup Triple Sec

1 pineapple

San Pellegrino Limonata (or plain seltzer with a squeeze of fresh lemon), for serving

Crushed ice, for serving

1. Pour the wine into an extra-large pitcher or punch bowl. Stir in the triple sec.
2. Place a cutting board on a stable surface. Use a sharp knife to shave off the spiny outer layer of the pineapple and cut it into dainty chunks. Transfer any juice on the cutting board to a bowl. Add the juice and pineapple chunks to the pitcher or punch bowl and swirl to combine.
3. To serve the punch, pour it into a cup filled with a scoop of crushed ice. Top with a spritz of Limonata.

Gent's Rosemary Gin Fizz

This is our take on the classic Ramos Fizz, invented in the 1880s by Henry C. Ramos in the crescent city of New Orleans. It was Mr. Ramos's innovation to add cream to this concoction. No doubt he felt his patrons were not getting enough calcium to make them grow big and strong (and able to shake this drink for the two solid minutes it requires for a proper fizz). Well, mixing dairy with one's gin is certainly our preferred way to achieve sturdy bones and a dazzling smile. We took the liberty of garnishing with rosemary to give the sophisticated city cocktail a rural charm.

PROVIDES 1 COCKTAIL

2 ounces gin

2 to 4 dashes orange bitters, according to one's appreciation of bitterness

2 tablespoons Lemon Confectionery Syrup (page 77)

2 tablespoons heavy cream

1 large farm-fresh egg white, optional

2 dashes orange flower water, optional (see

Edible Entomology

We love serving tiny bites along with our cocktails, and cocktail hours in the great outdoors are no exception. Whilst one prepares a bountiful platter of nibbles, one may look about the forest floor and see insects and think, "Hmmmm, that wriggly creature wouldn't look half bad skewered on a foil-tipped cocktail stick."

To be perfectly candid, we must admit that we have never proffered edible entomology as hors d'oeuvres. But we have an open mind about such matters—one does meet all kinds in the wilderness. And a little research shows that revulsion at the eating of insects is misguided. They are packed with protein and loads of vitamins and iron, just what one needs to feel fit and healthy and ready for an evening of fireside fun.

Naturally, there are a few caveats when dining on foraged bugs. Seek creepy-crawlies well away from urban areas, roads, or farms, as they may be contaminated by pollution or pesticides. Furthermore, although caterpillars may appear a particularly juicy and flavorful mouthful, we cannot recommend consuming them on account of our passion for butterfly hunting. If one eats all the caterpillars, from whence will the butterflies come? And finally, there are some brilliantly colored insects that will disagree with one's digestion. Those who regularly enjoy the delights of a multilegged buffet have an easy-to-remember saying: "Red, orange, yellow: forget this fellow; black, green, or brown: wolf him down."

Cicada (Order Hemiptera). Cicadas, with their obtrusively loud singing, are easy to find on any outdoor holiday. They are best harvested just after they molt, when they have a more pliable exoskeleton, similar to a softshell crab. Though they can be served plainly roasted, cicadas have more crunch than flavor and benefit from a spicy dipping sauce.

Grasshopper (Order Orthoptera). Grasshoppers are plentiful in spring and summer and not at all difficult to catch. They are often considered the prawns of the land; simply place them in a bowl of cold water with a generous sprinkling of baking soda to purge, then prepare them as one would shrimp. While they are delicious when served in a chilled crystal glass accompanied by cocktail sauce, they are also declared to be quite tasty when roasted and dipped in fragrant honey.

Termite (Order Isoptera). Termites can be a mite tricky to locate in the wild. Try looking for a telltale mound of the hard-working critters near fallen, rotting trees. Termites love the rain and will swarm out of their home to enjoy the precipitation. One might carry a watering can on one's nature walks, sprinkle the suspected termite abode, and try to catch a snack. Termites are marvelously simple to prepare. One need only place them in a hot skillet over the fire and sprinkle them with a good pinch of salt. They will soften and create their own, er, sauce. Serve them on crackers or flatbread, as one would tapenade.

Ants (Order Hymenoptera). As anyone who has ever set out picnicking can attest, all one needs to trap a battalion of ants is a crumb of food. We recommend a trap of one large leaf sprinkled with something delicious; this makes it much easier to lift the army straight to its doom. One can eat ants raw or lightly toast them in a skillet over a fire's embers. We've been told that after toasting, they can be ground, seasoned, and baked into a cake, but we find the pests unworthy of such trouble. A sprinkling of salt and chili powder post-roast ought to suffice.

Advisement)
1 fresh orange wedge
1 sprig fresh rosemary

Place the gin, bitters, confectionery syrup, and cream, as well as the egg white and orange flower water, if desired, in a shaker. Close the lid securely and shake vigorously until the drink is fizzy and foamy, about 2 minutes. Pour the mixture into a chilled highball glass and add a squeeze of orange. Use a sharp knife to remove the peel from the orange and skewer the fruit with the rosemary sprig. Plop the sprig into the glass and serve immediately, before the fizz dissipates.

Advisement: Be judicious with the orange flower water; a little of this elixir goes a long way. If one uses too much, the cocktail will be more suitable for decanting into a lady's cut-crystal perfume bottle than into a glass.

Beyond the Clock Face

TELLING TIME BY THE SUN AND STARS

When one is comfortably ensconced in the woods, what signify the hours of the day? Upon every moment hangs eternity. Whilst occupying Mother Nature's bower, one is permitted to dine when hungry, imbibe when thirsty, rest when weary, and frolic as one chooses. One becomes so in tune with the timepiece of innermost desire that one may neglect the winding of one's watch. This may prove problematic if one has invited guests from a neighboring encampment for cocktails and nibbles. What if they turn up just before sunset as one is about to commence serious frolicking? Social faux pas are inevitable. For those in a pinch, we offer simple instructions for determining the hour by careful observation of the firmament—and shrewd employment of mathematical science.

> "THE HOURS OF FOLLY ARE MEASURED BY A CLOCK, BUT OF WISDOM NO CLOCK CAN MEASURE."
>
> —*William Blake*

BY THE LIGHT OF THE SUN

We'll start simply. If the sun is positioned in the exact center of the sky, it is noon. If she is in the eastern half of the sky, it is morning; if in the western half, it is afternoon.

Does one need a more specific sense of the hour? Put on one's thinking cap. Estimate the number of hours from sunrise to sunset, keeping in mind that summer daylight lasts about fourteen hours and winter daylight about ten hours, whereas spring and autumn days endure for around twelve hours. Now, imagine the sun's path from the eastern horizon to the west as a great arc. Visualize dividing that arc into a number of segments corresponding to the number of hours in the present day. The number of segments to the east of the sun's position represents how many hours have passed since sunrise.

BY THE LIGHT OF THE STARS

This is of great use if one's wristwatch ceases ticking in the northern hemisphere. First, gaze skyward and locate the Big Dipper. The two pointer stars in the dipper (the two stars furthest from the handle) are directly in line with the North Star. Imagine the pointer stars are showing the hand of a clock, with the North Star as its center; direct one's gaze northward. Twelve will be at the top of the clock face, and six at the bottom. Take note of the hour on the imaginary clock face to which the imaginary hand points. This is the "raw time." Now it starts getting tricky, so do try to keep up.

Because it takes the Earth 365 days to rotate around the sun, and a circle is only 360 degrees, the celestial clock runs a little fast for most of the year—every year on March 7, it is dead correct. Therefore, one must add an hour to the raw time for every month after March. Likewise, one must subtract an hour for every month prior to March. What if this calculation results in a number higher than twelve? Simply convert it to military time thus: double the time and subtract twenty-four.

Now take into account daylight savings and time zone variations. If daylight savings is in effect, add an hour to the celestial clock. If one is presently at the western edge of the time zone, add half an hour, and, naturally, if one is at the eastern edge of the time zone, subtract half an hour. If the sums have been done properly, one now knows the correct time. Please feel free to celebrate with additional cocktails.

"One cannot think well, love well, sleep well, if one has not dined well."

—FROM A ROOM OF ONE'S OWN, VIRGINIA WOOLF

CHAPTER SIX

CAMPFIRE MAIN DISHES

IF EVER THERE WERE A TIME FOR QUIET CON-
TEMPLATION IN THE WILD, DINNERTIME IS NOT
IT. At breakfast, one may fall upon the excuse of
bleariness; at teatime, the afternoon haze summons
serenity; at cocktails, thoughtful squinting into dim-
ming skies intimates sagacity. But at dinner, one's
calling card ought to be engaging conversation and
witty banter.

To maintain lofty spirits, it is best to view the
progression of a meal as a slow crescendo, with the
main course as its cheerful climactic note. One's
companions might overlook a lukewarm consommé
or deflated meringue as dinner's bookends, but it is
difficult to feel glad when, at the very moment one
wishes to soar, a supper plate of gristly meat lands
upon the lap with a disappointing thud.

Fortunately, this catastrophe can be avoided. The
woods, fields, ponds, and pastures of nature are
chockablock with exceptional eats. Why line the walls
of one's study with frightening taxidermy when the
furred, feathered, and finned are so usefully employed
in the skillet? We put no stock in hanging our hats
upon antlers—we'd much prefer venison scattered
with treetop-plucked pine nuts, or fresh bass bedded
upon saffron-scented rice, or rabbit simmered in an
olive-studded tomato sauce. These are the things that
stimulate appetite and discussion alike!

Of course, wild game does not set every heart
aflutter, and outdoor etiquette dictates that everyone
in a party ought to dine comfortably or no one should
dine at all. To that end, we have provided simple
favorites, like a decadent burger, a peppery grilled
pork chop, and a seared Cornish hen (the bon vivant
camper's answer to classic roast chicken). For companions who have no taste for a joint of meat (or for
evenings when lighter fare beckons), we suggest meat-
less dishes such as a caramelized tomato tart, a creamy
springtime risotto, and a belly-warming stew of white
beans, sage, and pumpkin.

A main dish well prepared requires none of the
affected flourishes too often employed to distract—no
butler to lift a lid, no architectural plating, no strol-
ling string quartet. Beneath a chandelier of stars, amid
the perfume of wood smoke, one need only present
one's best self: convivial, clever, and hungry.

CARAMELIZED TOMATO TARTE TATIN à LA CLARK

OUR FRIEND, THE GIFTED FOOD SCRIBE MELISSA CLARK, INSPIRED THIS DISH. She prepares a similar version in the oven and tops it, decadently, with a puff pastry crust. Alas, fire cookery has its boundaries, and unfortunately, puff pastry pushes them. Here we've substituted her brilliant pie crust recipe, which is equally divine. When summer comes, and ripe, sweet tomatoes drip from the vine like gems on a countess's décolletage, do not overlook this recipe. It is a worthy use for Nature's bounty.

- 2 tablespoons unsalted butter
- 2 red onions, halved and thinly sliced
- 3 tablespoons plus 1 pinch Demerara or raw sugar
- 1½ pounds mixed heirloom cherry tomatoes (4 to 5 cups)
- ¼ cup chopped pitted kalamata olives
- 2 tablespoons chopped fresh thyme leaves
- 1 tablespoon extra-virgin olive oil
- 1½ teaspoons sherry vinegar
- 1 large pinch each kosher salt and freshly milled black pepper
- Melissa Clark's Pie Crust Unparalleled (page 78), rolled out to a 10-inch diameter

1. *Prepare a medium-high-heat fire, with the flames occasionally licking the grill grate. Let it burn steadily until it begins to form glowing, ash-covered coals and embers, about 45 minutes. Then use a coal shovel or like implement to scrape a bed of embers off to the side of the fire pit. Nestle the skillet's lid into the flames to heat.*

2. *Place the skillet upon the cooking grate. Add the butter and melt completely. Stir in the onions and a pinch of sugar. Cook, stirring occasionally, until the onions are dark golden and caramelized, about 20 minutes.*

3. *In the meantime, in a bowl, combine the tomatoes, olives, thyme, olive oil, vinegar, and salt and pepper. Stir the tomato mixture into the skillet with the caramelized onions.*

4. *Quickly rake hot coals from the embers of the fire to form an even bed at the side of the fire pit (be sure to save some coals for one's lid). Place the skillet atop the bed of coals. Unwrap the pie crust and arrange it neatly on top of the tomato mixture, tucking the edges into the sides of the skillet. Using a knife, cut several vents in the pastry lid so that steam may escape. Remove the hot lid from the fire and place it on top of the skillet. Generously heap additional red coals onto the lid. It is important that the coals on the lid remain blazing hot during baking; should they cease to glow, heap on a fresh batch. Bake until the crust is golden and firm to the touch, about 20 minutes.*

5. *Increase the heat of one's fire to high; Return the skillet to the cooking grate and let simmer until the juices beneath the surface of the pastry begin to bubble thickly through the vents and take on a jamlike appearance, 15 to 20 minutes. Let cool 5 to 10 minutes in the skillet before slicing into wedges and serving, crust side up, or flipped, crust side down, onto a plate.*

Fruits of the Sea

Herman Melville once wrote that "there is, one knows not what sweet mystery about this sea, whose gently awful stirrings seem to speak of some hidden soul beneath." And indeed, when balanced aboard a sailing schooner, wind battering the face and the cry of seagulls overhead, the pursuit of those teeming mysteries seems worth any consequence, even should these include a greenish complexion, a quivering bowel, and a case of vertigo.

Inland, where one experiences the sea only through consumption of its bounty, nothing—no matter how deliciously mysterious—is worth even a smidgen of seasickness. Improperly selected, stored, or prepared seafood might bear microscopic toxic critters who would like nothing more than to curse one's lively party. To prevent mass ailment, please devote a moment to studying the following advice on proper seafood management.

PURCHASING

· Seafood should not be procured in back alleys or dingy saloons. Either haul one's own fish from safe waters near camp or part with one's pennies at busy, brightly lit fishmongers' establishments purveying seafood that has been sustainably harvested. Shellfish, in particular, should always wear a tag identifying its provenance.

· The freshest seafood will seem the least corpselike. Fish will have bright, clear eyes, gleaming cherry-red gills, sparkling scales, and firm flesh. Its scent should carry only a refreshing whiff of the ocean. Shellfish should smell mildly of seaweed and have no sliminess or stickiness. Mollusk shells should be tightly closed and unbroken.

· Do not purchase endangered seafood; who could bear the guilt of eliminating an entire species merely to fill one's supper plate? The Monterey Bay Aquarium's Seafood Watch program publishes information on which fish are most apt to sully one's soul and which will earn one angel's wings.

STORING

· Use seafood promptly. In the wild, our inaugural dinner is always some sort of seafood. This is because, in the culinary world, nothing perishes more readily. Until that festive hour, store seafood in its original packaging in one's fully iced icebox, which should register no higher than 41 degrees on a thermometer, and keep it for no longer than a day or two. Change the ice frequently. Ideally, seafood and other meats will occupy their own icebox, away from fresh produce, dairy, and prepared foods. Should that not be possible, do at least tuck the former in a corner opposite the latter.

· Keep fresh-caught fish on ice. If one has the good fortune to find a fishing hole, fresh, whole fish can be packed on beds of crushed ice. We recommend the ice first be placed in a perforated pan so any fish juices can drain into the bottom of one's icebox. Change the ice often.

PREPARING

· Avoid consuming raw seafood in the wild. Although we adore oysters gargled with Champagne as much as the next bon vivant, one must make certain sacrifices outdoors. Moreover, we've found that Champagne goes just as brilliantly with . . . well, everything.

· Cleanliness, as they say, is next to godliness. When preparing seafood, maintain cutting boards, knives and utensils separately from those used for fresh produce. We also never embark on an outdoor adventure without a misting bottle filled with vinegar water, so that we can give our work area and tools the occasional sanitary spritz. And one final, gentle reminder—do wash one's hands often.

SCAPE RISOTTO with CURED HAM

IF WE HAD OUR DRUTHERS, WE WOULD CONSUME RISOTTO AFTER ALIGHTING FROM A GONDOLA, HAVING DRIFTED ALONG THE WINDING CANALS OF VENICE, KERCHIEFS ROUND OUR NECKS AND BRAWNY BOATMAN BY OUR SIDE. But eating a bowl of the stuff next to a crackling outdoor fire is a close second, particularly if this version is on offer—its combination of creamy rice, salty ham, and garlicky scapes is perfection. On a cool late-spring evening, it reconciles one's residual wish for warming comfort food with the clean, crisp flavors of warmer days to come.

Cooking risotto over a campfire is much simplified if one takes the following measures: Find a comfortable spot beside the fire, as the stirring will take a good twenty minutes or more. Bring a long-handled spoon, so that one need not loom directly over the flame, dripping perspiration into one's dinner. Lastly, enlist the aid of one's companions (children especially enjoy this task, we have heard). A party is most appreciative of risotto when all have helped to churn it.

1. Prepare a medium-high-heat fire, with the flames occasionally licking the grill grate. Let it burn steadily until it begins to form glowing, ash-covered coals and embers, about 45 minutes. Then use a coal shovel or like implement to scrape a bed of embers off to the side of the fire pit. Pour the stock into a Dutch oven. Cover the pot and place it upon the coals. Heat until it is bubbling, then uncover it and maintain a steady simmer, adding or removing coals as necessary.

2. Return one's attention to the fire. It should continue to blaze at medium-high heat, with the flames just licking the grill grate. Place a large skillet upon the fire. Add 3 tablespoons of the butter and let it melt. Stir in ⅓ cup scapes and cook, stirring, until the scapes are slightly softened, about 5 minutes. Stir in the rice and cook until the grains are slightly opaque, about 2 minutes. Pour in the wine and let simmer, stirring, until most of the liquid has been absorbed, about 1 minute.

3. Now is the time to flex one's arms and prepare for more diligent stirring. Ladle in about a cup (no need to be terribly precise here) of the simmering stock. Stir constantly, in a wide figure-eight fashion until the liquid has mostly evaporated. Add another ladleful of stock and repeat the process. The liquid should bubble gently, not vigorously. If the liquid begins to boil, adjust one's grate or dampen one's flames. Continue in this fashion,

2 quarts chicken stock, as needed

6 tablespoons (¾ stick) unsalted butter

⅓ cup plus ¼ cup garlic scapes (see Advisement, page 156), very thinly sliced

1 pound arborio rice (2½ cups)

⅔ cup dry white wine, such as Pinot Grigio

3 ounces Parmigiano-Reggiano cheese, grated (about ¾ cup)

3 ounces thinly sliced cured ham, such as prosciutto, torn into bite-size strips

1 teaspoon kosher salt

Freshly milled black pepper, to taste

stopping only to trade stirring duties with one's companions, until the risotto has a creamy consistency and the rice is al dente—tender, but with bite. Do not wait until the rice is soft; it will be too far gone to salvage.

4. *Remove the pan from the heat and immediately stir in the cheese, the remaining 3 tablespoons butter, prosciutto, salt, and pepper. Taste and adjust any seasonings. Sprinkle with the remaining ¼ cup scapes and serve.*

ᔪ **Advisement:** *We happen to be mighty devotees of scapes, the green shoots of the garlic bulb that appear in early June. Upon spying their tangled tendrils, one might suspect them to be unruly; but the young curls are cherubic, with a flavor much gentler than their pungent progenitors'. Should one have the good fortune to cross them in the wild, harvest them in the heat of the afternoon—the wound inflicted upon the garlic plant will heal more quickly in the sun.*

ᔪ *Let us suppose, as might well be the case, that one misses the brief window of scape season. Do not despair. Substitute ¼ cup chopped scallion (white and light green parts) and 2 minced garlic cloves for cooking in the skillet; garnish with thinly sliced dark green scallion tops.*

Fishing Lure & Lore

There is no tastier meal to be made over the open fire than that of a fish one has caught one's self. And every fisherman and woman has their own secret method of pulling a pescatarian delight from the rivers, lakes, stream, and ponds that are to be found a stone's throw from the very best campsites. Following are a few top tips culled from our angling companions, but *caveat emptor*! The universally acknowledged first rule every fisherperson learns is to keep their stratagems secret. Who is to say if the tips they shared are lure or lore?

FINE JEWELS, FINE CATCH

It's no secret that fish are attracted to bright and shiny things. Didn't fishhook earrings get their name from the splendid bait affixed to a fisherman's line? If one wants to attract the tastiest trout in the brook, one must bait the hook with one's most precious jewels. Simply tie one's diamond ring to the end of one's line and wait for an underwater tug. Reel in one's catch with care, but if one does lose a bauble or two to a scaly belly, take heart: The person who eventually lands that swimmer will have an unforgettable meal.

THE SNEAKY SALMON TICKLE

This is a technique developed by those opportunistic naturalists some call poachers. They needed a silent method of catching the delicious salmon who were swimming upstream on the warden-patrolled property of greedy land barons, the types who would never dream of sharing their watery blessings with the common folk. These wily anglers swear by immersing an arm in the rushing stream and tickling the pink underbelly of passing salmon. The fish, delighted, stop swimming and are easily snatched out of the water with no additional fuss.

APPLES, NO WORMS

As mad Prince Hamlet said, "A man may fish with a worm that hath et of a king and eat of the fish that hath fed from the worm to show how a king may go progress through the guts of a beggar," but we say skip the worm altogether and use the apple as bait. No one needs to contemplate digesting a king; it is just not appetizing.

AUDITORY BAIT

Freshwater fish are attracted to the basso profundo of reed instruments such as clarinets, oboes, or bassoons, or brass instruments such as the French horn or tuba. Bring along one of these orchestral music-makers and play a mournful air or two. The fish will leap into the boat with such reckless abandon that one may need to throw the smaller ones back if there are to be any fish left for the next excursion. Nota bene: Never play a stringed instrument whilst angling. Fish are repelled by the sound of a lute, harp, or banjo, and one will surely find oneself supping on Bon Vivant Burgers (page 182) rather than the catch of that day. Which is certainly an admirable alternative if these fishing lures are no more than fishing tall tales.

LEMONY SKILLET-SEARED RAINBOW TROUT

WHILST DIGGING A FIRE PIT, ONE IS SURE TO TURN UP A FEW EARTHWORMS. Although we fling most of them into the forest to continue performing their duty for our ecosystem, we always save a few for the fishing pole, in hopes of luring tasty rainbow trout from the cool, clean waters near camp. When fishing for trout, one must always plant one's feet firmly upon the riverbank, as their shimmering, colorful skin is uncannily similar to a mermaid's sequined sheath. While the former is destined for the frying pan, the latter draws unassuming fishermen toward tragedy with irresistibly beautiful songs, this flaky, white fish, with a simple lemon-butter dressing, requires only a few moments upon the grill to shine.

2 lemons

Four 8- to 10-ounce whole rainbow trout, cleaned (see page 161, or ask the fishmonger to perform this task)

2 teaspoons extra-virgin olive oil

Kosher salt, to taste

Freshly milled black pepper, to taste

4 small garlic cloves, very thinly sliced

1 small bunch fresh thyme

2 tablespoons unsalted butter, cubed

2 tablespoons capers, rinsed and patted dry

1. Prepare a high-heat fire, with the flames licking the grill grate. Let it burn steadily for 30 minutes.

2. Slice 1 lemon very thinly; cut the remaining lemon into wedges.

3. Coat the outside of the fish with oil. Season the fish all over, inside and out, with salt and pepper. Stuff each fish with lemon slices, garlic slices, and thyme. Top with butter cubes and capers.

4. Heat a cast-iron skillet over the grill grate until very hot. Carefully arrange the stuffed trout in the skillet and cook until the skin is crisp-golden and the flesh is opaque and flakes easily with a fork, 4 to 5 minutes per side.

5. Serve hot, with lemon wedges for squeezing over the fish.

STRIPED BASS

with

GRILLED FENNEL & SAFFRON-CITRUS PILAF

Striped Bass:

3 tablespoons extra-virgin olive oil

1½ teaspoons finely grated orange zest

1½ teaspoons freshly milled black pepper

¾ teaspoon crushed fennel seed

Six 6-ounce striped bass fillets

Kosher salt, to taste

For the Fennel and Pilaf:

1 large fennel bulb, cut into ¼-inch-thick slabs, fronds reserved and chopped for garnish

2½ tablespoons extra-virgin olive oil

Kosher salt, to taste

Freshly milled black pepper, to taste

1 tablespoon oil

1 shallot, finely chopped

2 cups long-grain white rice

¾ teaspoon crushed saffron threads

4 oranges peeled (see note, page 87) and cut into segments

⅔ cup slivered almonds, fire-toasted (see Advisement, page 206)

IT IS SAID THAT CLEOPATRA ENJOYED A SAFFRON-SPIKED BATH AFTER A LONG DAY OF BERATING SLAVES AND WRITING LOVE LETTERS TO MARC ANTONY. We quite understand why—one whiff of the transcendent, floral spice loosens our limbs. We wish we could endorse scattering a pinch into the nearest spring for an end-of-day dip, but fret that it's a terrible waste of provisions. Instead, we bring the sea to the saffron, serving meaty, mildly sweet striped bass (sometimes called "striper") atop a bed of scented rice. The result is akin to a refined paella, smoky with fish and fennel, perfumed with spice.

The beauty of this dish is that one may prepare it all together for a luscious feast or make only one part (fish, fennel, or pilaf) to accompany other dishes.

1. Prepare a high-heat fire, with the flames licking the grill grate. Let it burn steadily for 45 minutes, or until it forms glowing, ash-covered coals and embers. Then use a coal shovel or like implement to scrape a bed of embers off to the side of the fire.

2. In a bowl, whisk together the oil, orange zest, pepper, and fennel seed. Place the fish in a bowl and turn to coat well with the marinade; cover it tightly and return it to one's icebox.

3. Toss the sliced fennel with 1½ tablespoons of the oil and season with salt and pepper. Place it upon the grill grate and cook until it is charred and tender, 4 to 6 minutes per side. Let the fennel cool, then chop it into bite-size pieces and reserve. (The fennel is now ready to serve on its own as a side dish.)

4. Adjust the grill grate or tamp down the flame to medium-high heat. Place the Dutch oven upon the grill grate. Add the remaining 1 tablespoon oil and heat until shimmering. Add the shallot and cook, stirring, until it is just translucent, 2 to 3 minutes. Stir in the rice and cook for a minute or so, until it is well coated with oil. Pour in 3½ cups water, the saffron, and ¼ teaspoon salt.

5. Rake a bed of coals to one side of the fire pit. Place the pot upon the coals; cover and simmer, removing or adding coals as necessary, until most of the liquid has evaporated, 17 to 20 minutes. Remove the rice from the heat and let stand, covered, for 5 minutes.

HOW TO
Clean a Fish

The true test of any outdoorsman or woman is guts—more precisely, fish guts. For although one must never discount visceral abilities like courage, in the Great Outdoors one is measured just as seriously by his or her ability to eviscerate. Cleaning fish has an unwarranted reputation for being a difficult endeavor and a somewhat warranted reputation for being a messy one. However, we find that being armed with a thimbleful of know-how, a sharp knife, and a clean apron swiftly resolves both concerns.

1. Rinse the fish with fresh, clean water to rid it of any gritty silt or blood.

2. Use the dull back of a knife blade or the handle of a spoon to remove the scales: in short, quick strokes, run the knife from tail to the head, taking care not to pass over the areas around the fins. The scales should hail down upon one's work area like rain in Spain falling mainly on the plains. (If no scales fall, the fish is of a breed that does not need scaling. Proceed to step 3.) Continue until the fish has the silken texture of a clean-shaven cheek.

3. Hold the fish with the backside in one's palm and the pale belly facing upward. Locate the vent, a small hole close to the tail. Slip the tip of one's knife into this hole and slit the fish cleanly up to the gills, located just behind the jaw. Cut shallowly, to avoid puncturing the entrails. The cavity of the fish should now gape open.

4. Plunge one's fingers into the opening and remove the innards, snipping them close to the fish's head. Carefully scrape out the dark red kidney line hugging the length of the spine.

5. Carefully slice or snip off the sharp fins, head, and tail, if one wishes. Rinse the fish once more with cold water, inside and out. Dry well before cooking.

6. *While the rice cooks, place a skillet upon the grill grate and get it very, very hot. Season the fish fillets all over with salt. Add the fillets, skin side down, to the pan and cook until the flesh is just opaque and flakes easily with a fork, 7 to 8 minutes per side.*

7. *To serve, fluff the pilaf with a fork and stir in the chopped grilled fennel, orange segments, and almonds. Arrange the fish prettily on top and scatter with chopped fennel fronds.*

PINE-SMOKED & MAPLE-GLAZED WILD SALMON

FOR ALL THE ROBUSTNESS OF THE INGREDIENTS OF THIS DISH, THE END RESULT IS NOTABLY DELICATE. One might ask, "Oh, but won't the bracing scent of pine make the dish taste of Christmas fir or, worse, freshly waxed parlor?" It will not. The smoked needles impart a light, balsamic flavor akin to rosemary (indeed one might substitute a bundle of that herb in this recipe), and the light glaze allows the pine flavor to shine through. The overall effect proves an excellent complement to the moist, flaky fish this cooking technique yields. Should one desire a more intensely flavored glaze, one might make a bit extra to brush over the fish before serving.

1. *Prepare a medium-high-heat fire, with the flames occasionally licking the grill grate. Let it burn for at least 30 minutes. Whilst the fire heats, soak the pine needles in the bourbon.*

2. *In a bowl, whisk together the syrup, mustard, and pepper. Season the salmon generously with salt and coat with the glaze.*

3. *Place a large cast-iron skillet upon the grill grate. Let it heat until very hot. Using tongs or one's own gloved hand, press the needles into the bottom of the skillet, taking care not to drizzle combustible bourbon into the flames, and place the rack on top of the needles. Place the fish on top of the rack and cover the pan. Cook until the fish is just opaque, about 15 minutes for medium. Serve, brushed with additional glaze, if desired.*

1 to 2 large handfuls green pine needles

½ cup bourbon

½ cup grade-B, freshly tapped maple syrup

3 tablespoons Dijon mustard

2 teaspoons freshly milled black pepper

Four 6-ounce salmon fillets, patted dry

Kosher salt, to taste

One 9-inch round wire cooling rack

CLASSIC GARLICKY STEAMED MOULES

WE MIGHT NEVER HAVE FALLEN SO HARD FOR MUSSELS HAD A HANDSOME MAR-SEILLAISE SAILOR NOT ONCE OFFERED US A LUSTROUS BLACK BIVALVE WITH A PEARL GLISTENING INSIDE. After that, it seemed only proper to have a taste, which is when the love affair truly began. (With mussels, that is. To our great relief, the sailor ran off with a cancan dancer the following day.)

At camp, our tradition is to whip up a bowl of plump, briny mussels wading in an aromatic, garlic-studded broth the moment we arrive. While several among the party rig up our tents, pour glasses of Lillet, and polish the binoculars, the rest of us set to work building a fire. Shellfish being quite perishable (see Minding One's Fruits of the Sea, page 154), this is a prudent way to use them at their freshest and finest. We also love the speed with which they can be prepared, since one ought always begin outdoor revelry as quickly as possible. Be sure to include a crusty baguette in one's camp larder; it is a heavenly vehicle for soaking up the mussels' cooking juices.

3 tablespoons unsalted butter

1 shallot, finely chopped

2 fat garlic cloves, finely chopped

1 cup dry white wine

½ teaspoon kosher salt

2 pounds freshest mussels, rinsed and well drained

¼ cup chopped fresh parsley, for garnish

Crusty baguette, for serving

1. Prepare a medium-high-heat fire, with flames occasionally licking the grill grate. Let the fire burn for 45 minutes, until glowing coals and embers form. Then use a coal shovel or like implement to scrape a bed of embers off to the side of the fire.

2. Melt the butter in a Dutch oven over the high heat until bubbling. Add the shallot and garlic and cook, stirring, until fragrant, about 30 seconds. Carefully pour in the wine and add the salt. Add the mussels and give a quick stir. Cover the pot and cook until most of the mussels have opened, 3 to 5 minutes. Remove the pot from the heat and discard any unopened mussels. Sprinkle with parsley and serve with crusty bread for soaking up the delicious mussel liquor.

STONE-SEARED CORNISH GAME HENS WITH BOMBAY SPICE

Two 2-pound Cornish Game Hens, rinsed, patted dry, and butterflied (see Advisement)

1 tablespoons garam masala (see Advisement)

2 teaspoons extra-virgin olive oil

Kosher salt, to taste

Freshly milled black pepper, to taste

Zestful Yogurt Sauce (page 65), for serving

Chopped fresh cilantro, for garnish

Rhubarb Chutney or Apricot-Cherry Chutney (page 54–55), for serving

Several heavy, preferably flat, stones or bricks wrapped in foil

FINDING A MEAL UPON WHICH AN ENTIRE COMPANY AGREES CAN BE A THORNY PROSPECT. One might insist on grilled lamb, while another craves roast pheasant; a third will hear of nothing but chilled seafood in aspic. At times like these, we find the only sensible way to quell a brewing squabble is to offer perennially popular chicken. This simple dinner of Cornish hen (a type of small chicken, more manageable over a fire), enlivened with a rub of Indian spice, always satisfies. One's party is free to move on to more pressing questions, such as which side dish to serve (we prefer our Orchard Pear & Watercress Salad, page 223).

Without an oven or spit, it is not easy to develop the crisp, golden skin that makes roast chicken so pleasing. Thus, we've borrowed a page from the Italian peasants, who employ a clever technique called *pollo al mattone*, or "chicken under a brick." One wraps a brick or two in foil and uses the bundle to weight down butterflied birds. The technique yields a crackling mahogany crust and tender, juicy meat. If one does not intend to build one's fire at the city brickyard, we suggest borrowing heavy forest stones instead. If possible, use two skillets for this dish; one might otherwise need to draw lots for first dibs, which is liable to begin the discord anew.

1. *Prepare a high-heat fire, with the flames licking the grill grate. Place 2 large cast-iron skillets (alternatively, cook the hens in batches and serve them hot, warm, or cold) upon the grill grate to preheat.*

2. *Rub the hens all over with garam masala, then coat them with the oil. Season them generously with salt and pepper. Transfer the hens to the pan, skin side down. Place the foil-covered stones on top. Adjust the heat to medium-high. Cook, turning the hens once halfway through with*

tongs or one's own gloved hand, until the skin is no longer pink and the juices run clear when pierced with a knife, 20 to 25 minutes. Let rest 5 minutes, while one prepares the yogurt sauce.

3. *Arrange the meat on china plates and garnish with cilantro. Add a dollop each of yogurt and chutney.*

↬ ***Advisement:*** *Once one becomes comfortable with the tidy art of butterflying chickens, the temptation will be to do so*

often. It's an excellent way to make quick work of the bird. Begin by trimming the first two wing joints on each wing with a chef's knife or a cleaver. Using kitchen shears, cut along each side of the backbone and remove it. Flip the bird over. At the base of the breastbone, locate the white knob of cartilage on top of the long, spear-shaped keel bone. Cut a small slit in the knob, then flatten the chicken. The keel bone should pop out. Remove it completely with one's fingers or trim it with a knife. Now cut the bird completely in half down the center. Voilà—butterfly.

↬ **Advisement:** Although garam masala can be purchased from Asian markets for a song, one might prefer the vibrant flavor of a fresh spice blend, as we do. To make one's own, combine the following in a dry skillet over a medium-high heat: 1½ tablespoons cumin seed, 1½ tablespoons coriander seed, 1½ teaspoons black peppercorns, 1½ teaspoons cardamom seed (green hulls discarded), 1 teaspoon whole cloves, 2 cinnamon sticks (broken into pieces), and 1 bay leaf. Toast the spices until they are lightly fragrant, 1 to 2 minutes. Grind the mixture in a spice grinder, then stir in ¾ teaspoon freshly grated nutmeg. Tip the mixture into an airtight jar and store it in a cool, dark pantry for a period of up to 3 months.

Novice Rock Gardening

A return to the city can feel awfully gloomy after a blissful stretch of time in the outdoors. Urban soot does not freshen one's lungs like the clean country air, and though a manicured lawn might match one's elegantly pared fingernails, it is no match for the wild tangle of prairie grass. If, like us, one's thoughts perpetually return to those far-off rugged horizons and mossy glens of yore, we recommend our favored post-holiday remedy: the Japanese Rock Garden.

Rock gardens make ideal urban monuments to camping holidays—as anyone who has ever read the signposts at the local botanical society is aware, their purpose is to capture, on a minute scale, the serene essence of large natural landscapes. Why spend hours squinting fondly at grainy picture postcards when the memories are alive and well just beyond the garden gate? We also see something pleasantly paradoxical in the marriage of stones—those reliable, everlasting lumps—and plant life, as delicate and apt to disappear with the first frost as a frivolous holiday romance.

The word "garden" might leave the black-thumbed among us panicked at the thought of tedious hoeing and mortally wilted blooms. But what enchants about the rock garden is its undemanding nature, particularly once the initial terrain has been set, which is done in the following manner:

1. Select the garden plot. This might be an underutilized patch of yard or a bed at the local community garden, but ideally, it will be on a natural slope or terrace to allow for proper drainage (and to facilitate the sense of majestic mountain ranges).

2. Clear away any weeds from the area and overturn the dirt. Investigate the soil. While typical rock garden plants don't require dry soil necessarily, they tend to perish in naturally damp soil. Therefore, ideal soil is moist, but well drained. If this does not describe one's yard space, concoct a mixture of soil that is equal parts loamy topsoil, peat, and coarse sand or bits of stone. Dig up a good six inches of original dirt and fill it with this mixture.

3. Install the rocks. Let us be somewhat realistic here, because one does not want to spend an afternoon huffing, puffing, and pushing tremendous boulders about like some modern-day Sisyphus. Whether the rocks are procured from one's own yard or the local gardening shop, choose specimens that are as large as one can comfortably move about the yard. We also find rock gardens look most natural if the rocks are varied in size and of the same geological pedigree; limestone, sandstone, and shale are all excellent choices for most rock gardens (excepting the desert-inspired). Nestle the rocks one-third of the way into the soil so that they look as if a glacier set them there several millennia ago. Scatter them close together, but somewhat haphazardly, and be sure to leave enough space between them for one's greenery.

4. Install the greenery. Remember that the objective is to imitate nature, so plants should be those that would actually hunker down in mountain or woodland crevices. Excellent choices include perennials like primrose, wall rockcress, forget-me-nots, phlox, creeping baby's breath, and wooly thyme; dwarf conifers like creeping juniper, hillside creeper Scotch pine, and cypress; and bulbs like crocus, cyclamen, and ornamental onion. Plant them close to the rocks so that as they grow, their leaves and blossoms will tumble down the hill in a most becoming and natural way.

5. Scatter an even layer of tiny pebbles around the base of the plants and in between the rocks. This will prevent erosion, discourage weeds, help plants drain properly, and give one's garden a less contrived air. As one's tiny Eden thrives, take care to see that its windswept peaks remain clear of weeds, overzealous plants, and meditating gurus.

DUCK BREAST WITH PORT AND DRIED PLUMS

FRANKLY, WE HAVEN'T THE STOMACH FOR WATERFOWL HUNTING. One can hardly be expected to toss bread to mallards in the park one morning and set up decoys the next. Moreover, we feel a particular kinship with the migratory birds, who gorge themselves on long journeys so as to develop a protective layer of fat. We find our own vacation girth serves nicely as a mattress when sleeping upon a pebble-strewn forest floor.

We may refuse to take part in the wretched pursuit (unless it is to pet the birds, see box), but we never refuse the delicious meat. To reach it, one must first render nearly all of the fat in a scorching skillet. Next, the rich red meat beneath (quite lean from all that strenuous flying) is cooked to an ideal medium rare. We've heard that many flavorings complement duck, but blind adoration for our own sauce has thus far inhibited experimentation. More addictive than opium or snuff, the claret-colored glaze boasts a sweet-savory-piquant brilliance that makes a fine match for duck.

Two 12- to 16-ounce duck breast halves, patted dry

Kosher salt, to taste

Freshly milled black pepper, to taste

2 tablespoons extra-virgin olive oil

¼ cup finely chopped shallots

⅓ cup port wine

¼ cup chicken broth

¼ cup packed, chopped dried plums

1 tablespoon good balsamic vinegar

1 tablespoon unsalted butter

1 tablespoon chopped fresh thyme

1. *Prepare a medium-high-heat fire, with the flames occasionally licking the grill grate. Let it burn steadily for 30 minutes. Place a large cast-iron skillet upon the grill grate and let it heat until very hot.*

2. *Score the fatty skin of the duck in a ¾-inch diamond pattern, taking care not to cut through to the flesh. Season the duck all over with salt and pepper. Transfer the duck, skin side down, to the hot skillet and cook until it is honey-brown and crisp, 5 to 8 minutes. Pour off all but 2 tablespoons of fat into a heatproof container (reserve it for Duck Eggs with Rosemary Salted Potatoes, page 107).*

3. *Turn the duck and adjust one's grill grate or tamp one's flames so that the fire provides medium heat. Cook to the desired doneness, 4 to 7 minutes (depending upon the size of the breast) for medium rare. Transfer the duck to a work surface, tent it with foil, and let rest for 10 minutes.*

4. *Again pour off and reserve all but 2 tablespoons of the fat drippings. Return the skillet to the heat. Stir in the shallots and cook 30 seconds. Add the port, broth, plums, and vinegar. Simmer until the mixture thickens slightly, 2 to 3 minutes. Whisk in the butter and fresh thyme; season to taste with salt and pepper.*

HOW TO CALL A DUCK

When loitering at the local marsh, one might presume the squawks of waterfowl to be no more than haphazard clamor. In fact, to draw a duck near (either for petting or hunting), one must perform a convincing mimicry of the bird, and, like the Portuguese language or a Verdi aria, imitate duck calls that brim with nuance. While newfangled duck-calling contraptions exist, we encourage the use of one's built-in instruments: the mouth and lungs. The best way to learn is to set out with a serious calling master so that one can hear the vast gradations of sound, but the following tips will help one begin:

- A common beginner's mistake is calling too frequently and too noisily. Desperation is not an attractive quality among any of the earth's creatures. Aficionados know that ducks, like people, find the occasional silence golden. Consider it an act of seduction—call once, twice, then sip one's cocktail and wait.

- A number of patented calls exist, such as the greeting, feeding, comeback, and lonesome hen, but all are moot if one cannot master the basics. Many erroneously believe that elementary quacking is more convincing when one honks a nasal-sounding *qua, qua, qua*, but it is imperative to not omit the final *-ck*. One wants to mock a duck's sound, not make a mockery of its intelligence.

- Advanced duck calls are not so different from practicing one's vocal scales at the pianoforte; instead of running up and down a scale, duck calling demands that one always begin high on the scale and work down smoothly. For example, the greeting call should be a series of five or six descending quacks, called in even rhythm: *QUACK, QUACk, QUAck, QUack, Quack* . . . .

- Most importantly, do not become discouraged. Many factors will sway success, including the direction of the wind, the amount of cloud cover, the time of year, and one's proximity to the flying formation.

5. *To serve, thinly slice the duck crosswise against the grain of the meat. Transfer the slices to one's finest camp plates and spoon the sauce on top.*

OPEN-FLAME MOROCCAN MERGUEZ & RED PEPPER BROCHETTES

PROVIDES
4-6
PORTIONS

1 large red bell pepper, seeds and veins removed

1 tablespoon extra-virgin olive oil

Kosher salt, to taste

Freshly milled black pepper, to taste

2 pounds merguez sausages, cut crosswise into 2-inch lengths

Smoky Green Olive & Almond Relish (page 52)

Zestful Yogurt Sauce (page 65), optional

Metal skewers

WE HAVE EVERY INTENTION OF VOYAGING TO MOROCCO, BUT SO FAR HAVE NEVER MADE IT ANY FURTHER THAN THE SPANISH FERRY PORT OF MALAGA, WHERE THE PULL OF MEDITERRANEAN SANDS AND BULLFIGHTING MATADORS PROVE TOO ENCHANTING FOR OUR SYBARITIC SOULS. But a quick dusting off of our history books reveals the following: nearly every civilization in the world has ruled Morocco at one time or another, including the Berbers, Phoenicians, Romans, Arabs, Turks, French, Portuguese, and Spanish.

Naturally, this has given rise to a hodgepodge cuisine assembled from the best each culture has had to offer. In this spirit, we hope our readers will forgive us for presenting a dish that is not (to our knowledge) strictly faithful to Moroccan cookery. Rather, it is a blend of delicious North African ingredients well-suited to the open flame, such as spicy fresh sausage, tangy olives, and smoky harissa sauce. If one wishes to go a bit more native, we suggest following the Moroccan disregard for cutlery: eat with one's hands, using warm bread to scoop up the (vaguely authentic) meat, vegetables, and sauces.

1. Prepare a medium-high-heat fire, with the flames occasionally licking the grill grate. Let it burn steadily for 30 minutes.

2. Cut the bell pepper into 1½-inch chunks; toss them with 2 teaspoons of the oil and sprinkle lightly with salt and pepper. Brush the sausage chunks with the remaining oil. Thread the sausages and peppers onto the skewers, alternating between the two.

3. Transfer the skewers to the grill grate. Grill them, turning them once halfway through, until the sausages are cooked through and the peppers are beautifully charred, about 5 minutes per side.

4. Slide the meat and vegetables from the skewers onto fine china plates. Serve with relish and, if desired, the yogurt sauce.

Pan-Roasted Squab
with Pâté-Walnut Bread Stuffing

PROVIDES
4
PORTIONS

WE ADMIT TO A BLATANT, INEXPLICABLE HYPOCRISY ON THE MATTER OF THIS DISH.
In the city, there nests a certain nefarious bird called the pigeon. The bane of urban dwellers, these winged vermin belong in a category with sewer-dwelling rodents, Tweed Ring politicians, and grubby-fingered pickpockets. In the country, however, where these birds bear the genteel title of "squabs," we consider them worthy of such embellishments as superior pâtés and fortified wines.

Squabs are young pigeons, and are therefore rather small; the meat is dark and fine-textured, with a gamy appeal. In this dish, we enhance its inherent richness by filling the birds' cavities with a pâté-inspired stuffing. If, after a long day in the sun, one wishes to reduce the effort involved, we suggest skipping the stuffing (the bird will cook in less time, so watch it carefully) and serving the squab with pâté-slathered toast and a drizzle of the syrupy port sauce.

1. Prepare a medium-high-heat fire, with the flames occasionally licking the grill grate. Let it burn steadily for 30 minutes.

2. Place a large skillet upon the grill grate. Add the bread cubes and toast, stirring occasionally, until golden, 3 to 5 minutes. Tip them out into a large bowl.

3. Return the skillet to the heat and melt the butter in it. Add the shallot and cook, stirring, until softened, about 3 minutes. Add the squab livers, 1 teaspoon each salt and pepper, and herbs. Cook, stirring briskly, until the livers are firm, but still pink. This will take 30 seconds or less, so watch it carefully. Chop the livers and add them, along with shallot-butter, stock, and Cognac, if using, over the bread and toss to coat well. Take a nibble

of a bread cube and add more Cognac or salt and pepper, if needed.

4. Rinse each squab and pat it dry. Coat the skin with oil and season the squab all over with salt and pepper. Pack the stuffing loosely into each bird. Tie the legs shut with cooking twine or pin them together with a skewer.

5. Add enough fuel to the fire so that it burns at high heat. Place a large skillet upon the flame and let it get very, very hot. Place the squabs into the skillet. Cook, turning occasionally, until the birds are dark golden on all sides and the juices run clear, 15 to 20 minutes. Adjust the flame if necessary. Using long-handled tongs transfer the squabs to a cutting board to rest. If a light sauce is

2 cups ¼-inch cubes Crusty Walnut Bread (page 226), or other crusty bread

4 tablespoons (½ stick) unsalted butter

3 tablespoons finely chopped shallot

4 whole squabs, about 1 pound each (see Advisement), livers rinsed, chopped, and reserved

Kosher salt, to taste

Freshly milled black pepper, to taste

1 teaspoon dried herbes de Provence or chopped fresh thyme

¼ cup chicken stock

2 teaspoons Cognac, optional

2 tablespoons extra-virgin olive oil

⅓ cup port, Madeira, or sweet red wine, optional

desired, pour the port into the skillet and let it bubble for 30 seconds.

6. *To serve, use kitchen shears to cut along either side of each squab's backbone. Flip each bird over and cut the breasts up the middle. Arrange the birds and stuffing on fine china plates. Drizzle with sauce, if using, and serve.*

Advisement: As the old adage goes, birds of a feather flock together. When cooking these plumed creatures, one's flock might include any bird of similar size, so long as one is willing to make some adjustments. As a substitute for squab, any bird weighing about one pound will do, such as poussin, small Cornish hen, or small Guinea fowl. Guinea fowl shares the gamy flavor of squab, but can be dry, so rub the exterior with an extra drizzle of oil before cooking. Cornish hen and poussin—both small chickens—have a lighter flavor than squab; one might do well to use a young ruby port in the sauce and drizzle it sparingly upon the chicken. Since cooking times may vary, check the birds occasionally by inserting an instant-read thermometer into the thickest part of the thigh. Strive for an internal temperature of 165 degrees.

A WORD ON THE

Artful Pairing of Wine & Food

May we be frank? One of our chief pleasures in an outdoor holiday is the delightful juxtaposition of civilization and wilderness. We adore the clink of silver on china backed by the song of cicadas, relish a hint of smoky char on a bittersweet chocolate cake, and—joy of all joys—we love seeing a vintage claret unstoppered and left to breathe on the stump of a lightning-felled pine. These delicious incongruities seem to open the soul to the limitless possibility of the natural world, indeed to life itself.

Wine is essential to the enjoyment of food, and as food is essential to life, it is necessary to bring along a selection of bottles before setting out on any culinary adventure. But which bottles to include? Plan for one variety to serve at each day's luncheon. Choose a light wine that will blend judiciously with all courses. At the dinner hour, one might offer a flight of wines, ranging from dry to sweet, rising in a crescendo that may be subtly smoothed over as digestifs are passed around. Of course, the general rule of chilled white wine with fish and fuller-bodied reds with butcher meat or game is sound practice and has the added benefit of ease of remembrance. Simply match the color of the flesh to the color of the wine. Poultry can be a bit of an oenological wild card, as some swear it goes better with a dry white, while others prefer a fruity red. We say chicken's ideal partner is Champagne; the *ch* sounds so charming upon repetition. Of course, when one is serving squab, such alliterative flourishes are spoilt. Never mind! One can't taste alliteration.

Time was, Society would only tolerate wines from France's Bordeaux and Burgundy regions or a glass of very dry sherry to be drunk at table. Today we are presented with a host of choices from nearly every grape grown on the globe. So here we humbly offer our menu and wine-pairing suggestions with the international connoisseur in mind. As a reminder: one needn't be shy about calling higher-end, fully pedigreed bottles into service with those of a lesser provenance. It is only the vulgarian who desires to imbibe solely the great wines at every meal. And, really, if one makes the effort to pour every wine into suitably pretty glasses, one can be assured of a well-appointed and appreciated table regardless of the monetary value of its contents.

Caramelized Tomato Tarte Tatin à la Clark (page 152)	One can't go amiss with a Pinot Noir from the Pacific Northwest with this dish; to really make an impression, serve a nice dry Gewürztraminer from the Pfalz region of Germany.
Lemony Skillet-Seared Rainbow Trout (page 158)	Try a sparkling wine like Prosecco, a lighter-bodied South African or Californian Chardonnay, or a semichilled bottle of Pouilly-Fumé.
Pine-Smoked & Maple-Glazed Wild Salmon (page 163)	A white Burgundy or young Viognier will set off the maple glaze, and Sancerre with salmon is always a safe bet. If it is the season, a Beaujolais Nouveau would be a surprising yet apt choice.
Pan-Roasted Squab with Pâté-Walnut Bread Stuffing (page 173)	Something bold is needed to stand up to a game bird. We like Italian Barbaresco or Barolo, perhaps an aged Rioja from Spain. This may even be a meal worthy of unstoppering the good claret.
Stone-Seared Cornish Hen with Bombay Spice and Orchard Pear & Watercress Salad (page 166)	A late-harvest Riesling (which needn't be French or German in origin; there are excellent Rieslings from Australia and certain areas of the United States) or a demisec Champagne, or cru Beaujolais would be a fitting complement to the hen and spice.
Open-Flame Moroccan Merguez & Red Pepper Brochettes (page 172)	A light Sémillion, Chablis, or Spanish Albariño will serve to cut the heat, whereas one may savor the burn with a ruby red, super-Tuscan.
Brandied Steak au Poivre served with Mustard Mashed Potatoes with Mushrooms (page 180)	One cannot help but recommend a Napa Cabernet Sauvignon here. Do uncork multiple bottles to take advantage of that marvelous peppery bouquet. In an economical pinch, a Chilean Malbec will do nicely as well.
Rabbit Ragù with Green Olives (page 190)	Châteauneuf-du-Pape blanc is a fruit-forward white partner to stewed rabbit as is an Alsatian Pinot Gris, and either will be lovely when splashed into the ragù. Any dry rosé will partner well with green olives, especially a sparkling pink Cava.

"Wine is one of the most civilized things in the world . . . and it offers a greater range for enjoyment and appreciation than, possibly, any other purely sensory thing which may be purchased."

—FROM **DEATH IN THE AFTERNOON**, ERNEST HEMINGWAY

Leg of Lamb Lavished with Mint

One 6-pound boneless, butterflied leg of lamb (ask one's butcher to perform this task)

½ cup extra-virgin olive oil

Finely grated zest of 2 lemons

⅓ cup freshly squeezed lemon juice

¼ cup chopped fresh oregano

¼ cup chopped fresh rosemary

¾ cup chopped fresh mint

10 garlic cloves, finely chopped

1½ teaspoons freshly milled black pepper

Kosher salt, to taste

Zestful Yogurt Sauce (page 64), for serving, optional

8 to 12 long metal skewers

THIS IS THE SORT OF DISH ONE SERVES WHEN THE OUTDOOR NEIGHBORS POP IN FOR A FEAST. It makes a tremendous amount of meat. As the immense butterflied leg tends toward unwieldiness, we cut it crosswise into two equal-sized hunks before skewering it, which allows for easier handling.

For years, we'd heard from fashionable people that leg of lamb was divine with mint jelly. First we tried our lamb with store-bought jelly. It was vile. Next, we made mint jelly from scratch, and it was viler. Never ones to give up, we made it a third time, and it was its most vile yet. As we believe the Shakespearean motto "to thine own self be true" ought always to prevail, we now smother the lamb with fresh mint, grill it, and then, for good measure, smother it with some more. Be as heavy-handed as feels true to one's party.

1. *With a sharp knife, clean up the lamb, cutting away any dangling bits and filleting off the long, shiny, slightly fibrous looking silver skin running the length of the leg. Some say to trim the fat, which one may do if desired; we fall firmly into the fat-is-flavor side of things and leave it more or less intact. Cut the leg in half crosswise, then cut ½-inch-deep slits all over each slab, essentially creating a pleasant haven for the flavorful marinade one is about to whisk together.*

2. *Whisk together the oil, lemon zest and juice, oregano, rosemary, ½ cup mint, garlic, and pepper. Place the meat in a large container and pour the marinade over it, turning the meat until it is well coated. Cover the container and place it in one's icebox for at least 1 hour or*

overnight (bring it to air temperature before cooking).

3. *When one is ready for the lamb, prepare a medium- to medium-high-heat fire, with the flames only occasionally licking the grill. Let it burn for 30 minutes.*

4. *Remove the lamb from the marinade, scraping off any excess, and transfer both pieces to a clean cutting board. Run skewers horizontally through each piece of meat about 2 inches apart, first lengthwise (2 to 3 skewers), then crosswise (2 to 3 more) to form a grid. (Skewering the meat greatly facilitates the turning of it.) Sprinkle generously with the salt.*

5. *As the fat on the lamb renders, it will likely cause some flare-ups. Should this happen, adjust the grill grate as*

ALTERNATIVES TO DINING IN A DOWNPOUR: FIVE SPLENDID TENT-FLOOR PICNIC MENUS

When Henry Wadsworth Longfellow wrote that "Into each life some rain must fall," we presume he meant to scribble, "Into each *light* some rain must fall," meaning of course, his campfire. But perhaps he was rushing off to the post office or a dentistry appointment and allowed his penmanship to go a bit off the rails. His editor, not being able to make out the hastily formed curlicues, botched the transcription, and that was that.

Over time, we have determined a dependable menu of mealtime options for those tempestuous occasions when food must be prepared by the glow of a lantern rather than a crackling flame. We acknowledge that a few of the following meal suggestions might require some opening of tins and a pinch of leniency in cookery standards, but the results make for splendid and elegant tent-floor picnicking.

Sun-Drenched Terrace Breakfast	Sliced ripe apricots tossed with freshest ricotta, Sevillian Orange & Honey Marmalade or Strawberry-Champagne Jam (pages 57), chopped almonds, and thinly sliced lemon verbena
Fisherman's Spring Luncheon	A salad of flaked smoked trout, paper-thin ribbons of raw asparagus (made using one's vegetable peeler), sliced radishes, and coarsely chopped walnuts, tossed with olive oil and freshly squeezed lemon juice and served with Crisp Fired Crackers (page 73)
Extraordinarily Rustic Tomato Soup	Fresh tomatoes (only the ripest and juiciest), chopped and left to marinate in a bowl with a generous pinch of salt until the juices are plentiful; mashed gently with a fork and tossed with torn bread bits, chopped garlic, ample fresh basil, olive oil, and a splash of balsamic vinegar. Served at room temperature, or with an ice cube from the icebox
The Strapping Woodsman Supper	Smartly arranged platter of best-quality venison, buffalo, or beef jerky, artful chunks of aged cheddar, fig jam, mixed with a dollop of The Colonel's Mustard (page 49), Spicy Dill Pickles (page 50), and crusty wholesome brown bread
The Spanish Shepherd Sandwich	Crusty bread drizzled with oil, rubbed with garlic, and sprinkled with smoked paprika, then stuffed with slices of Manchego cheese, thinly sliced onion, and any available foraged wild greens

necessary to continue cooking yet prevent charring. Cook, turning once halfway through, until the meat reaches the desired doneness, 25 to 30 minutes for medium rare (at which point it will register 125 degrees on an instant-read thermometer). Let the meat rest on a cutting board at least 5 minutes before thinly slicing against the grain. Sprinkle with the remaining ¼ cup mint and serve with generous spoonfuls of yogurt sauce, if desired, or mint jelly, if one would rather.

CHARRED LEMON-PEPPER PORK CHOPS
SERVED WITH PIPÉRADE SALAD

THE PIG IS SUCH AN EXQUISITE CREATURE—ITS HANDSOME UPTURNED NOSE, ITS USEFULNESS IN TRUFFLE HUNTING, THE WAY IT ROLLS ABOUT IN THE MUCK WITH FREE-SPIRITED ABANDON. And culinarily speaking, a hog's charms are infinite, from lardons, terrines, and sausages to confits, galantines, and roasts. Truth be told, we would gladly trade our silk purses for sows' ears.

In spite of our serious dedication to the swine, until recently the successful preparation of the humble pork chop eluded us. That was a grave oversight, since remedied. The secret to succulent pork chops is uncomplicated: do not overcook them. Use thick-cut, bone-in chops for tender, juicy results. We season ours with a homemade lemon-pepper rub that shames any stale bottled version, and serve it with a colorful pepper salad for a swift summer supper.

1. *Prepare a high-heat fire, with flames licking the grill grate. Let it burn steadily for 30 minutes.*

2. *While the fire preheats, rub garlic all over each pork chop, making sure to grind the clove into the bone, which will help release the garlicky juices, thereby scenting the meat. Rub a little of the lemon zest onto each pork chop. Season with pepper and salt. Brush the chops with oil.*

3. *Place the pork chops directly upon the grill grate. Grill for 4 minutes, then turn and cook them an additional 3 minutes. Let stand 5 minutes before serving, topped with Pipérade Salad.*

1 garlic clove, cut in half

Four 8-ounce, bone-in, center-cut pork chops, about 1 ¼-inch thick

2 teaspoons finely grated lemon zest

1 tablespoon freshly cracked black peppercorns

Kosher salt, to taste

1 tablespoon extra-virgin olive oil

Pipérade Salad, for serving (page 203)

BRANDIED STEAK AU POIVRE
SERVED with MUSTARD
AND MUSHROOM MASHED POTATOES

IT'S TRUE THAT THERE IS VERY LITTLE ABOUT THE WILD THAT RESEMBLES A FRENCH BISTRO—NO CHECKERBOARD FLOOR, NO CURLICUE CHAIRS, NO ART- FULLY TARNISHED MIRRORS LOOMING OVERHEAD. But that does not mean one cannot conjure the Left Bank at camp. Steak au poivre, classic bistro fare, was made for the outdoors. The richness of the tender meat marries wonderfully with the pungent peppery crust and the smoky flame. To highlight these attri- butes, we skip the traditional cloak of creamy mustard sauce, choosing instead to inject those same flavors in a side of fluffy mashed potatoes.

We believe steak tastes finest cooked rare or medium rare, so determining its doneness is paramount (see *Cuit à Point*, page 183). Please do not wreck one's lovely dinner by cutting into the meat to check it; the dish will lose its bis- tro appeal—though one can always recover by throwing a few cutting remarks, French waiter–style, at one's companions.

1½ tablespoons black peppercorns

¼ cup extra-virgin olive oil

1½ tablespoons brandy or Cognac

1 tablespoon finely chopped fresh rosemary

4 garlic cloves, thinly sliced

Four 5- to 6-ounce strip steaks

Mustard and Mushroom- Mashed Potatoes (page 210), for serving

Kosher salt, to taste

1. In a mortar and pestle, crush the pep- percorns. If one does not have a mortar and pestle, place the pepper in a reseal- able plastic bag and bang upon it with the bottom of a cast-iron skillet until the pep- percorns are crushed. Set them aside.

2. In a large bowl, whisk together the oil, brandy, rosemary, and garlic. Place the steaks in the marinade, turning each one to ensure that it is well coated. Cover tightly and return to one's icebox for at least 1 hour. Let the meat come to air tem- perature before grilling.

3. While the steak marinates, prepare a high-heat fire, with the flames licking the grill grate. Let it burn steadily for

30 minutes. This is an excellent time to prepare the mashed potatoes.

4. Scrape off the excess marinade from the steaks; season them generously with salt and press the crushed peppercorns into the meat on all sides. Transfer the steaks to the grill. The flames should be almost licking the steak. Cook, turning once with long-handled tongs, until the steaks reach the desired doneness, 2 to 3 min- utes per side for medium rare. Transfer the steaks to a fine china platter to rest for 5 minutes before serving them with heaping spoonfuls of mashed potatoes alongside.

THE BLUE-BLOODED
BON VIVANT BURGER

10 ounces bison meat or prime ground beef

5 ounces ground brisket (ask one's butcher to perform this task) or prime ground beef

5 ounces ground rib beef (ask one's butcher to perform this task) or prime ground beef

1 teaspoon kosher salt

½ teaspoon freshly milled black pepper

1 ounce crumbled Stilton or other good-quality blue-veined cheese

4 Portuguese rolls, split, for serving

The Colonel's Mustard (page 49) or Dijon mustard

½ shallot, minced

WE FIND THAT A GOOD BURGER CAN BE JUST AS NOBLE AS A PREMIER STEAK. Even Apicius, that ancient Roman epicure, enjoyed minced meat every now and again. Whilst embracing the bold tastes of the Great Outdoors, we seek out meat with big game flavor—hence our choice of bison. Unfortunately, when cooked over a searing flame, bison can become as dry as a teetotaler. An injection of deliciously fatty brisket and rib beef provides the ideal alchemical solution. If one hasn't the inclination to trot about town in search of three different ground meats (though we insist it is worthwhile), then by all means, substitute prime ground beef for the whole thing, so long as it has a meat-to-fat ratio of 80 percent to 20 percent.

We also sometimes serve this burger without the cheese but with a hefty dollop of our World's Fair Catsup (page 48) and Sweet Cucumber-Pepper Piccalilli (page 52).

1. *Prepare a high-heat fire, with the flames licking the grill grate. Let it burn steadily for 30 minutes.*

2. *Gently combine all the meats, the salt, and the pepper. Form the mixture into* four 1-inch-thick patties. Transfer the burgers to the grill grate and cook them to the desired doneness (see Cuit à Point, page 183), 2½ to 3 minutes per side for medium rare. Crumble the cheese on top for the last 30 seconds of grilling. Transfer the burgers to a platter to rest while one toasts the buns.*

3. *Place the bun halves, cut sides down, upon the grill grate and toast until light golden, 1 minute or less. Sandwich the burgers between the buns and garnish with mustard and minced shallot.*

QUADRILLAGE It is quite easy to *quadriller*—that is, make the crisscross branding upon meat that marks a cook's mettle over the fire. Simply place the food upon the grill grate; then, halfway through its cooking time, rotate the meat at a 90- or 45-degree angle to create intersecting lines. Do not shift the meat more than the two times necessary to form the distinct lines. One might also perform *quadrillage* one grill line at a time, with a scorching hot skewer.

Cuit à Point:

DETERMINING THE DONENESS OF MEAT

Perhaps the most marvelous reward for embarking on an adventure is that one never knows what other nature lovers might be bunking down among the pines. Over the years, our adjacent campsites have been peopled with a motley crew, including a trapeze artist, a milliner, a bordello proprietress, a Chilean cricketer, and one rather sozzled poet laureate. Truly, there is no guessing what miscellany one might suddenly be asked to discourse upon. A Gypsy might request a palm reading, or a schoolmaster might conduct a lightning round of multiplication tables. Lest one appear a dilettante, we suggest a modicum of preparedness. Therefore we present:

		DETERMINING THE DONENESS OF STEAK IN THE COMPANY OF A SNOOTY FRENCH WAITER* **(A SKILL ALSO QUITE USEFUL IN FIRE COOKERY)**		
FRANÇAIS	ENGLISH	APPEARANCE	THERMOMETER TEMPERATURE	BY TOUCH
Bleu (blü)	Black and Blue	Indisputably rare	115 to 120 degrees	Positively spongy
Saignant (senyân)	Rare	Cool, bloody pink center	125 to 130 degrees	Soft and jiggly
Moyen-saignant (mwayan senyân)	Medium Rare	Predominantly rosy center fading to chestnut	130 to 140 degrees	Fleshy and relaxed
Cuit à Point (küee ah pwan)	Medium	Predominantly chestnut edges fading to a blushing center	140 to 150 degrees	Firm, but giving
Bien Cuit (byan küee)	Medium Well	Taupe, mahogany, and the barest streaks of pink	150 to 155 degrees	Taut and scarcely yielding
Très Bien Cuit (tre byan küee)	Well Done	Grayish brown and haggard	Above 160 degrees	Suitable for flagstones

* Although one's companions will likely be too staggered by one's erudition to inquire, we imagine one will receive extra flattery if aware that pork should be cooked to an internal temperature of 170 degrees and poultry to an internal temperature of 165 degrees (check for this in the thickest part of the bird's thigh).

Wildflower Lore

Wandering about on our nature walks produces many delights, not the least of which is the panoply of petals that intermittently carpet the wilderness floor. We think wildflowers are more beautiful than any hothouse bloom one may purchase in a shop—but before one gathers these buds into a nosegay take a moment to peruse this guide to the language and lore of wild flora.

Bluebells

What a treat to come upon a field of bluebells in the sweet air of a forest clearing! These bright blue blooms are commonly thought to be the provenance of woodland sprites, and certainly, there is more than a bit of fairy magic in the azure beauty of their bell-shaped blossoms. Ancient stories caution one never to tread on or, indeed, to pluck a bluebell or bad luck will ensue. This is a wildflower that is not to be tamed. Enjoy bluebells on one's walk only—never arrange them in a vase or even bring them indoors, or the wrath of the woodland folk may be one's reward.

Daisies

In the language of flowers, daisies symbolize sweetness and innocence. They may be gathered at will, but remember, they are fragile and their blooms never last long.

Honeysuckle

This supple white flower with a heady, honey-ish fragrance brings to mind wild summertime romance. But take care! Legend has it that a wedding ceremony will take place within a year under the same roof as a bouquet of honeysuckle. We recommend exercising caution when bestowing this as a wildflower corsage.

Ivy

This robust plant may be found growing on the side of the forest's most stately arbors. It makes a delightful addition to any wildflower arrangement and is hearty enough to withstand the journey back to camp without so much as a spritz of water.

Moss

Prized for its emerald green color and a texture akin to a velvet gown, moss is symbolic of nurturing, motherly love.

Wild Heather

Ancient peoples have found this lively pale purple or dove gray flower to be good luck, and no wonder—heather is magnificently useful and has been employed from time as roof thatch, outdoor bedding, and fuel to ignite a campfire.

Anemone

These orangey-red blossoms are said to have sprung from the tears of a lovelorn Aphrodite. Despite such a grievous beginning, this flower is thought to bring luck and protection from evil. Certainly, it is a useful plant to see on an outdoor holiday. The anemone's pretty petals close up just before sunset—or before a rainstorm. If one sees them shut in the daylight reach for an umbrella and thank the goddess of yore for her early warning bloom.

Water Hemlock

This wildflower has a prim and delicate appearance very similar to Queen Anne's Lace, but is actually extremely poisonous, even to the touch. A water hemlock bouquet is a harbinger of ill fortune, and that's no legend.

LOIN OF VENISON WITH ESCOFFIER PINE NUT SAUCE

PROVIDES
4-6
PORTIONS

WE WONDER WHETHER ESCOFFIER HAD MANY DINING COMPANIONS. For although it is human nature to flock like bears to the honey pot upon receiving a dinner invitation, what hungry creature ever possessed the stamina to wait while this celebrated gourmand finished up in the kitchen? An anecdote: When we happened upon his recipe for pine nut sauce, we thrilled to the idea of a novel use for foraged pinecone nuggets. But after meandering through pages of mirepoix, roux, clarified butters, blanched bones, brown stock, poivrade sauce, and Espagnol sauce—all prerequisites for the desired pine nut sauce—we accepted that sometimes one must embrace the essence of a thing and not the thing itself. Adaptability, especially on an adventure, is a virtue. We are brazenly proud of the results.

On the point of brazenness, we should also mention that venison's rich, gamy flavor is complemented by musky juniper berries and black currants. Because it becomes gamier the longer it cooks, we prefer it a subtle medium rare.

4 garlic cloves

Kosher salt

Six 5-ounce bone-in venison loin chops

Freshly milled black pepper, to taste

1½ tablespoons extra-virgin olive oil

½ cup Madeira

1 cup chicken or beef stock

Several dried juniper berries

2 tablespoons black currant jam

1 sprig fresh rosemary

3 tablespoons heavy cream

3 tablespoons pine nuts, lightly fire-toasted (see Advisement, page 206), for garnish

1. Prepare a high-heat fire, with the flames licking the grill grate. Let it burn steadily for 30 minutes.

2. Finely chop 2 garlic cloves. In a mortar and pestle or with the back of a knife, mash the chopped garlic with 1½ teaspoons of the salt. Smash the remaining two garlic cloves with the back of a knife and reserve. Rub the garlic paste all over the venison chops. Season the meat generously with pepper and rub each chop with oil. Cover and transfer the meat to one's icebox for 30 minutes, then let it come to air temperature before cooking.

3. Place the cast-iron skillet upon the grill grate and heat until very, very hot. Add the venison chops and cook to the desired doneness, 2½ to 3 minutes per side for medium rare (145 degrees). Transfer the chops to a platter to rest, tented with foil, while one prepares the sauce.

4. In the same skillet, combine the Madeira, stock, juniper berries, jam, rosemary, and reserved garlic cloves. Simmer until syrupy, stirring occasionally and crushing the berries lightly against the side of the pan, about 6 minutes. Adjust the flame as needed. Stir in the cream and remove from the heat. Season with salt and pepper. Discard the rosemary branches and garlic cloves.

5. Serve the venison, with spoonfuls of sauce, a garnish of pine nuts, and a blessing upon the head of Escoffier.

DUTCH OVEN STEWS

WHEN CAMPING NEOPHYTES ASK US TO DIVULGE OUR MOST FOOL-PROOF FIRE COOKERY RECIPES, WE ALWAYS STEER THEM TO DUTCH OVEN STEWS. They are nearly impossible to ruin. Sometimes these friends will peruse the stew recipe and stammer, "Oh, but it's long!" Perhaps, but it is also simple. For while the ingredient lists can ramble on, the work itself requires only an initial flurry of activity, mostly chopping (which one might even do at home and carry along), followed by a long period of relaxation, during which a party can pull out a fiddle, collect moss for a home terrarium, or spin a few yarns by the fire. Meanwhile, fragrant layers of spice, meat, vegetables, and wine commingle in the stewpot, and the aroma of food—hearty and complex—wends its way through camp.

Stews are ideal for ingredients that thrive on long simmering, such as dried beans or tough cuts of meat, filled with fat marbling and connective tissues that slowly dissolve into moist, juicy morsels. Lean meats and fish are not meant for this technique. We've provided a collection of favorites here, but one could cobble together an impromptu and delicious stew with little more than some scraps of meat and vegetables, a splash of wine, and fresh herbs. Just be sure to pat the meat dry and brown it well on all sides (tagines being the exception to this rule) before adding any liquid, as this will strongly enrich one's broth.

Our favorite part of any stew is that it always tastes better the following day. Simply stash it in one's icebox and return it to the stewpot for an easy afternoon luncheon. Note, however, that stew thickens as it sits, and one might need to add an additional cup or so of water to restore its unctuous texture.

Lamb Tagine with Preserved Lemon & Dates

WE HEAP PRAISE UPON THE FIRST NORTH AFRICAN COOK, WHEREVER HE MAY BE, WHO BRAVELY BLENDED SUCH A MYRIAD OF FLAVORS IN ONE DISH. As tagines cook, the heady scent grows redolent of adventures in places long ago and far away. If one wishes to arrive in those places more quickly, by all means whisk together the spice mixture at home before the trip; it is easier than fiddling with teaspoons by the fire.

Traditional tagines also do not require much browning of the meat, and we are not inclined to argue with tradition, particularly when it serves as a time-saving measure. We serve this over steamed couscous, with a crisp green salad.

1. *Prepare a medium-high-heat fire, with the flames occasionally licking the grill grate. Let it burn steadily for 45 minutes, or until it begins to form glowing, ash-covered coals and embers. Then use a coal shovel or like implement to scrape a bed of embers off to the side of the fire pit.*

2. *In a bowl, toss together the lamb, onion, oil, garlic, ginger, salt, and all the spices, except for the saffron.*

3. *Place a Dutch oven upon the cooking grate and heat until very hot. Tip the lamb mixture into the pot and brown it lightly, stirring, for 2 to 3 minutes. Pour in enough water to cover about two-thirds of the lamb (1 to 1½ cups) and crumble in the saffron.*

4. *Place the Dutch oven upon the coals and cover it. Keep it at a steady simmer, adding or removing coals as necessary, until* the lamb is buttery tender and falling apart, 1½ to 2 hours. Stir it occasionally, skimming off any excess fat that rises to the surface. Finely chop the lemon rind and stir it into the tagine; stir in the dates. Simmer the stew, uncovered, 15 minutes longer. Taste and adjust the seasonings, as needed. Spoon couscous into fine china bowls and ladle stew on top. Strew with chopped almonds.

Advisement: Preserved lemon is a North African condiment consisting of lemons pickled for some weeks in a brine of lemon juice, water, and salt. They are frequently available at Middle Eastern groceries or in the ethnic section of large markets. If one cannot locate any for this dish, we recommend substituting chopped pitted green olives to taste. Although this not quite an even trade, in this recipe it works nicely.

1½ pounds lamb stewing meat

½ onion, finely chopped

3 tablespoons extra-virgin olive oil

1 fat garlic clove, finely chopped

1 teaspoon fresh ginger, peeled and chopped

1½ teaspoons salt

1½ teaspoons ground coriander

1½ teaspoons ground cumin

¾ teaspoon sweet paprika

½ teaspoon ground cinnamon

½ teaspoon freshly milled black pepper

¼ teaspoon ground turmeric

1 pinch ground cloves

1 large pinch saffron threads

1 preserved lemon (see Advisement), quartered, with flesh and seeds removed

⅓ cup chopped pitted dates

Couscous, for serving

Chopped almonds, for garnish

BŒUF BOURGUIGNON

3 pounds boneless beef chuck or other beef stewing meat, cut into 2-inch chunks

Kosher salt, to taste

Freshly milled black pepper, to taste

¼ cup all-purpose flour

⅓ pound thick-cut bacon, cut into 1-inch pieces

2 tablespoons extra-virgin olive oil, as needed

3 tablespoons unsalted butter, as needed

1 pound white button mushrooms, quartered

1 pound pearl onions, peeled

3 stalks celery, chopped small

2 carrots, peeled and sliced into ¼-inch-thick coins

1 large yellow onion, finely chopped

4 garlic cloves, finely chopped

1½ tablespoons tomato paste

One 750-milliliter bottle dry red wine, such as Burgundy or Côtes du Rhône

3 sprigs fresh parsley, plus chopped parsley leaves for garnish

2 sprigs fresh thyme

2 bay leaves

Boiled potatoes or buttered noodles, for serving

SOMETIMES WE ENJOY SLUMMING ABOUT THE CAMPSITE, PRETENDING WE ARE FRENCH PEASANTS, HAVING A RUSTIC MEAL. This is our first choice for that diversion, since we can also slake our thirst with very good (or, admittedly, sometimes very mediocre) Burgundy wine in the process.

Although those determined French country folk blanch the pearl onions in water to remove the skins, we find it more convenient to use a paring knife when fireside. At certain rebellious moments, we have even been known to substitute one large onion, cut into bite-size chunks. Serve this with boiled potatoes, or even a large bowl of buttered noodles.

1. Prepare a medium-high-heat fire, with the flames occasionally licking the grill grate. Let it burn steadily for 45 minutes, or until it begins to form glowing, ash-covered coals and embers. Then use a coal shovel or like implement to scrape a bed of embers off to the side of the fire pit.

2. Season the beef pieces all over with salt and pepper and toss to coat with the flour. Place a Dutch oven upon the cooking grate; cook the bacon until crisp. Transfer it with a slotted spoon to a paper towel–lined plate. Heat the fat remaining in the pot until it shimmers like a mirage in the Sahara. Working in batches (one mustn't crowd the pan—the aim is to allow sufficient heat to flow around the meat so that it browns and does not steam), cook the beef until a golden crust forms on all sides. Add oil, 1 tablespoon at a time, if needed, to keep the meat from sticking. Transfer the meat to the platter with the bacon.

3. If one's pot looks dry, add 1 tablespoon butter. Add the mushrooms and a pinch of salt and pepper. Cook until the mushrooms are golden and tender, 3 to 5 minutes (add enough fuel to the fire to increase the heat to high, if necessary); remove with a slotted spoon and reserve. Drop in 1 tablespoon butter and add the pearl onions; cook until golden in places, about 3 minutes. Drop in 1 tablespoon of butter and let it melt. Stir in the celery, carrots, onion, and garlic and cook until almost tender, about 5 minutes. Stir in the tomato paste and cook 1 minute. Return the beef and bacon to the pot. Stir in the wine, parsley and thyme sprigs, and bay leaves.

THE BEAUTY OF FIRESIDE TERRARIUMS

Terrariums are man-made, miniature landscapes confined in glass, a temporary decoration for one's fireside home. Let us show you how they are done.

1. Find any small, clean glass container lying about. Jam jars will do, as will a brandy snifter.

2. Fill the bottom of the jar with a healthy layer of miniature pebbles. In a home terrarium, this would facilitate proper drainage. In ours, it just looks proper.

3. Move on to the moss layer (collected from rocks and logs). We arrange the moss directly on top of the pebbles.

4. Next, cover the moss with an inch or so of dirt. This is the landscaping layer, so any terraces or valleys one would like to convey in one's jam jar should be contoured here.

5. Finally, having laid all the necessary groundwork, one is free to embellish one's landscape. At camp one should feel free to decorate with whatever twigs, blossoms, leaves, nuts, or stones one finds strewn about camp. Even a whittling project, such as a tiny statuette, makes a grand addition.

6. Cover one's terrarium with a lid. Since the plants are likely plucked flowers and therefore lacking roots, one's fireside terrarium should need no watering, but do keep all terrariums out of direct sunlight. Admire one's work over a bowl of hearty, steamy stew.

4. *Place the Dutch oven upon the coals and cover. Keep at a steady simmer, adding or removing coals as necessary and stirring occasionally, until the beef is buttery tender and falling apart. Stir in the mushrooms and let them warm through. Taste and adjust seasonings, if necessary.*

5. *Bed one's finest camp bowls with boiled potatoes, ladle the stew on top, and garnish with parsley.*

Rabbit Ragù with Green Olives

IF ONE HAS MASTERED THE ART OF FALCONRY, CATCHING A HARE FOR THE STEW-POT IS A SIMPLE MATTER. One need only stretch out one's arm and wait while the predatory bird does one's bidding. If not, a hunt for rabbit holes always provides ample opportunity for excitement, if young Alice is any authority. As a last resort, we find rabbit increasingly abundant in city butcher shops. Serve this dish of goodness over a steaming bowl of creamy, soft polenta.

Two 28-ounce tins San Marzano tomatoes, drained and juices reserved, coarsely chopped

Two 1½-pound rabbits, each cut into 8 pieces (ask one's butcher to perform this task)

½ teaspoon kosher salt

½ teaspoon freshly milled black pepper

¼ cup extra-virgin olive oil

1 yellow onion, finely chopped

2 carrots, chopped

2 celery stalks, chopped

1½ teaspoons tomato paste

1 cup white or red wine

2 sprigs fresh thyme

1 bay leaf

⅓ cup chopped pitted green olives

2 tablespoons cold, unsalted butter, cut into pieces

Creamy, soft polenta, for serving

1. *Prepare a medium-high-heat fire, with the flames occasionally licking the grill grate. Let it burn steadily for 45 minutes, or until it begins to form glowing, ash-covered coals and embers. Then use a coal shovel or like implement to scrape a bed of embers off to the side of the fire pit.*

2. *Place a Dutch oven upon the grill grate and let it heat until very, very hot. Meanwhile, pat the rabbit pieces dry and season them generously with salt and pepper. Add 3 tablespoons of the oil and heat until it shimmers like a mirage in the Sahara. Working in batches (one must not crowd the pan—the aim is to allow sufficient heat to flow around the meat so that it browns and does not steam), brown the rabbit until light golden on both sides. Transfer the meat to a paper towel–lined platter.*

3. *Add the remaining 1 tablespoon oil to the pot. Stir in the onion, carrots, and celery, and cook, stirring occasionally, until the vegetables are tender, about 5 minutes. Adjust the heat if necessary. Stir in the tomato paste and cook 1 minute. Pour in the chopped tomatoes with their juices, and the wine; drop in the thyme, bay leaf, and the salt and pepper. Give the mixture a hearty stir, then gingerly arrange the rabbits in the pot. The pieces will not all fit in one layer; stack them as cozily as possible. If necessary, add enough water for the liquid to come two-thirds of the way up the sides of the rabbit.*

4. *Place the Dutch oven upon the coals and cover. Keep it at a steady simmer, adding or removing coals as necessary, until the rabbit is buttery tender and falling apart, about 1½ hours. Be sure to stir the stew occasionally, rotating the rabbit pieces inside the pot. Stir in the olives and cook, uncovered, for an additional 15 minutes.*

THE QUIET JOY OF A SOLITARY WALK

In our experience, campfire mealtimes are a robust and lively affair. Eating, drinking, and merrymaking are activities best enjoyed surrounded by a coterie of one's favorite friends. As long as one's fire is lit and one's plate (or glass) never stands empty, there need be no end to the group jollity. Spectacular as this group amusement may be, we humbly suggest that it is even better when balanced out by time spent alone.

Each camper ought to try and wrest an hour away from the clamoring of campfire companions every day. Set out on a journey away from the fire; any direction will do, so long as the walk is undertaken in solitude. How else is one to think up jokes and stories to share with the folks back at the fire unless one takes some time to walk in the wild and think without being interrupted?

Listen to the cicada song, to the running stream, to the sound of the grass growing. When surrounded by the munificent splendor of the great outdoors, one is sure to concoct grand plans, recover from old wounds, or simply breathe in the beauty of the present moment. Perhaps that is all that one can ask of a holiday in nature. That, and a full stomach, are worth all the treasures in an emperor's coffer—and yet can be had for free.

5. *If the meat is tender but one wishes a thicker sauce, let stew cook, uncovered, until it reaches the desired consistency. Taste and adjust seasonings, if needed.*

6. *Now, at this point, one can either whisk in the butter and serve the mixture, bones and all, over polenta or fastidiously remove the meat from the bones, returning the meat to the pot and the bones to the fire (do not fling them into the forest unless one wishes to invite a visit from furry nighttime scavengers), before* *whisking in the butter and serving over polenta. We've done both, and have been content either way—the former makes for less complicated cookery; the latter makes for less complicated dining.*

WHITE BEAN STEW WITH PANCETTA & PUMPKIN

WE SET OUT TO CREATE THIS NOURISHING DISH SO THAT WE MIGHT INCLUDE A NICE VEGETARIAN OPTION FOR ANY PYTHAGOREAN COMPANIONS. But as soon as we'd decided it, our untamed imaginations strayed again and again to savory chunks of pancetta, which we thought could only improve the taste of the stew. This of course, is our own prejudice, the result a powerful dependence upon pork. One can feel certain comfort that it could be omitted from this dish to no great detriment—the pumpkin, beans, and sage have flavor to spare. We serve this over mountains of our Garlicky Sautéed Dandelion and Wild Spinach (page 212).

½ pound dried white beans such as Great Northern, navy, or cannellini (see Advisement)

1½ pounds pumpkin, such as sugar or peek-a-boo, or butternut squash

½ pound pancetta, cut into ½-inch cubes (about 1½ cups), optional

3 tablespoons oil, optional

½ medium onion, peeled and diced

1 celery stalk, finely chopped

2 garlic cloves, finely chopped

1 bay leaf

6 sprigs fresh parsley

1 sprig fresh thyme

1½ tablespoons chopped fresh sage

Kosher salt, to taste

Freshly milled black pepper, to taste

1. *Well before one needs to prepare the stew, pick over the beans and discard any that are shriveled, discolored, or in any way deformed. Place the remaining bean booty in a large bowl and cover generously with cold water. (The beans will expand more than one might expect as they soak. Allow them the space to do so.) Do not use one's Dutch oven for this task, as the standing water is liable to cause rust to the cast iron. Soak at least 8 hours or overnight.*

2. *Prepare a medium-high-heat fire, with the flames occasionally licking the grill grate. Let it burn steadily for 45 minutes, or until it begins to form glowing, ash-covered coals and embers. Then use a coal shovel or like implement to scrape a bed of embers off to the side of the fire pit.*

3. *Peel the pumpkin and scoop out the seeds and pulp (reserve the seeds for Fire-Toasted Squash Seeds, page 139). Cut the pumpkin into ½-inch chunks.*

4. *Place the Dutch oven upon the grill grate and heat it until hot. Add the pancetta, if using, and cook, stirring, until the meat is golden, 8 to 10 minutes. For a vegetarian stew, heat the oil instead. Stir in the onion, celery, and garlic. Cook until golden, about 5 minutes. Stir in the pumpkin or squash and cook 2 minutes longer.*

5. *Drain the beans and add them to the pot. Top with 2 quarts of fresh water, and the bay leaf, parsley, and thyme.*

6. *Place the Dutch oven upon the coals and cover it. Bring the liquid to a simmer and*

FORAGING FOR PINE NUTS

Climbing trees is part and parcel of outdoor living. Treetops provide a wonderful perch for bird-watching, offer unrivaled views of the surrounding countryside, and are the last resort to safety after stumbling upon a bear. But scrambling up a tree can be taxing, and it is only natural that eventually a person will crave a snack, preferably one packed with energy for the long climb down.

We first learned the trick of foraging the nuts of pine cones as children, when grown-ups showed us that the rough petals of the cones could be plucked like artichokes, revealing tiny, tasty nuts within, perfect nibbles when hiking, or when stuck in tree boughs. Here we share our expertise.

- While many pine trees bear edible nuts, in North America one's best choices are pinyon pines, gray pines, sugar pines, and ponderosas. We've also encountered excellent foraging trees in Italy, Greece, and Russia.

- The best time of year for foraging is late summer to late fall, when the pinecones are well developed but have not yet dropped all their nuts.

- Slightly open pinecones are best for snacking in the wild. They are easier to peel. Peeling pinecones is a fine activity for youngsters, as their small fingers can reach right into the tiny openings.

- If bringing cones back to camp to make pesto or the Escoffier Pine Nut Sauce (page 185), look for tightly packed cones, which contain the most nuts.

- Once back at camp, place the cones near the fire, where the heat will open their petals. Shake the cone over a burlap sack, letting the nuts shower into the bag. If this does not work, throw the cones into the sack and smash the sack lightly against a log to loosen the nuts. Pour the nuts into a fine-mesh screen or strainer and shake, to rid them of debris.

- The resinous sap of pinecones smells divine, but it is sticky. Though we never bother, more fastidious campers might wish to wear kid gloves.

---

uncover. Continue to simmer, adding or removing coals as necessary, and stirring the stew occasionally, until the beans are tender and most of the liquid has evaporated, 1 to 1½ hours. Stir in the sage, season generously with salt and pepper. Taste and adjust seasonings if necessary.

Advisement: It has happened, on an occasion or two, that we became wrapped up in a morning round of croquet and completely forgot to soak our beans. While prevailing wisdom claims that a long soak yields softer and more easily digestible beans, we've cut corners now and again to no disappointment: bring a Dutch oven full of beans and water to a boil over the fire, cook them for 2 minutes and let them stand in the cooling water, uncovered, for 1 hour. Proceed with the recipe as instructed.

"Everybody needs beauty as well as bread, places to play in and pray in, where nature may heal and cheer and give strength to body and soul alike."

—JOHN MUIR

CHAPTER SEVEN

CAMPFIRE SIDES & VEGETABLES

WHENEVER AND WHEREVER ONE SITS DOWN TO A MEAL, ONE EXPECTS IT TO BE WELL BALANCED. Like the scales of Justice, it should not be weighted in the favor of any single flavor, texture, or color. To achieve this delicate harmony, we count on the side dish to be the great plate equalizer. Side dishes give us a bit of crispy along with the tender, green and leafy to back up the charred and meaty, and, above all, a hot, bready conveyance by which we can (somewhat) politely sop up all that jus.

When one dines in the wilderness, one needn't give up the notion of balance. Quite the contrary; whilst basking in nature it is of the utmost importance to honor the hard-won détente between flora and fauna—by eating a good deal of both. With a few exceptions made for those who forgo meat, our menu of main courses features faunae of all varieties. Of course, before these succulent beasts shuffled off their mortal coils, they were flamboyantly different in appearance (as different as fur, feathers, and scales can be), but over the cooking fire, all become monochromatic. Varying shades of brown are appetizing, to be sure, but may lack flair. Best to liven things up with a side of Seared Minted Courgettes for a dose of the green stuff, or perhaps peppery Pipérade Salad to add sunnier hues. Remember, when setting a wilderness table, one ought to live up to that pageant-quality beauty herself—Mother Earth.

Fortunately for those with a hearty appetite, forest florae are not only beautiful, they can be delicious as well. For those adept at foraging (a brief study of wild edibles may suffice), endless riches to supplement the feast may be found just off the beaten path. If one is lucky in a foraging stroll, what more pleasurable way to share forest plunder than with our Greens of the Wilderness Salad or Foil-Roasted Mushrooms with Hazelnuts & Chives? Should one lack the know-how, or simply not feel terribly lucky, we recommend a stop at a farmers' market, where one is sure to find the necessary ingredients for these delightful sides.

In this chapter we have devised simple dishes that may be prepared at the same time as the main course, if one can embody a spirit of adventurous organization. For example, our pretty Charred & Herbed Heirloom Cherry Tomatoes can be assembled in a flash and roasted in a quaint foil packet nestled in the fire's embers, and our Classic Buttered Cob Corn will cook over the grill in the time it takes meat to rest before carving. A bit more planning is required to serve Rustic Pain de Campagne and Crusty Walnut Bread. But, as one will see, it is only the time that is wanted to make this yeasty bread rise. Little extra effort is involved.

After all, one is on holiday. And a plate of balanced beauty ought only to call for a minimum of fuss and, perhaps, a maximum of nerve.

GREENS OF THE WILDERNESS SALAD

8 cups mixed wild greens, such as purslane, dandelion (best used sparingly, as it is bitter), arugula, sorrel, or miner's lettuce

Sprightly Lemon Vinaigrette (page 68)

Kosher salt, to taste

Freshly milled black pepper, to taste

Edible flowers (see box), for garnish, optional

THE WILDERNESS IS FILLED WITH GREENS, FROM GRASSY GLADE AND MOSSY ROCK TO THE LEAVES UPON THE TREES. But how to celebrate this verdant splendor, when one eats neither grass nor moss, neither leaf-lined branch nor bud? The salad bowl is just the place for a pageant of greenery, as one can fill it with a tender mix of lush edibles scooped from the field. We prefer a wild salad to be austerely dressed; too much accessorizing can distract from its simple beauty. A drizzle of lemon and oil and perhaps a scattering of edible blooms are all that are needed here.

Tear the greens into bite-size pieces and drop them into a large salad bowl. Pour enough dressing over the salad to lightly coat the greens. Taste and adjust seasonings, if necessary. Garnish with edible flowers, if one strives for fanciness.

EDIBLE BLOOMS

If the notion of eating flowers calls to mind a pasture cow chomping on clover, it is time to revise one's thinking. A colorful blend of delicate blossoms instantly makes a salad of simple mixed greens more elegant, and depending upon the chosen blooms, will add lemony, peppery, tart, or honeyed flavor. Before dashing off to the nearest meadow, take note: *not all flowers are edible.* Pluck only those one is certain can be safely digested, such as violet, hyssop, borage, calendula, lilac, nasturtium, dandelion, pansy, and marigold. Remove all pistils and stamens before eating and avoid any flowers suspected to have received pesticide treatment.

Foraging For Greens of the Wilderness

The seventeenth-century poet Robert Herrick famously implored us to "gather ye rosebuds while ye may." For, he explained, "Old Time is still a-flying; and this same flower that smiles to-day, To-morrow will be dying."

Trade "salad greens" for "rosebuds," and we couldn't agree more.

We are a society said to have evolved from groups of hunter-gatherers, yet we now spend our time hunting for parking spots at the supermarket, then gathering cartloads of prepackaged goods. Much more pleasant to take a walk on the wild side, with a canvas satchel ready to be filled with the edible forest foliage one spies along the way.

The shocking truth is that tasty roughage such as purslane, miner's lettuce, wild arugula, or dandelion greens is so prolific in the great outdoors that certain government agencies have classified them as pernicious weeds. But what do bureaucrats know of the joys wilderness greens can bestow? Flavors peppery to sweet are the signature of these discovered delicacies. But take warning: when foraging for forest greens, do go wild but not with abandon. Adhere to the forager's code: Never take more than is necessary; leave at least two-thirds of one's verdant quarry for the next lucky salad seeker. Never rip the plants out by the roots, but snip off the tops with a dainty pair of shears so the harvest will return the next season. And to answer the question, Should one bother to wash one's foraged greens? We reply with a question of our own: Does a bear wee in the woods?

Naturally, one ought never to eat what one cannot absolutely and positively identify. To that end, we present a truncated guide to greens of the forest. We hope it will inspire one to invest in a more comprehensive encyclopedia to further the quest to gather ye salad greens while ye may (for tomorrow they may be encased in plastic and sold for a small fortune at a boutique market).

1. **Purslane (Portulaca oleracea).** Its distinctive, paddle-shaped leaves are smooth and branch off from reddish stems. When in doubt, give the stem a snap—if it is filled with a waterlike liquid, it's purslane. If a milky substance leaks out, exercise caution. That plant could be the poisonous spotted spurge, which is not so good.

2. **Miner's Lettuce (Claytonia perfoliata).** This lovely green, also sometimes called spring beauty, emerges from February to June in shady areas of North America. It is known for its rosettelike leaf adorned by a tiny white bloom at the center. It got its name because it was so widely enjoyed by those who journeyed to California in a rush for gold. They sought riches of gilt and found a leaf rich in vitamin C. The forty-niners may have suffered financial disappointment, but at least they didn't have scurvy.

3. **Wild Arugula (Eruca sativa).** This wild green will certainly give its cousin, domesticated arugula, an inferiority complex. For it is everything that tamed arugula is, but more so. Its radishlike flavor is even bolder; its looks are similar, but it has more jagged leaves, a more pronounced stem, a deeper, more emerald color. It is mostly found in the Mediterranean, where the ancients sang its praises as an aphrodisiac. Gather ye wild arugula for wild amour.

4. **Dandelion Greens (Taraxacum officinale).** The telltale yellow flower is easily spotted, though the greens are really at their most tender and flavorful just as they emerge from the earth, before they have had a chance to blossom. The name dandelion comes from the French dent de lion ("lion's tooth") and, indeed, the leaves are reminiscent of jagged rows of predatory fangs. This is a green with bite; its bitter, piquant flavor is at its best after with a gentle sauté over the fire (see page 212).

5 **Chicory (*Cichorium intybus*).** Closely related to the dandelion green, chicory also has leaves with toothy edges; it can be distinguished by the bright blue flowers and sparse down upon its leaves. For salad, one should harvest chicory leaves early in spring, before its tender shoots have been corrupted by sultry summer. Like dandelion, chicory leaves are also good sautéed. The roots may be roasted, ground, and used as a convincing substitute for coffee, if one doesn't mind the missing jolt of caffeine.

6 **Sorrel (*Rumex acetosa*).** Should one wish to lunch like a butterfly, sorrel would be one's first choice; certain species' larvae feast on this tangy green. The plant boasts juicy stems and leaves shaped like arrowheads—appropriate, considering sorrel's sharp taste. It makes an excellent, lemony soup, though we enjoy the vibrancy it lends to an otherwise mild mix of salad greens. It flourishes in grassy fields and woods.

7 **Watercress (*Nasturtium officinale*).** Once a domesticated plant, watercress is such an enthusiastic breeder that it now thrives in the wild. As its name suggests, watercress can be found growing in streambeds and creeks, and even in damp roadside ditches, though we imagine ditch cress to be rather steeped in petrol fumes. Watercress consists of a thick stem that can be eaten or not, and small, roundish leaves. It is an astoundingly nutritious plant and can be served nearly any way one wishes sautéed, steamed, boiled, or raw. We find its flavor mildly peppery.

GRILLED RADICCHIO INSALATA
with
BLOOD ORANGE-DATE VINAIGRETTE

ALTHOUGH WE CONSIDER OURSELVES ADVENTURERS IN THE WILDERNESS, WHEN WE JOURNEY TO GREAT CAPITALS ABROAD, WE OFTEN FEEL OBLIGED TO STICK TO OUR BAEDEKERS. Still, every so often, we abandon obligation, toss our guidebooks aside, and go off on a jaunt with only our wits and perhaps a pack animal at our service. So it was on a sight-seeing trip to Rome that we found we had tired of the madding crowd. (Not to mention, all that lovely gelato had wrought havoc upon our delicate constitutions.) We hired a mule, loaded her up with our valises, and tramped off in search of a really cracking salad. We are pleased to share the result, which we find eminently suitable for any outdoor adventure.

2 blood oranges

1 small head radicchio, quartered lengthwise, with some core still attached to each piece

Extra-virgin olive oil, for drizzling

Kosher salt, to taste

Freshly milled black pepper, to taste

1 large head romaine lettuce, coarsely chopped

2 ounces Parmigiano-Reggiano cheese

Blood Orange & Date Vinaigrette (page 67), to taste

¼ cup torn basil leaves, for garnish

1. *Prepare a medium-hot fire, with the flames occasionally licking the grill grate. Let it burn steadily for 30 minutes.*

2. *Use a sharp knife to slice off the top and bottom of the orange. Stand the fruit on its flat end and slice off the rind, removing as much of the bitter white pith as possible (see Advisement, page 76). Slice the fruit crosswise into thin, elegant "wheels." Repeat with the remaining orange. Transfer the fruit to a plate and keep covered until ready to use.*

3. *Drizzle the radicchio wedges with olive oil and sprinkle with salt and pepper. Arrange the radicchio directly upon the grill and cook, turning once with one's tongs, until the leaves are wilted and lightly charred, 2 to 3 minutes per side. Use the tongs to carefully transfer the radicchio to a resting place to cool*

slightly, then chop it into bite-size pieces. Toss it in a large bowl with the lettuce.

4. *Finely grate half of the cheese. Use a vegetable peeler to shave the remaining cheese into fanciful curls. Whisk the grated cheese into the vinaigrette; season with salt and pepper. Add just enough vinaigrette to the salad to lightly coat the greens.*

5. *If one has a platter to spare, this is a wonderful time to use it. If not, a salad bowl will do. Arrange the dressed greens on the platter and slip the orange slices in amongst the greens. Strew parmesan curls and basil across the top. Drizzle the orange slices very lightly with oil. Serve, allowing one's guests to help themselves.*

SEARED MINTED COURGETTES

THE FIRST SIGN THAT ONE HAS CROSSED FROM AN URBAN INTO A RURAL ENVIRON-MENT IS THE SIGHT OF GARDENS BLOOMING WITH PRODUCE. And the courgette (which some call zucchini) is notoriously the bloomingest of the lot—gardens positively burst at the seams with this tasty squash. If one is blessed with choice, select the daintiest specimens from the vine. The smallest are the sweetest, and their natural sugars are set off best by a good sear in the skillet. Served with a generous sprinkle of fresh mint and a squeeze of lemon, the common courgette becomes the kind of rarefied side dish any country squire might call upon to dazzle his city cousins.

1½ tablespoons extra-virgin olive oil

¾ pound (about 2 small) courgettes, trimmed and cut into 1-inch chunks

1½ tablespoons fresh mint leaves, cut into fine ribbons

Kosher salt, to taste

Freshly milled black pepper, to taste

Lemon wedges, for serving

1. *Prepare a medium-high-heat fire, with the flames occasionally licking the grill grate. Let it burn steadily for 30 minutes. Place a cast-iron skillet upon the grill grate and heat it until very hot. Drizzle the oil into the skillet and heat until it begins to sizzle without smoking, 2 to 3 minutes.*

2. *Drop the courgettes into the skillet and allow them to sear without stirring until they begin to brown, about 2 minutes. Continue to cook the courgettes, stirring once or twice, until they are just tender when pricked with a long-handled fork, 1 to 2 minutes longer.*

3. *Transfer the skillet to a resting place and toss in the fresh mint. Season the courgettes with the salt and pepper. Carefully transfer them to a platter and serve with lemon wedges.*

PIPÉRADE SALAD

IF ONE HAS THE MEANS, WE HIGHLY RECOMMEND A SUMMERTIME JOURNEY TO THE PYRENEES. Yes, it can be a bit of a challenge carting one's cast-iron skillet up the passes in those Basque-region Alps, but this reward is enough to spur one on: a smoky-sweet blend of grilled peppers, tomatoes, and onion. Although by tradition pipérade is sautéed and served over eggs or ham, here we've transformed it into a colorful salad, made all the better by a dash of good sherry vinegar. We quite like it served atop our Charred Lemon-Pepper Pork Chops (page 179), but naturally it is best enjoyed if one can persuade a swarthy Mediterranean to convey it by the spoonful to one's mouth.

1. *Prepare a high-heat fire, with the flames licking the grill grate. Let it burn steadily for 30 minutes.*

2. *Brush the peppers with olive oil. Place the peppers directly upon the grill grate, turning them occasionally with tongs, until the skin is evenly charred and blistered, 7 to 10 minutes. Use the tongs to transfer the peppers to a bowl and let them rest, covered, until cool enough to handle, about 5 minutes.*

3. *Slide the charred skin off the peppers and remove the seeds. Slice the peppers into ¼-inch-thick strips and place in a bowl.*

4. *Brush the tomatoes with olive oil and season with salt and pepper. Place the tomatoes directly upon the grill grate and cook, turning once, until they are evenly charred and slightly softened, about 5 minutes. Transfer the tomatoes to a resting place to cool, then chop them into bite-size pieces. Add the tomatoes to the peppers, tossing gently to combine.*

5. *Brush the scallions with olive oil and season with salt and black pepper. Place them directly upon the grill grate and cook, turning occasionally, until they are evenly charred and tender, 3 to 4 minutes. Transfer the scallions to a resting place to cool, then give them a rough chop. Add the scallions to the tomatoes and peppers and toss gently to combine.*

6. *Drizzle in 1½ tablespoons of olive oil, the sherry vinegar, piment d'Espelette, and basil. Toss to combine, and serve.*

*❧ **Advisement:** Should a pilgrimage to the south of France be in one's future, one will certainly encounter piment d'Espelette. Bundles of the drying pepper adorn every sunny terrace there, like bunting. If one cannot find it, a good sprinkling of paprika or cracked black pepper will suffice; we often use a mix of the two when our piment d'Espelette supplies run low.*

1 red bell pepper

1 yellow bell pepper

1 green bell pepper

1½ tablespoons extra-virgin olive oil, plus additional for brushing

3 plum tomatoes, halved lengthwise

Kosher salt, to taste

Freshly milled black pepper, to taste

1 bunch scallions, rinsed and trimmed

1 teaspoon sherry vinegar, plus additional to taste

¼ teaspoon piment d'Espelette (see Advisement)

2 tablespoons chopped fresh basil

CHARRED & HERBED
HEIRLOOM CHERRY TOMATOES

1 pint mixed heirloom cherry tomatoes

1 tablespoon extra-virgin olive oil

2 teaspoons chopped fresh thyme

2 teaspoons chopped fresh basil

1 teaspoon chopped fresh sage

½ teaspoon kosher salt

½ teaspoon freshly milled black pepper

THIS ATTRACTIVE SIDE DISH PUTS US IN MIND OF THE PRETTY YOUNG THINGS WHOM SOME OF OUR POWERFUL AND, ER, RATHER LONG-IN-THE-TOOTH COMPATRIOTS ESCORT TO OUR WILDERNESS SOIREES. Like that lovely arm candy, this dish is sweet, just a little salty, and oh so simple. And while it really doesn't make much of an impact on its own, it enhances the value of the main course it accompanies. Truly, these hot tomatoes are a marvelous enhancement—and we mean, of course, that they go well with fresh fish, sautéed greens, or tossed into a salad.

1. *Prepare a medium-heat fire, with the flames just under the grill grate. Let it burn steadily for 30 minutes.*

2. *Place the tomatoes, olive oil, herbs, salt, and pepper in a bowl and toss gently to combine. Turn the mixture out onto a large sheet of foil, making sure that the tomatoes are in a single layer. Fold the edges of the foil securely over the tomatoes, leaving no tears or gaps in the enclosure.*

3. *Nestle the foil packet in a bed of glowing embers near to, but not in, the fire. Allow the tomatoes to roast until slightly charred and very juicy, 15 to 20 minutes.*

THE HEIRLOOM SEED

One glance at a basket of heirloom tomatoes, with its pretty mix of shapes and candy-sweet hues of golden yellow, sunburst orange, and classic red, will show that these are no more like bland supermarket tomatoes than cheap paste baubles are like the treasures in Grandmama's jewel box. Before the advent of industrialized agriculture, produce of all kinds was available in a much greater variety of colors, shapes, and flavors. With a nod toward modernity, laboratory-created hybrid seeds that bloomed into longer-lasting (but less flavorful) fruit and vegetables became the norm. Bland conformity filled our salad bowls until heirloom seeds, passed down from generation to generation among family farmers, began their determined comeback. Heirloom crops tend to be smaller and not as portable (they are often available only at specialty shops and farmers' markets), but they have flavor that puts the hybrids to shame.

"Science is an edged tool, with which men play like children, and cut their own fingers."
—FROM **GRYLL GRANGE**, THOMAS LOVE PEACOCK

Roasted Garlic in Foil

PROVIDES AS MANY GARLIC CLOVES AS ONE WISHES

ONLY A FOOLISH COOK WOULD DEPART FOR THE WILD WITHOUT A HEAD (OR FIVE) OF GARLIC IN THE SUPPLY TRUNK. Raw, it lends lively kick to anything (or anyone) it kisses; roasted, as here, its flavor mellows, and it becomes an ideal condiment for warm bread, vinaigrettes, mashed potatoes, and dips. If one's journey leads to Transylvania—which we've been told is stunningly green and picturesque—one might even make a garland of raw or roasted cloves to ward off certain nocturnal nuisances. A hot-burning fire with good coals is needed for this dish, which is cooked in the embers.

1. Prepare a high-heat fire, with the flames licking the grill grate. Let it burn steadily for 30 to 45 minutes, until it forms ash-covered coals.

2. Peel away the papery outer layers of the garlic bulbs, but do not remove the skins from the individual cloves, and do not separate them. Cut off the top fourth of each head of garlic.

3. Place each head on a large square of foil. Drizzle it with oil and fold the edges of the foil securely over the garlic, leaving no tears or gaps in the enclosure. Tuck each packet into the embers and roast until the cloves feel soft when pressed, 30 to 40 minutes. Check occasionally to make sure they are not so close to a flame that they might scorch.

4. Allow the garlic to cool enough for easy handling, then use a cocktail fork or one's own fingers to pull or squeeze the roasted cloves from their skins.

Whole heads of garlic

Extra-virgin olive oil, for drizzling

FOIL-ROASTED MUSHROOMS WITH HAZELNUTS & CHIVES

WHAT THIS SCRUMPTIOUS SIDE DISH LACKS IN LOOKS, IT MORE THAN MAKES UP FOR IN FLAVOR. And, really, who could imagine that a handful of squidgey brown things dug from the forest floor would taste so transcendently delightful? It just goes to show that merit ought never be judged by appearance alone. It also shows that crunchy toasted hazelnuts are advantageously employed in the service of the savory as well as the sweet—and that a mushroomy morsel is improved by a good bit of butter and fresh herb. One does learn so many life lessons in the forest! (For additional tutorials, see Foraging for Mushrooms of the Wilderness, page 208.)

8 ounces mixed wild mushrooms, such as hen of the woods, cinnamon caps, yellow cap chanterelles, black trumpets, and hedgehog mushrooms, wiped clean with a soft, dry cloth and sliced (about 4 cups)

4 tablespoons (½ stick) unsalted butter, cut into cubes

2 tablespoons chopped fresh chives

¾ teaspoon kosher salt

½ teaspoon freshly milled black pepper

½ cup chopped hazelnuts, fire-toasted (see Advisement)

1. Prepare a high-heat fire, with the flames licking the grill grate. Let it burn steadily for 30 minutes.

2. Place the mushrooms in the center of a large sheet of foil. Dot the mushrooms with the butter and sprinkle on the chives, salt, and pepper. Fold the edges of the foil securely over the mushrooms, leaving no tears or gaps in the enclosure, and place the packet upon the grill grate. Cook until the mushrooms are tender and turning golden, about 15 minutes. Unwrap the foil and continue roasting upon the grill grate or, if one desires, nestle the packet in hot embers to the side of the fire until the juices thicken and evaporate, 10 minutes longer. Transfer the mushrooms to a bowl and toss in the toasted hazelnuts to serve.

↝ **Advisement:** To toast hazelnuts, place a cast-iron skillet over a medium-high flame. Add the hazelnuts and cook, shaking the pan occasionally, until the nuts are golden and the skin has begun to crackle and flake loose, 7 to 10 minutes. Keep the nuts under vigilant observation to ensure that they do not scorch. Let them cool completely before chopping.

FORAGING FOR MUSHROOMS OF THE WILDERNESS

Foraging for wild mushrooms is not for the faint of heart. It is an undertaking to be considered only when in the company of a foraging expert along the lines of Friar Tuck, Robinson Crusoe, Sancho Panza, or perhaps, if one is feeling particularly fanciful, the caterpillar from *Alice's Adventures in Wonderland*. The golden rule for wild mushroom dining is this: if one cannot positively identify the fungus, then one should not eat it. Words to live by, to be sure. That rule is for survival, but there are a few more for common sense. Firstly, always harvest the mushroom by cutting it away from its base with a sharp knife. Simply pulling it out at the root will inhibit the progress of subsequent mushroom generations. Secondly, place one's harvested mushrooms in a wicker basket whilst one continues foraging. Not only is a basket an attractive means of fungus portage, the open weave of the wicker will allow space for the mushrooms spores to scatter themselves along one's merry forest path. With luck, these may spawn new foraging sites next season. Lastly, do remember to clean one's mushroom with a cloth or (if one must) a paper towel before cooking it. Rinsing it with water will dampen the flavor of the wild edible—one might as well purchase a cellophane-wrapped button cap from the local box store.

Morel (*Morchella esculenta, elata,* and *semilibera*). Morels are among the easiest wild mushrooms to identify, with caps that look like a beige, sea coral chapeau. Depending on the precise type, the cap may be tall and slender or short and squat, but all have the same distinctive knobbiness. One will find them blooming with the first flowers of spring in groves of apple, cottonwood, and elm trees, especially in the moist and sandy soil near streambeds.

Golden Chanterelle (*Cantharellus cibarius*). Golden chanterelles are the flashiest of the edible fungi and are therefore easily spotted. As the moniker indicates, this is a golden-hued fungus, with a cap color that ranges from bright orange to lemony yellow. Its gills extend from the cap's underside halfway down the firm stem. If one is uncertain about its identity, it helps to consult one's nose. A Golden chanterelle has a fragrance that resembles apricot and a creamy, buttery flavor.

King Bolete (*Boletus edulis*). This mushroom appears frequently in the repertoire of urban chefs and is also known by its Italian name, porcini, and its French name, cèpe. It is often scarce in the natural forest habitat, where it has been greedily overforaged. One will know it not by its color—which ranges from deep ruby red to a nondescript tan—but by its smooth cap, which is shaped like a hamburger bun. The king bolete has no gills, but rather is textured like a sponge under its cap. It is smooth, sometimes shiny, but never slimy.

Hen of the Woods (*Grifola frondosa*). Do bring an extra-large wicker basket (and at least one muscular companion) whilst hunting for hen of the woods. A massive thing, made up of tightly clustered caps, it can weigh up to fifty pounds. It looks like a cascade of ruffles bubbling up from the forest floor, and can be green, tan, brown, or pure white. The firm flesh has a marvelous flavor and is said to have mysterious properties that benefit the immune system. What is certain is that lugging the hen of the woods back to one's forest abode makes for a sound fitness regimen. Or, if one is not up for lugging the entire fungus, simply use one's pocket knife to cut off a cluster of its ruffled edge.

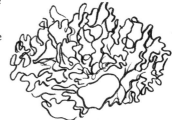

MUSTARD AND MUSHROOM MASHED POTATOES

WE ONCE BECAME SO CAUGHT UP IN OUR EVENING MERRIMENT THAT WE STUMBLED OFF TO BED WITHOUT TAKING ANY MEASURES TO DISCOURAGE CURIOUS CRITTERS FROM OUR ENCAMPMENT (SEE STRATEGEMS FOR THE THWARTING OF CURIOUS CRITTERS, PAGE 42). We awoke the next day to a ransacked larder and telltale pawprints trailing into the trees. Fortunately, though we gave ourselves a stern admonishment, we were not so poorly off—the burglars had left us a sack of potatoes (silly woodland beasts!). We turned the tasty tubers into a banquet of fluffy mashed potatoes studded with wild mushrooms gathered in a hungry haste.

One can play with this recipe by omitting the mushrooms or the hazelnuts or even (gasp!) the tangy mustard. And though we prefer the natural creaminess of yellow-fleshed potatoes, some prefer the airy quality of fine-textured russets. Just remember that russets are thirstier spuds and will likely beg for another splash of cream. If the larder has not been invaded, serve the potatoes with Brandied Steak au Poivre (page 180).

2 pounds yellow-fleshed potatoes, such as Yukon gold or yellow Finn, cut into large chunks

3½ teaspoons kosher salt

2 tablespoons the Colonel's Mustard (page 49) or good Dijon mustard

6 tablespoons heavy cream

3 tablespoons unsalted butter

1 teaspoon freshly milled black pepper

Foil-Roasted Mushrooms with Hazelnuts and Chives (page 206)

1. Prepare a medium-high-heat fire, with the flames occasionally licking the grill grate. Let it burn steadily for 30 to 45 minutes, until glowing, ash-covered coals and embers form. Using a coal shovel or like implement, rake a bed of coals to the side of one's fire pit.

2. Place the potatoes in a large Dutch oven. Add enough water to cover the potatoes and add 2 teaspoons salt. Place the lid on the Dutch oven and transfer it to the bed of coals. Bring the water to a boil and remove the lid. Continue to boil, adding or removing coals as needed to maintain steady heat, until the potatoes are tender, 20 to 25 minutes. If one has not yet done so, this is an excellent time to prepare the mushrooms.

3. Remove the pot from the coals and drain the potatoes. Drop in the mustard, cream, butter, remaining 1½ teaspoons salt, and pepper; mash with a potato masher or fork. Fold in the mushrooms.

RIESLING-BRAISED PARSNIPS

WE LOVE TO WHILE AWAY AN EVENING ENJOYING FOOD AND DRINK AND READING HENRY DAVID THOREAU'S _WALDEN_ AROUND THE FIRE. And everyone just adores the song he quotes: "We can make liquor to sweeten our lips of pumpkins and parsnips and walnut-tree chips." One can take only so much inspiration from a man like Mr. Thoreau (he did have a tendency to put a toe over the line with his esthete's hermit abode), but the man knew a thing or two about the poetic combination of sweet wine and root vegetables. If only he had attempted our recipe for parsnips braised over the fire with shallot, dill, and a nice helping of Riesling wine bubbling in the mix! Surely, he would have attracted a romantic prospect or two to his lonely home in the woods. Though even if he had found a parsnip-tempted lady knocking at his makeshift door, it is likely she would have been put off at the sight of his neck whiskers.

1. _Prepare a medium-high-heat fire, with the flames occasionally licking the grill grate. Let it burn steadily for 30 minutes._

2. _Drop the butter in the cast-iron skillet and place it upon the grill grate. When the butter has melted, add the shallot and cook, stirring occasionally, until almost translucent, 2 to 3 minutes. Stir in the parsnips and continue cooking, until they are slightly golden around the edges, 1 to 2 minutes. Stir in the wine, stock, and ¼ teaspoon each salt and pepper. Place the lid on the skillet and_ simmer over a medium heat until the vegetables are tender and beginning to caramelize, 15 to 20 minutes. By this time, most of the liquid in the skillet will have evaporated. Transfer the skillet to a resting place to cool slightly. Stir in the dill and taste, adjusting the salt and pepper, if necessary. Spoon the parsnips onto china plates to serve._

2 tablespoons unsalted butter

1 shallot, finely chopped

2 pounds parsnips, peeled and cut on the bias into ½-inch chunks

⅓ cup Riesling

¼ cup chicken stock

Kosher salt

Freshly milled black pepper

2 teaspoons minced fresh dill

GARLICKY SAUTÉED DANDELION & WILD SPINACH

WE SOMETIMES WONDER WHAT SOCIAL FORCES PERMIT ONE VEGETABLE TO BECOME A COMMON KITCHEN INGREDIENT, WHILE ANOTHER, JUST AS TASTY, REMAINS SHUNNED AS A GARDEN NUISANCE. Such is the case with wild spinach, also known as lamb's-quarters, goosefoot, and sometimes, quite unkindly, as pigweed. Its blunted, triangular leaves have jagged edges and a silver-green cast, and one finds them proliferating in barren fields from midspring through autumn (we have also spied them at farmers' markets). Less delicate than spinach, but still tender, one need neither treat them with kid gloves nor parboil them to reduce toughness. We enjoy the contrast of astringent dandelion with wild spinach, but one can substitute domestic spinach, chicory, kale, or any hardy green in this dish to no ill effect.

3 tablespoons extra-virgin olive oil

2 garlic cloves, smashed

½ teaspoon kosher salt

½ teaspoon red pepper flakes

1 pound dandelion greens or chicory, hardy stems removed, leaves cut crosswise into bite-size morsels

1 pound wild or domesticated spinach

1. Prepare a medium-high-heat fire, with the flames occasionally licking the grill grate. Let it burn steadily for 30 minutes.

2. Place a skillet upon the grate and add the oil. Heat it until it shimmers like a mirage in the Sahara. Do not wait until the oil smokes, as this will impart a foul flavor to one's greens and is liable to burn the garlic.

3. Add the garlic cloves to the hot oil and cook until they are fragrant and just beginning to color, about 30 seconds. Sprinkle the salt and pepper flakes into the bottom of the skillet. Add the greens, a handful at a time, allowing each batch to wilt slightly before proceeding to the next.

4. Cook the greens, tossing them with a pair of long-handled tongs, until the liquid has fully evaporated, 3 to 4 minutes.

WARM ROASTED FINGERLING POTATO SALAD

CONSIDER, FOR A MOMENT, THE POTATO. It has been celebrated for its beauty—well, not the actual tuber, but its blossom was a favorite *fleur* of no lesser fashion plate than Marie Antoinette. Coquettish maidens of the imperial court showered the unlucky French queen with bouquets of the little lilac-colored flowers. It must have been a lovely life in the days before *la guillotine*! And, of course, when one thinks of that dreadful blade which made Frenchmen's shoulders shrug for good reason, one is disinclined to slice the potatoes for the salad. That is but one of the reasons we make this dish with fingerlings. They need much less attention from the knife than russets and have a deliciously sweet taste when roasted. Toss them with Moutarde Vinaigrette (page 67), which can be made in advance, for a potato salad really worth losing one's head over.

1. Prepare a medium-high-heat fire, with the flames occasionally licking the grill grate. Let it burn steadily for 30 minutes. Place a 12-inch, cast-iron skillet over the fire to heat whilst one prepares the potatoes.

2. Use a sharp knife to split the potatoes in half lengthwise. Cut any large potatoes in half again, this time crosswise. Leave smaller potatoes whole to maintain a size symmetry. Put the potatoes in a bowl and toss them with the olive oil and ¼ teaspoon each salt and pepper.

3. Place the potatoes in the hot skillet in a single layer. Cover the pan and return it to the grill grate. Roast the potatoes, lifting the lid to toss them occasionally, until they are tender and dark golden, 35 to 45 minutes. Transfer the skillet to a resting place to cool slightly.

4. Tip the potatoes into a bowl, drizzle in Moutarde Vinaigrette, and sprinkle in the basil. Season with additional salt and pepper to taste. Allow one's guests to help themselves whilst the salad is still warm.

1 pound fingerling potatoes, scrubbed and rinsed

2 tablespoons extra-virgin olive oil

Kosher salt

Freshly milled black pepper

Moutarde Vinaigrette (page 67), for serving

3 tablespoons freshly chopped basil leaves, for serving

CLASSIC BUTTERED COB CORN

COUNTRY-FRESH CORN ON THE COB, DRIPPING WITH BUTTER AND HOT OFF THE GRILL IS A SIMPLY IDYLLIC TREAT AND IS UNIVERSALLY REGARDED AS THE HEIGHT OF CAMPFIRE CULINARY ACHIEVEMENT. If any one thing could persuade us to give up the joys of urban living, it would be these sweet ears, which are so plentiful in the bucolic hinterlands. Do oneself and one's dining companions a favor and stop to purchase some from a family farm en route to an outdoor holiday. Don't dillydally about—grill it up at one's earliest convenience. Fresh corn is at its best the moment the cob is plucked from the stalk. As the days pass, the natural sugars turn to starch. Remember, dear readers, when it comes to grilling fresh corn, the goddess Fortuna favors the speedy.

1. Prepare a high-heat fire, with the flames licking the grill grate. Let it burn steadily for 30 minutes.

2. Using one's bare hands, peel the husks away from the corn, leaving them attached at the base; remove and discard the silk. Push the husks back up to envelop the ears and soak them in cold water for about 10 minutes.

3. Whilst the corn soaks, drop the butter into the skillet and place it upon the grill grate. When the butter has completely melted, transfer the skillet to a resting place and allow it to cool slightly.

4. Transfer the corn directly from the water to the grill grate. Grill the corn, turning it occasionally with tongs, for about 10 minutes. Carefully turn back the husks and return the ears to the grill grate until the kernels are charred and tender, an additional 5 to 7 minutes.

5. Generously brush the corn with butter and sprinkle it with salt before arranging it on a platter. Allow one's guests to help themselves to the golden ears.

Advisement: *A premier salt will take this humble dish to higher planes. We adore coarse gray sea salt, which hails from Brittany and harkens back to seaside summers along the windswept coast of France. One needn't be put off by the salt's purple-gray hue; those are traces of the minerals in the clay from whence it came.*

8 ears sweet corn, of the freshest possible quality

½ cup (1 stick) unsalted butter or Chive Butter (page 63), cut into pieces

Coarse gray sea salt, fleur de sel, or kosher salt (see Advisement)

Heirloom Apple and Cheddar Dumplings

IS ANY SIDE DISH MORE BELOVED THAN THE DUMPLING? All the world boasts a favorite dumpling to serve alongside a range of dishes from stews to salads, and we are no different. Ours is this apple-and-cheddar-stuffed version, which we often share with our fireside companions and consider a worthy member of the dumpling pantheon. It is delicious on its own and transcendent when paired with a juicy main course.

Now, when it comes to apples, we advocate the careful selection of heirloom fruit. We confess to a smidgen of aversion to newcomer varietals, which seem mass-produced and display a conformity of appearance, bland taste, and durability for shipping better suited to that Fritz Lang film. Apples grown in heirloom orchards have a pleasing eccentricity of color and flavor—they are a breath of fresh air in these modern times. Certainly time will march on, but we hope it does so with the spirit of unconventional fruitiness such as one finds in these dumplings.

1 cup all-purpose flour

1½ teaspoons sugar

½ teaspoon baking powder

1 pinch kosher salt

4 tablespoons (½ stick) unsalted butter, cubed

2 ounces (1 cup) white cheddar cheese, grated

1 apple such as Macoun, Honeycrisp, or Cortland, peeled, cored, and cut into ⅛-inch dice

4 smooth stones, for lining the pot

1. *First, make the dumpling dough. In a large bowl, gently combine the flour, sugar, baking powder, and salt. Use a fork or pastry cutter to mash in the butter until crumbs the size of chickpeas form. Mix in cold water 2 tablespoons at a time, using no more than necessary (likely between 8 and 12 tablespoons total), until the mixture comes together into a dry, crumbly dough. Knead the dough gently in the bowl.*

2. *Turn the dough out onto a lightly floured surface and divide it into 8 lumps. Use a rolling pin or wine bottle to roll each lump into a circle about ⅛ inch thick.*

Divide the cheese and apple amongst the dough circles, mounding about 3 tablespoons cheese and ¼ cup diced apple in the center of each. Brush the rim of the dough circles with cold water and fold the edges inward in pleats over the filling. Wrap the dumplings in foil and chill them in the cooler until ready to bake.

3. *Prepare a medium-high-heat fire, with the flames occasionally licking the grill grate. Let it burn steadily, until glowing, ash-covered embers begin to form, about 45 minutes. Then use a coal shovel or other like implement to scrape a bed of embers to the side of the fire pit.*

4. *Rest the Dutch oven on top of the bed of glowing embers and place the lid near the flames for 5 to 10 minutes. Place the baking stones inside the Dutch oven and cover them with a sheet of foil. Arrange the dumplings in a single layer on the foil. Carefully place the lid on the pot and shovel glowing embers on top of it. Use the shovel to mound more embers around the sides of the Dutch oven.*

5. *After 10 minutes, rotate the Dutch oven 180 degrees. Let the dumplings bake for another 10 minutes, then use the coal shovel to scrape the embers and ash off the lid to check them. If they are golden brown, remove the Dutch oven from of the fire and replace the lid, allowing the radiant heat to continue baking the dumplings for another 5 minutes. If the dumplings are still pale, cover the pot and leave it on the embers for another 5 to 10 minutes. The dumplings are done when they are firm to the touch and golden brown.*

6. *Transfer to a plate to serve.*

The Storage Of One's Provisions

We can become overzealous when assigned the duty of shopping for camp provisions. For while it may be insensible to pack more than a small case of baubles, frocks, and feathered chapeaux, one always needs food to eat—and a market basket piled high with frilly lettuces and glittering berries is a highly tempting way to slip some bona fide (but unobjectionable) beautification into our adventures. It is only several days later, when the icebox bulges from the strain of containing several dozen clementines, a peck of potatoes, and a fleet of pineapples that we fret over our eagerness besting us yet again.

Keeping a firm grasp on one's provisionary needs prior to shopping is the obvious remedy for such dilemmas. Barring that, we suggest becoming acquainted with the ideal habitat for one's produce. It might come as a surprise to learn that many fruits and vegetables do not need the safe haven of the icebox; they are perfectly content—strike that, they *improve and ripen* when stowed away in the gentle open air rather than when packed away on ice. We provide here a guide for such items. However, a reminder: To deter the attention of bears and other critters, all food should be bundled and slung in a tree (see Strategems for the Thwarting of Curious Critters, page 42) at bedtime or when camp is temporarily deserted. To ward off hungry insects, we also suggest storing thin-skinned items, such as tomatoes or apples, in a brown paper sack at all times. Once a food item has been sliced, any remainders should always be wrapped and stored in an icebox. And use one's noggin—one ought not store anything at open-air temperature if the weather conditions are extremely hot, cold, damp, or otherwise harsh.

Avocados

It is perfectly fine to chill an avocado, but it will slow its ripening process. Should one inadvertently purchase a rock hard specimen, hasten its maturation by placing it in a paper bag or wrapping it in newspaper at open-air temperature until ripe.

Onions

Although it is entirely unnecessary to chill this allium, we strongly suggest sniffing out a cool, darkish place, such as an abandoned cave, to avoid rapid decay. This goes for other alliums as well, such as garlic and shallots.

Potatoes

Storage for the humble spud is trickier than one might imagine—chilling adversely affects its flavor, but sunlight turns its skin a mildly toxic shade of green. The best home for potatoes is in a dark, cool place.

Winter Squash & Pumpkins

Chilling degrades the natural sugars of these sweet autumn gems, but extreme heat is not friendly either. We tuck them into a cool, shady place, such as in the boughs of an old elm, or beneath a rocky overhang.

Bananas

Perhaps it is the way they are pitched about by muscular monkeys, but bananas appear awfully resilient. In fact, they are not. While it is fine to chill a banana once it has reached optimum ripeness, chilling unripe bananas disrupts the development of their flavors. Store them in the open air, wrapped in a paper bag or newspaper to hasten maturation.

Citrus

Storing lemons, limes, oranges, and grapefruit in a chilled environment might extend their life by a week or more (depending on the variety), but they are not particularly apt to spoil quickly at open-air temperature. They will certainly survive the length of most camping adventures with nary a blemish. Wrap them only in paper; plastic is a certain means of cultivating mold.

Papaya

If a papaya blushes a reddish-orange, it is ready for consumption, and ought to be immediately eaten or chilled. Those that are yellow-tinged or green have some maturation to complete; store these young specimens in the open air until their color changes and the fruit feels less firm.

Peaches

We always prefer the divine juiciness of tree-ripened peaches, but we admit they will continue to ripen in the open air if purchased a bit immature. Be sure to wrap them in a paper sack or newspaper.

Pears

For the sweetest fruit, leave pears at open-air temperature until ripened, then move them into the icebox, if one wishes.

Pineapple

Once a pineapple has been cut from its tree, it will never grow any sweeter, thus storing it at open-air temperature will not affect its flavor, though some believe they grow juicier this way. We tend to chill them unless we cannot afford the icebox space, in which case one can store them outside for a day or two.

Tomatoes

We feel quite firm on this matter: Never chill a tomato unless one is hoping to transform its meaty lusciousness into something bland and mealy. Store these "love apples" in the open air in a paper sack.

Watermelon

So long as it is not yet cut open, a whole, ripe watermelon is happy as a clam outside the icebox, and will last up to two weeks without chilling.

Skillet Pane Giallo
with
Fresh Corn & Myriad of Variations

DURING OUR GRAND TOUR OF ITALIA, WE ESCHEWED THE PRACTICE OF PICTURE POSTCARD COLLECTING. Those pasteboard reproductions couldn't possibly capture the dramatic colors painted by the Italian masters—the very idea was preposterous! When we wish to remember the fantastical colors of a Michelangelo, a Titian, or one of the many Venetian mosaics, we prefer to make this *pane giallo* right in our cast-iron skillet. This golden bread excites the eye as well as the palate, whether one prepares it with fresh corn, ruby-red tomatoes, or a smattering of wild berries. Or if one has been overdazzled with color, prepare the sausage variation; though it lacks the visual artistry of the others, it is every bit as tasty.

½ cup (1 stick) unsalted butter, cut into pieces

1 cup all-purpose flour

1 cup stone-ground yellow cornmeal

3 tablespoons sugar

1 tablespoon baking powder

1 teaspoon kosher salt

1¼ cups sour cream

1 large farm-fresh egg

¼ teaspoon baking soda

Kernels from 1 cob Classic Buttered Cob Corn (page 215)

1. *Prepare a medium-heat fire, with flames occasionally licking the grill grate. Let it burn steadily for 30 minutes.*

2. *Drop the butter into the cast-iron skillet and place it upon the grill grate. Place the skillet lid in the fire's embers to heat. While the butter melts, waste no time in preparing the pane giallo batter.*

3. *In a bowl, gently combine the flour, cornmeal, sugar, baking powder, and salt. In a separate bowl, whisk together the sour cream, egg, and baking soda. Let this wet mixture sit until the baking soda starts to foam slightly, about 1 minute. Scrape the wet ingredients into the dry and fold them together just until combined. Fold in the corn kernels.*

4. *By this time, the butter should be melted and the skillet and lid quite hot. While wearing one's fireproof gloves, carefully transfer the skillet to a resting place away from the heat. Scrape the batter into the skillet, on top of the melted butter. Cover it with the lid and nestle the skillet in a bed of glowing embers. Making certain the lid is firmly in place, shovel additional glowing embers on top.*

5. *After 20 minutes, gently scrape the embers off the lid and carefully check the pane giallo. If it is golden brown all over and firm in the middle, transfer the skillet to a resting place to cool. If it is the desired color, but not firm in the middle, cover the skillet and return it to the embers for an additional 5 minutes.*

6. Cool the pane giallo, then cut it into fat wedges and serve.

∽ **Sausage Pane Giallo Variation:**
Crumble 4 ounces Italian-style sausage into the skillet and place it over a medium fire, stirring occasionally, until the sausage is browned and cooked through, 7 to 10 minutes. Transfer the sausage to a bowl with a slotted spoon and have it ready to add to the batter in place of the corn kernels. Meanwhile, add 4 tablespoons unsalted butter to the sausage fat remaining in the skillet and place it over the fire to melt. Continue preparing the pane giallo in the usual fashion.

∽ **Herb-Charred Cherry Tomato Pane Giallo Variation:**
In place of the fresh corn, fold in 1 cup Charred & Herbed Heirloom Cherry Tomatoes (page 204) and continue preparing the pane giallo in the usual fashion.

∽ **Wild Berry Pane Giallo Variation:**
In place of the fresh corn, fold in 1 cup wild berries, rinsed and stemmed, from one's forest foraging expedition. We find wild blueberries and blackberries work best, wild strawberries being slightly too sweet for this side dish. Of course, continue preparing the pane giallo in the usual fashion.

CRACKED BLACK PEPPER BUTTER BISCUITS

PART OF THE ALLURE OF OUTDOOR HOLIDAYS IS THAT IN THE WILD INHIBITIONS CAN BE LOWERED, BOUNDARIES OF BEHAVIOR REDRAWN; it may seem as if anything is possible.

But wait! Only *almost* anything is possible, dear reader. No matter how delectable the sauce that accompanies the main course, we must insist that licking one's plate clean is not permissible. Therefore, lest our guests lament the loss of one drop of saucy goodness, we endeavor to serve these American-style biscuits at every meal. Their buttery layers are ideal for discreet sauce sopping, and the jolt of cracked black pepper adds a harmonious grace note to whatever it accompanies, even a humble plate of scrambled farm-fresh eggs.

1 cup all-purpose flour

1 teaspoon baking powder

½ teaspoon freshly cracked black peppercorns

¼ teaspoon kosher salt

½ cup (1 stick) cold unsalted butter, cut into pieces

½ cup heavy cream

4 smooth stones, for lining the pot

1. *Use a fork or pastry cutter to combine the flour, baking powder, pepper, and salt in a mixing bowl. Mash in the cold butter pieces until pea-size crumbles form.*

2. *Make a well in the dry ingredients and pour in the cream. Fold the ingredients using a spatula or wooden spoon until the dough just comes together.*

3. *Turn the dough out onto a lightly floured surface to gently fold over, as one would a puff pastry dough, making 4 to 6 turns. Pat the dough into a circle about 1½ inches thick. Dip the rim of a Champagne coupe in flour and use it to the cut out circles of the dough. Press the scraps together to cut out more circles, one should get 8. Wrap the circles 2 to a packet in foil and place them in the cooler or refrigerator while one readies the fire.*

4. *Prepare a medium-high-heat fire, with the flames occasionally licking the grill grate. Let it burn steadily until glowing, ash-covered embers begin to form, about 45 minutes. Then use a coal shovel or other like implement to scrape a bed of embers to the side of the fire pit.*

5. *Rest the Dutch oven for 5 to 10 minutes atop a bed of glowing embers and place the lid near the flames. Place the baking stones inside the Dutch oven and cover them with a sheet of foil. Arrange the biscuits in a single layer on the foil. Carefully cover the pot and shovel glowing embers on top of the lid. Use the shovel to mound more embers around the sides of the Dutch oven.*

6. *After 10 minutes, rotate the Dutch oven 180 degrees.*

7. *Let the biscuits bake for another 10 min-utes, then use the coal shovel to scrape the embers and ash off the lid. Check the biscuits. If they are golden brown, take the Dutch oven out of the fire and replace the lid, allowing the radiant heat to bake the biscuits for another 5 minutes. If the biscuits are still pale, cover the Dutch oven and leave it on the embers for another 5 to 10 minutes. The biscuits are done when they are firm to the touch; they should feel light when one lifts them (if they seem heavy, they may still have raw dough in the middle).*

8. *Transfer the biscuits to a plate to serve.*

ORCHARD
PEAR & WATERCRESS SALAD

Outdoor adventures ought not be reserved for the flush. If one wishes to feast the eyes upon the beauty of the land in parsimonious fashion, we recommend that one feast upon the land itself. For this dish, one need glean only two blushing pears from the orchard and a sackful of cress from the watery dale. If prosperity knocks upon one's door, we suggest serving the salad with juicy pieces of Stone-Seared Cornish Game Hens with Bombay Spice (page 166).

PROVIDES 4–6 PORTIONS

8 cups watercress , hardy stems removed

2 blushing ripe pears, cored and diced

⅓ cup almonds, fire-toasted (see Advisement, page 206) and chopped

Moutarde Vinaigrette (page 67), as needed

Drop the watercress leaves into a large bowl. Add the pears and almonds. Drizzle enough vinaigrette over the salad to lightly coat the greens. Toss well and serve.

RUSTIC PAIN DE CAMPAGNE

IF GREAT ART IS A MARRIAGE OF THE MAGICAL AND THE MUNDANE, THEN SURELY A LOAF OF THIS RUSTIC BREAD DESERVES AN EXHIBITION IN THE LOUVRE. For it is nothing less than magical that a few granules of yeast interact with flour, water, and salt to create a rustic loaf that satiates the most basic earthly hunger. Many recipes for country bread call for prolonged kneading, but we prefer not to get our hands dirty and so employ this no-knead method made popular by the contemporary baker Jim Lahey. It may take longer to rise, but is certainly less effort—perfect for a holiday, when one is disinclined to be tied to the upkeep of one's dough. The real trick to this loaf is in the baking, the careful heating of the embers so that the Dutch oven stays warm throughout, never too hot. Faithful tending of the oven nestled in the embers will be rewarded by a picturesque round loaf, a work of art that will not linger long enough to be appreciated by the ages. It will be gobbled up long before it has a chance to be matted and framed.

1 teaspoon active dry yeast

1 cup bread flour, plus additional for scattering

1 cup whole wheat flour

1¼ teaspoons kosher salt

1. The dough should be mixed about 8 hours before one intends to enjoy the bread. In a medium bowl, add the yeast to 1¼ cups tepid water and mix gently until the yeast dissolves. Let the mixture rest for 5 minutes.

2. Dump the bread flour, whole wheat flour, and salt into the liquid mixture and stir with a spatula or wooden spoon until it is well combined but still wet. Cover the bowl loosely with plastic wrap or a clean tea towel and allow it to rise until doubled, about 6 hours.

3. Scatter a light sprinkling of flour onto a clean, flat workspace and use a spatula to scrape the sticky dough out onto it. Shape the bread dough into a round; one's hands are the most appropriate tool for this task. Cover the shaped dough loosely with the plastic wrap or a tea towel and allow it to rise for 1 to ½ hours. The dough should almost double in size and will hold an indentation when lightly pressed.

4. Meanwhile, prepare a medium-high-heat fire, with the flames occasionally licking the grill grate. Let it burn until glowing, ash-covered embers begin to form, about 45 minutes. During the last 10 minutes of the rising time, preheat the Dutch oven by setting it alongside the fire.

5. Use a coal shovel or like implement to scrape a bed of embers to the side of the fire pit. Scatter a handful of bread flour into the bottom of the Dutch oven and nestle the pot into a mound of glowing

embers. *Plunk the bread dough into the Dutch oven, scatter a small amount of flour on top, and cover the pot. Shovel glowing embers onto the lid and let the bread bake for 30 minutes.*

6. *Use the shovel to carefully scrape the embers off the lid. With a gloved hand, remove the lid and check the bread. At this point, it should have risen into a nice pale loaf, but it will not be quite baked through. If the bread is very pale, replace the lid and shovel glowing embers on top again. If the bread is already dark, replace the lid but not the embers. Either way, allow the bread to bake an additional 10 to 15 minutes.*

7. *Check the bread by rapping it with one's bare knuckle. It should be ascertainably crusty and sound a hollow tone. When this is achieved, simply turn the loaf out of the Dutch oven and onto a cutting board to cool for at least 15 minutes before cutting into it. If it still does not sound hollow after 45 minutes of baking, take it off the ember pile but leave it in the covered Dutch oven for another 10 minutes to continue baking by radiant heat.*

CRUSTY WALNUT BREAD

PROVIDES **6–8** PORTIONS

ONCE ONE HAS MASTERED THE FINE ART OF CAMPFIRE BREAD WITH RUSTIC PAIN DE CAMPAGNE (PAGE 224), ONE MAY WISH TO ADORN THE LOAF WITH ADDITIONS OF TOASTED WALNUTS AND HONEY. For it is only natural to drape one's true love—whether made of flesh or flour—with adornments. This bread is marvelous when served at dinner; likewise, leftover slices make noteworthy sandwiches and stuffings (see Pan-Roasted Squab with Pâté-Walnut Bread Stuffing, page 173).

1 teaspoon active dry yeast

2 heaping tablespoons dark honey such as chestnut

1 cup bread flour, plus additional for scattering

1 cup whole wheat flour

1¼ teaspoons kosher salt

1 cup coarsely chopped walnuts, lightly fire-toasted (see Advisement, page 206)

1. The dough should be mixed about 8 hours before one intends to enjoy the bread. In a medium bowl, add the yeast to 1¼ cups tepid water and mix gently until the yeast dissolves. Stir in the honey and let the mixture rest for 5 minutes.

2. Dump the bread flour, whole wheat flour and salt into the liquid mixture and stir with a spatula or wooden spoon until the dough is well combined but still wet. Fold in the walnuts. Cover the bowl loosely with plastic wrap or a clean tea towel and allow it to rise until doubled, about 6 hours.

3. Scatter a light sprinkling of flour onto a clean, flat workspace and use a spatula to scrape the sticky dough out onto it. Shape the bread dough into a round; one's hands are the most appropriate tool for this task. Cover the shaped dough loosely with the plastic wrap or tea towel and allow it to rise for 1 to 1½ hours; the dough should almost double in size and will hold an indentation when lightly pressed.

4. Meanwhile, prepare a medium-high-heat fire, with the flames occasionally licking the grill grate. Let it burn steadily until glowing, ash-covered embers begin to form, about 45 minutes. During the last 10 minutes of the rising time, preheat the Dutch oven by setting it alongside the fire.

5. Use a coal shovel or other like implement to scrape a bed of embers to the side of the fire pit. Scatter a handful of bread flour into the bottom of the Dutch oven and nestle the pot into a mound of glowing embers. Plunk the bread dough into the Dutch oven, scatter a small amount of flour on top, and cover the pot. Shovel glowing embers onto the lid and let the bread bake for 30 minutes.

6. Use the shovel to carefully scrape the embers off the lid. With a gloved hand, remove the lid and check the bread. At this point, it should have risen into a nice pale loaf, but it will not be quite baked through. If the bread is very pale, replace the lid and shovel glowing embers on top

of it again. If the bread is already dark, replace the lid but not the embers. Either way, allow the bread to bake an additional 10 to 15 minutes.

7. *Check the bread by rapping on it with one's bare knuckle. It should be ascertainably crusty and sound a hollow tone. When this is achieved, simply plop the loaf out of the Dutch oven and onto a cutting board to cool for at least 15 minutes before cutting into it. If it still does not sound hollow after 45 minutes of baking, take it off the ember pile, but leave it in the covered Dutch oven for another 10 minutes to continue baking by radiant heat.*

Medicinal Plants

With each adventure comes a fair degree of risk; such is the nature of exploration. For every hidden waterfall, primordial ostrich, and indigenous tribe discovered, one must pay the tariff of the unknown and face the possibility of adversity. Which brings us to the subject of infirmity. We are well aware that apocryphal tales of mortal snake wounds and malarial mosquitoes travel, unbridled, along the campsite circuit; however, years of adventuring have taught us that most afflictions are far more pedestrian than serious, requiring only balms for upset bellies and itchy skin. Fortunately, Nature's medical kit is well equipped to handle health crises large and small. Many plants can provide temporary or permanent relief for what ails, so long as one knows where to look. Here we provide some of the most useful remedies. Please consult one's physician or local medicine man for more information on any of the following cures.

FOR POISON IVY, HIVES, MOSQUITO NIPS, OR OTHER ITCHY DISORDERS
Nature's Prescription: Jewel Weed (*Impatiens*)
This common plant is a natural antihistamine—rub the clear liquid contained inside its hollow stem on rashes, mosquito bites, bee stings, nettle stings, and other inflamed patches of skin for relief. Alternatively, one can smear a poultice of crushed leaves upon affected areas. Prior to a woodland hike, apply Jewel Weed to exposed skin as protection against poison ivy. Look for a green plant with oval, toothed leaves and yellow flowers spotted with red. Its leaves repel water, giving it a sparkling appearance when bedewed. Preferring damp, shady areas, Jewel Weed can grow up to five feet tall.

FOR CAMPFIRE BURNS AND OTHER SORES
Nature's Prescription: Cattails (*Typha*)
A wonderful plant from root to tip, each bit of the cattail has various culinary, medicinal, and other practical uses. For the purpose of first aid, boil its rootstock until tender, then mash it into a soothing salve for cuts and burns. We have also heard reports that spreading the burn with the mucilaginous jelly found between cattail's young leaves has the same effect. Most adventurers are familiar with its furry, fawn-colored, cob-shaped heads that bob on straight, slender stalks. It is a wetland plant, so expect to find it near swamps and brackish waters.

FOR INDIGESTION
Nature's Prescription: Dandelion (*Taraxacum*)
Although some botanists recommend chewing the resin of the Tamarack tree (a small, deciduous larch tree), we have more faith in the trusty dandelion. It is also so wonderfully easy to spot its butter-yellow blossoms, which multiply freely in fields and meadows (for more information, see Foraging for Greens of the Wilderness, page 198). After one has plucked its jagged leaves for the salad bowl, its root can be stewed into a tonic that gives swift liberation from bellyaches and constipation. Dandelion is also said to detoxify one's liver, which is excellent news for the oenophiles among us.

FOR HEADACHES AND ANXIETY
Nature's Prescription: Linden (*Tilia americana*)
When the incessant stimulation of camp life becomes too stressful for the hysteria-prone, we suggest settling their souls with a soothing tea made from the leaves, flowers, or buds of this common deciduous tree. It proliferates in woodland regions; look for its spreading, brown-gray branches lined with large, finely toothed leaves and yellow-white flowers. It is also said to alleviate coughs, colds, and fevers. Additional natural nerve-settlers include Valerian and Pink Lady's Slipper.

"IF YOU WISH TO MAKE AN APPLE PIE FROM SCRATCH, YOU MUST FIRST INVENT THE UNIVERSE."

—FROM COSMOS, CARL SAGAN

CHAPTER EIGHT

CAMPFIRE DESSERTS

IN THE WILD, ONE MUST HAVE COURAGE.

It's a simple fact that the first step outside one's door is the beginning of an adventure. Who's to say what dangers untold and hardships unnumbered may await? Or sprightly scenes of merriment and romance? A journey into the great outdoors is surely a journey into the unknown. To extract the utmost joy from every outdoor opportunity, each circumstance must be greeted with a spirit of passionate abandon, an anything-goes, live-for-the-moment kind of mindset with no room for timid apprehension or second-guessing. In short, dear readers, do not be afraid of dessert.

Just as the most oft-told fairy tales have sweet endings, so should one's meal have a similar confectionery conclusion. To partake of a ripe fig, grilled and glistening with honey, under the soft glow of the heavens would be enough to make the angels weep with joy. Should not one's guests, living on terra firma, be afforded this delight? For those occasions when one craves something on a slightly less celestial plane, we offer a pleasingly bitter, dark-chocolate cake, pungent with New World spice. Because sometimes the last course is necessary to sate our earthier tastes as well as our heavenly ones, and it would never do to overlook the bitter in favor of the sweet.

Naturally, one's fireside companions could not be expected to scoot off to slumber without an after-dinner cordial to settle the spirits within. Be it a glass of sweet Madeira, bitter amaro, or perhaps a shot of absinthe taken, medicine-like, with a spoonful of sugar, these little delicacies heighten the senses in preparation for a night of undisturbed repose or for frolicking in the firelight après the witching hour. To paraphrase at least one White Witch of lore, "It is dull to drink without eating."

So never skip the dessert course, if for no other reason than to entertain those things that go bump in the night. One wouldn't want them to make moonlight mischief through idleness.

PINEAPPLE-RUM BROCHETTE FLAMBÉ

AFTER A DECADENT MULTICOURSE MEAL, MANY GUESTS MIGHT ESCHEW THE NOTION OF A RICH AND CREAMY CONFECTION. "Oh, just a piece of fruit for me!" they might cry, giving their bulging bellies a pat. And a good host should be obliging to this request, though we can all agree that one could never be too rich or too, er, creamy. For occasions such as these, we recommend serving the fruit skewered brochette style, grilled with a bit of sugar and doused liberally with rum. Setting the pineapple on fire is a delightfully gratuitous display, designed to transform an abstemious dessert into a spectacle to remember.

1 medium pineapple (about 2 pounds)

½ cup firmly packed light brown sugar

½ cup dark rum

4 metal skewers

1. *Prepare a high-heat fire, with the flames licking the grill grate. Let it burn steadily for 30 minutes.*

2. *On a clean, flat surface, slice the top and bottom off the pineapple and stand the fruit on one end. Slice along the curve of the fruit to remove the prickly rind (see Advisement, page 87). Cut the pineapple into 1½-inch chunks.*

3. *Thread the pineapple chunks onto the skewers. Sprinkle the brown sugar onto a plate. Roll the skewered fruit on the plate, coating the pineapple in sugar.*

4. *Place the skewered pineapple directly upon the grill grate. Grill until the sugar begins to caramelize, about 3 minutes, then use the tongs or one's own gloved*

hand to flip the skewers and grill for an additional 3 minutes. Do expect to sacrifice some sugar to the fire. Transfer the skewers to a platter and work quickly to drizzle the booze onto the fruit. Return the skewers to the grill until the alcohol ignites (see Advisement). Serve while the brochettes are still aflame, keeping well away from foliage.

∾ ***Advisement:*** *Do keep a jug of water close at hand in case the pyrotechnic display should go awry. If one is dining in a particularly arid locale, the flambé step is best passed over. One must follow one's better angels and use sound judgment to prevent forest fires or other such catastrophe.*

Forest Fairy & Sprite Lore

We are fortunate to live in an age of reason. Folklore that speaks of diminutive, merrily magical beings hell-bent on making mischief does not trouble us. Simple logic dictates that fairy stories are nothing more than diverting tales spun from no matter at all, naught but imagination and fancy. Then again, whilst sipping our cordials by the fire, we have seen far-off glimmers of what could only be described as fairy lights and heard the otherworldly piping of a puckish tune. And, sure enough, when we awake our hair is so elf-locked the only possible explanation for its tangled appearance could be a nocturnal visit from Queen Mab. If for no other reason than to protect one's hairdo from the hazelnut-size chariot of Mercutio's fairy midwife, we recommend these simple procedures designed to limit visitations from creatures of the imagination.

It is offensive to call fairies by their proper names. One is unlikely to commit this distressing faux pas if the local fairy is named Titania, Oberon, or some other word not in everyday use. However, some fairies have names like Dog, Flower, or Willow Tree. If these words are spoken aloud as a sprite with the same name chances by, one might acquire a mightily disgruntled fairy foe. To avoid such a plight, one need only point at the dog, flower, or willow tree in question while saying the word, to signify no fairy name is being said.

Fairies loathe cast iron. Legend has it that the fairy kingdom flourished in the age of stone and was beaten underground by warriors who harnessed the power of iron. Consequently, modern fairies can't stomach the sight of most metal, iron in particular. Leaving a cast-iron skillet at the foot of one's bed-roll will ensure one a night of undisturbed sleep.

Fairies have an aversion to untidiness. Just the slightest bit of disarray in one's campsite may be enough to discourage fairy visitation. A caveat: a messy tent may attract the attention of helpful housecleaning imps, but this is not necessarily a bad outcome.

ABSINTHE, THE GREEN FAIRY

During the Belle Époque, the beautiful person's beverage of choice was absinthe. A spirit distilled from anise, fennel, and wormwood, absinthe was called "the Green Fairy" for both its verdant color and its tendency to prompt hallucinations that involved, presumably, winged and scantily clad women. It was also rumored to produce great artistic talent, a not entirely unfounded notion, since its devotees included the poets Charles Baudelaire and Arthur Rimbaud, the painter Henri Toulouse-Lautrec, and the great wit Oscar Wilde, amongst other notables. Sorry to say, absinthe is nothing neither more nor less than a tasty tipple, one that may inspire brilliance, but not provide it. However, its unforgettably ethereal taste is enough to merit inclusion at one's fireside gathering.

There are two widely used methods for the ceremonial presentation of this extraordinary liquor. Though some enthusiasts may strongly prefer one of them, we endorse both.

The Traditional Method:
Pour a dram of absinthe into a cordial glass. Place a sugar cube atop a specially made slotted absinthe spoon and set it over the glass. Slowly drizzle ice water over the sugar cube until it has dissolved, using three to five parts water to one part absinthe.

The Bohemian Method:
Pour a dram of absinthe into a cordial glass. Place an absinthe-soaked sugar cube in a demitasse spoon. Light the sugar cube on fire and drop it into the absinthe. Allow it to flame for a moment, then douse the blaze with a shot of spring water.

GRILLED FIGS with THYME HONEY

IN MORE CONTEMPLATIVE MOMENTS, OUR THOUGHTS TURN TO THE TERRIBLE PLIGHT OF ADAM AND EVE, COMPELLED TO DON WRETCHED GARMENTS OF FIG LEAVES WHEN CAST OUT OF EDEN. Why and wherefore, we ask, were they made to feel naked and ashamed? Most regrettable, we say. The noble fig is much better employed as a dessert, one best enjoyed with a liberal application of sticky honey and melted butter. Not to mention the hint of thyme—an herb whose pungent fragrance seems to banish negative thinking and create an air of joy and harmony in any gathering. (It also serves to cut the sweetness of the honey.)

Make no mistake; we are in firm favor of frolicking in the style of prelapsarian Adam and Eve during one's outdoor holiday. The naked human form is a testament to the beauty and wonderment of nature. But take note: when the time comes for dabbling in fireside culinary arts, a frock of some kind is in order, even if it's simply a fig-leaf smock. One needn't feel shame about placing a garment between bare skin and hot thyme honey, which might splatter.

3 heaping tablespoons delicately flavored honey such as orange blossom

2 tablespoons unsalted butter

1 tablespoon fresh thyme leaves, minced

12 ripe figs, trimmed and halved lengthwise

Mascarpone or vanilla ice cream, for serving, optional

4 metal skewers

1. Prepare a high-heat fire, with the flames licking the grill grate. Let it burn steadily for 30 minutes.

2. Drop the honey, butter, and thyme into a cast-iron skillet and place it directly upon the grill grate. Allow the butter and honey to melt together, 30 seconds to 1 minute. Transfer the skillet to a resting place to cool slightly and stir vigorously to combine.

3. Toss the figs in the honey mixture until they are completely coated. Slide 6 sticky figs onto each skewer, piercing them lengthwise and taking care that all the fruit faces the same direction.

4. Place the skewered figs, cut sides down, directly upon the grill grate. Grill for 2 minutes, then, using the tongs or one's own gloved hand, flip the skewers so the cut sides are facing up (see Advisement). Do expect to sacrifice some honey to the fire. Grill for an additional 2 to 3 minutes, then transfer the skewers to a plate to cool slightly. Place the figs on dessert plates with a generous dollop of mascarpone or quenelle of vanilla ice cream, if desired, and drizzle with the remaining honey straight from the skillet to serve.

Advisement: As the figs sizzle over the fire, they may lose a dram or two of their wonderfully sweet juice. Experience shows that if one grills them cut sides down first, they will get seared and browned. Then, when they are flipped, the husk will provide a barrier to keep as much of the bubbling juice as possible from dripping into the fire.

CaLVaDOS BaKeD APPLeS & PEARS ~with~ CaNDieD PECANS

Apples & Pears:

2 large baking apples, such as Winesap or Rome Beauty

2 large, firm Bartlett pears

2 tablespoons unsalted butter, cut into 8 cubes

¼ cup firmly packed light brown sugar

4 teaspoons ground cinnamon

¾ cup Calvados or other eau-de-vie, such as poire Williams

Candied Pecans:

¼ cup firmly packed light brown sugar

2 tablespoons unsalted butter

1 tablespoon ground cinnamon

1 pinch kosher salt

1 cup pecans

ONE OF THE MANY JOYS OF AN OUTDOOR HOLIDAY IS PARTAKING IN A RAMBLING COUNTRY WALK THROUGH MOSSY GLEN AND MUDDY DALE WITH THE SUN AT ONE'S BACK AND THE BREEZE FLUTTERING ATTRACTIVELY THROUGH ONE'S COIFFURE. Perhaps one's path may cross an orchard with low-hanging fruit, ripe for the picking. And if the apples and pears are not plucked at that moment, what is to become of them? Must they be left to rot? Far better that they find their way—stuffed with sugar and butter, spiced with a sprinkle of cinnamon—into a campfire feast, no? And a shot or two of Calvados makes them so appetizingly fruity, more so than if they were to be eaten sans enhancement. Do try these candied pecans; they provide precisely the crunch one needs to accompany soft baked fruit. It may be too much to hope for to stumble across an apple, pear, and pecan orchard, so we advise purchasing a bag of nuts prior to one's outing.

1. Prepare a medium-high-heat fire, with the flames occasionally licking the grill grate. Let it burn steadily until glowing, ash-covered embers begin to form, about 45 minutes. Then use a coal shovel or other like implement to scrape a bed of embers to the side of the fire pit.

2. Scrub and rinse the fruit. Slice off the top quarter of each apple and pear, setting the lid aside. Use a demitasse spoon scoop out the pips and core, taking care not to puncture the base. Stand the fruit in a Dutch oven.

3. Drop 1 cube of the butter into each hollow, then fill each fruit with 1 tablespoon sugar and 1 teaspoon cinnamon; top with the remaining butter cubes and replace the lids. Pour ½ cup tepid water and ½ cup Calvados into the Dutch oven. Drizzle the remaining ¼ cup spirits over the fruit and place the lid on the pot.

4. Place the Dutch oven upon the ember bed, then shovel additional embers onto the lid.

5. Cook until the fruit is fork-tender and most of the liquid has evaporated, 30 to 35 minutes depending on the softness one desires.

DIGESTIFS

If one has followed the recipes in this modest tome, one has no doubt enjoyed a rich and abundant repast. It may seem counterintuitive that a glass, however small, of the unusually potent potable known as a digestif might top off such a gustatory experience. But, in this instance, intuition may lead one astray. Truly, this little beverage will settle the stomach and lead to a more pleasant night's rest. What fortunate happenstance that overindulgence may be soothed by indulging just a little bit more! Do take advantage of this moment by serving one of these beverages.

- **Amaros.** A woodsy family of liqueurs born in the monasteries of the Apennine Peninsula, amaro is grain alcohol that has been aged for a minimum of twelve days with an herbal blend that may include flowering milk thistle, sweet calamus root, lemon verbena, lavender, and thyme, amongst others. The specific ingredient list for any variety of this bitter beverage will be a secret well kept; half the fun of tasting amaros is the lively discussion about what they may contain.

- **Eaux-de-Vie.** These clear-as-springwater spirits are distilled from a variety of fruits to give them a refreshingly intense flavor and (at 45 percent alcohol) a not-so-subtle kick. Because they are not aged in casks, eaux-de-vie have a purity of flavor that is particularly suited to an evening of outdoor drinking. The scent of a fine eau-de-vie made from strawberries is so evocative of a field of fruit that one may (rightly enough) want to keep a weary eye out for bears.

- **Cognacs.** This dear spirit is a type of brandy heat-distilled from wine in the Cognac region of southwestern France. The very best Cognacs are aged for more than six years and are labeled Grande Champagne. One needn't dilute this drink with water or ice. A clean snifter, a comfortable place to sit, and (at minimum) one good friend to share the experience are all that are called for. As Ralph Waldo Emerson said, "a friend may well be reckoned the masterpiece of nature." And we say any friend bearing a Cognac is well reckoned, indeed.

6. *While the fruit bakes, see to it that the fire is at a medium blaze and make the candied pecans. Combine the brown sugar, butter, cinnamon, and salt in a skillet and place it on one's adjustable tripod grill or grate. When the butter has melted, add the nuts and stir with a spatula. Cook for no longer than 3 minutes, roughly the time it takes to recite one sonnet. Tip the candied pecans out of the skillet and onto the fruit. Serve, drizzled with a bit of the remaining cooking liquid, accompanied by a cheese plate or a scoop of vanilla ice cream.*

GRILLED PEACH-AMARETTO SKILLET CAKES

Skillet Cakes:

2 cups all-purpose flour

½ cup granulated sugar

2 teaspoons baking powder

½ teaspoon kosher salt

¼ teaspoon baking soda

5 tablespoons (½ stick plus 1 tablespoon) unsalted butter, cut into pieces

4 tablespoons almond paste, cut into pieces

¾ cup sour cream

2 large farm fresh eggs, lightly beaten

2 tablespoons amaretto liqueur

Demerara sugar, for sprinkling

Peach Topping:

4 large, ripe peaches, cut into eighths, stones removed

2 tablespoons unsalted butter

2 tablespoons firmly packed light brown sugar, or to taste

1 pinch kosher salt

Crème fraîche or vanilla ice cream, for serving, optional

THE PAIRING OF SENSUOUSLY SWEET PEACH AND DELICATELY BITTER ALMOND IS ADVOCATED BY NO LESS A LOVER OF NATURE THAN CHARLES DARWIN, WHO CLASSIFIED THE FRUIT AS AN EVOLVED FORM OF THE ALMOND. Certainly, the two complement each other when served fresh from the fire with this pancake-like confection. Early- and late-season peaches alike benefit from a buttery caramel sauce—and what, one may inquire, would happen if a ripe height-of-season peach were to be grilled? Oh, sublime magnificence! Would one dare to eat such a peach?

1. *Prepare a medium-high heat fire, with flames occasionally licking the grill grate. Let it burn steadily for 30 minutes. In the meantime, make the skillet cake dough.*

2. *In a medium bowl, gently combine the flour, granulated sugar, baking powder, salt, and baking soda. Use a fork or pastry cutter to mash in 4 tablespoons of the butter and all of the almond paste until crumbs the size of chickpeas form.*

3. *In a separate bowl, whisk together the sour cream, eggs, and amaretto. Use a spatula to make a well in the dry ingredients and scrape the sour cream mixture into it. Fold the ingredients with the spatula until a crumbly dough comes together. Knead the dough several times inside the bowl until it sticks together enough to be shaped. Turn it out onto a lightly floured surface and divide it* into two spheres. *Pat each sphere into a thickness of ½ to 1 inch and cut each into 4 equal wedges. Place the wedges on a plate to bake immediately or wrap them in foil and chill until one is ready to proceed. They will keep overnight.*

4. *Place a cast-iron skillet upon the grill grate. Drop in the remaining tablespoon butter and wait for it to melt. Whilst wearing one's gloves, pick up the skillet by its handle and swirl the melted butter to coat the pan. Return the skillet to the grill grate.*

5. *Place 4 wedges in the skillet and sprinkle the Demerara sugar on top. Allow them to cook for 5 to 10 minutes (this will take longer if the shortcakes are chilled). Use the fire-safe spatula to flip the skillet cakes and sprinkle on more Demerara sugar. Continue cooking for another 5 to*

MERRY-MAKING FLOATS

From time to time, one's fireside repast may be enriched by the presence of the very young or even, shockingly enough, those who choose not to partake of alcohol. It won't seem quite right, as one merrily raises one's glass of absinthe, to see them solemnly sipping water. We propose providing a selection of merry-making floats to enliven the teetotalers' post-meal experience.

WEST INDIES SPARKLER

Drop 2 scoops of coconut sorbet, or vanilla ice cream into a chilled pint glass. Pour in ginger beer, filling almost to the top of the glass. Garnish with toasted coconut shavings and crystallized ginger.

FRAISES DES BOIS FLOAT

Drop 2 scoops of strawberry ice cream into a chilled pint glass. Pour in seltzer, filling almost to the top of the glass. Garnish with wild strawberries.

LEMON FIZZ FLOAT

Drop 2 scoops of lemon ice or strawberry ice cream into a chilled pint glass. Pour in San Pellegrino Limonata. Garnish with fresh mint or basil.

10 minutes. Transfer the skillet cakes to a plate and allow them to cool in the open air. Cook the remaining skillet cakes in the same fashion.

6. While the skillet cakes are cooling, grill the peach topping. Carefully place the peach slices, butter, brown sugar, and salt in the still-hot skillet and return it to the grate. Stir the mixture occasionally, until the butter melts. Keep the peach topping over the fire for 8 to 10 minutes, until the peaches are caramelized and slightly crispy. Transfer the skillet to a resting place to cool slightly.

7. Arrange the skillet cakes on dessert plates, providing one or two wedges to a serving as appetites dictate. Spoon on the piping-hot peach topping and add a dollop of crème fraîche or vanilla ice cream if desired.

WILD BLUEBERRY STEAMED PUDDING

THIS IS A TREAT BEST ENJOYED FROM JULY TO OCTOBER, WHEN ONE'S PAIL OF FRESHLY PICKED WILD BLUEBERRIES RUNNETH OVER. The wild blues that stud this fluffy cake greet the eye like so many sparkling jewels plucked from a maharajah's box. It's a lovely cake to bake in the glowing embers. Set it to cook as the main course is served and, as if by magic, it will be ready by meal's conclusion.

4 tablespoons (½ stick) unsalted butter, cut into pieces, plus additional for baking

1 cup sugar

½ cup whole milk

1 large farm-fresh egg

1 teaspoon vanilla extract

Finely grated zest of 1 lemon

1 cup all-purpose flour

1 tablespoon baking powder

½ teaspoon kosher salt

1 cup wild blueberries, gently rinsed and stemmed

4 smooth stones or a folded tea towel, for lining the pot

1. Prepare a medium-high-heat fire, with the flames occasionally licking the grill grate. Let it burn steadily until glowing, ash-covered embers begin to form, about 45 minutes. Then use a coal shovel or other like implement to scrape a bed of embers to the side of the fire pit.

2. Drop the butter into a metal bowl and place it directly upon the grill grate. Allow the butter to melt, about 1 minute, and transfer the bowl to a resting place to cool slightly.

3. Add the sugar, milk, and egg to the butter and whisk until the mixture is light and frothy. Mix in the vanilla and lemon zest.

4. In a separate bowl, gently whisk the flour, baking powder, and salt just to combine. Dump the dry ingredients into the wet ingredients all at once, and fold with a spatula to form a batter. Don't be troubled if the texture is still a little lumpy, so long as there are no dry patches.

5. Generously butter a 1-quart metal bowl and scatter half the blueberries in the bottom of it. Scrape the batter on top of the berries. Scatter the remaining berries on top of the batter.

6. Place the baking stones or tea towel in the bottom of the Dutch oven. Rest the batter-filled bowl on top of the stones or towel. Pour enough water into the Dutch oven to reach halfway up the side of the bowl. Cover the pot and rest it on the bed of glowing embers. Shovel additional glowing embers on top of the lid. Allow the pudding to steam for 40 to 50 minutes, or until it is firm to the touch and a wooden skewer inserted in the center comes out clean. Allow the pudding to rest in the pot, uncovered, for 15 minutes before turning it out onto a platter. Cut the pudding into slices and serve.

Foraging for Wild Berries

A walk in the woods is not only pretty—it can also be profitable, if one keeps a sharp eye out for wild berries ripe for picking. During the summer months in the North American woodlands, one may chance upon wild strawberries, blueberries, blackberries, and raspberries. Each of these is easily recognized, as it looks much like what one finds in the shops, only a bit smaller and brighter in color. The flavor of these untamed treats is far and away more decadent than their cultivated, store-bought counterparts. And they're available at the right price, too. For a happy berry-foraging excursion, we proffer the following advisements:

MOTHER NATURE FROWNS ON GLUTTONY.

While an orgy of berry eating would be a fun, if sticky, way to while away an afternoon, it is no way to behave in the woods. Unless one is a hermit living rough and contemplating life's mysteries in a secluded cave, one is a guest in the forest. It would never do to eat one's generous host out of house and home. One may politely pick one-third of the berries from each bramble, leaving one-third for the birds and the remaining third for the beasts.

A GENTLEPERSON DOESN'T FORAGE AND TELL.

Neither lady nor gent should divulge the whereabouts of a fruitful find. This privileged information ought to be kept close to the heart of the lucky woodland explorer, lest word get out and other, less scrupulous foragers denude the branches of their bounty.

BE AWARE OF OTHER FOREST FORAGERS.

Creatures great and small are known to enjoy a nice plump berry, but perhaps none more than the bear. Please be on the lookout for this ravenous denizen of the wild, for his appetite is not limited to what grows on the bramble.

THE BEST BERRIES ARE OFF THE BEATEN PATH.

While berries may thrive in the brightly lit clearings along busy roadsides, those specimens are bound to carry the taint of automotive or other pollution and are best left alone.

TO FIND THE BRAMBLES, FIND THE BIRDS.

The seeds of wild berries are sown by our feathered friends; thus, one will find the most abundant berries where birds congregate. Look for traces of birdlife around the bases of trees, especially those near standing water. Or simply follow the sound of twittering.

DARKLY BITTER CHOCOLATE SPICE CAKE

PROVIDES
6–8
PORTIONS

THE INSATIABLE DESIRE FOR SPICE LAUNCHED AN ARMADA'S WORTH OF SAILING SHIPS IN SEARCH OF THE MOST PRECIOUS COMMODITY OF THE AGE. And when those rakish privateers returned bearing chocolate as well, they truly had the world at their feet. This densely dark and piquant cake is a tip of a tricornered hat to culinary explorers everywhere.

1. *Generously butter a 1-quart metal bowl and set it aside until ready to bake. Prepare a medium-high-heat fire, with the flames occasionally licking the grill grate. Let it burn steadily until glowing, ash-covered embers begin to form, about 45 minutes. Then use a coal shovel or other like implement to scrape a bed of embers to the side of the fire pit.*

2. *Drop the butter into a metal bowl and place it directly upon the grill grate. Allow the butter to melt, about 1 minute, and transfer the bowl to a resting place to cool slightly.*

3. *In a separate bowl, combine the flour, cocoa powder, sugars, baking powder, salt, cinnamon, nutmeg, and cayenne. When the butter is no longer hot, whisk the sour cream and eggs into it. Fold the dry ingredients into the wet until just combined. Fold in the chocolate pieces. Scrape the batter into the buttered 1-quart bowl.*

4. *Place the baking stones or tea towel in the bottom of the Dutch oven. Rest the batter-filled metal bowl on top of the stones or towel. Pour enough water into the Dutch oven to reach halfway up the side of the bowl. Cover the pot and rest it on the bed of glowing embers. Shovel additional glowing embers on top of the lid. Allow the cake to steam for 40 to 50 minutes or until it is firm to the touch and a wooden skewer inserted in the center comes out clean. Allow the cake to rest in the pot, uncovered, for 15 minutes before turning it out onto a platter. Cut it into slices and serve.*

5 tablespoons (½ stick plus 1 tablespoon) unsalted butter, plus additional for the bowl

1½ cups all-purpose flour

⅓ cup cocoa powder

⅓ cup granulated sugar

⅓ cup firmly packed dark brown sugar

1 teaspoon baking powder

½ teaspoon kosher salt

½ teaspoon ground cinnamon

½ teaspoon freshly grated nutmeg

1 pinch cayenne pepper

⅔ cup sour cream

2 large farm-fresh eggs

6 ounces dark chocolate, crumbled or coarsely chopped (about ½ cup)

4 smooth stones or a folded tea towel, for lining the pot

INDIAN SUMMER PLUM TARTE TATIN

THE APPLE TARTE TATIN HAS BECOME UBIQUITOUS AT STAID URBAN FRENCH RESTAURANTS. One may wish to serve something more extraordinary to dazzle fireside companions, and this delightfully syrupy, crisp and flaky, plum tart is sure to exceed all expectations. The plums, which ripen in late summer, have had nearly the whole season to bask in the glow of the sun's bright rays and are sweeter and more flavorful than those plucked early in the summer. If one's stars align so fortuitously as to enable a gathering around the blaze just before the autumn chill, this is the ideal dessert with which to celebrate the end of a glorious season.

3 tablespoons unsalted butter

1 quart ripe plums (about 1½ pounds), washed, pitted, and quartered

½ cup firmly packed light brown sugar (or less, according to taste)

Melissa Clark's Pie Crust Unparalleled (page 78), rolled out to a 10-inch diameter

1. *Prepare a medium-high-heat fire, with the flames occasionally licking the grill grate. Let it burn steadily until it begins to form glowing, ash-covered coals and embers, about 45 minutes. Then use a coal shovel or like implement to scrape a bed of embers off to the side of the fire pit. Nestle the skillet's lid into the flames to heat.*

2. *Place the skillet upon the cooking grate. Add the butter and melt it completely. Add the plums and sprinkle the sugar over them. Cook, without stirring, until the plums are dark golden and caramelized, about 20 minutes.*

3. *Quickly rake hot coals from the embers of the fire and form an even bed to the side of one's fire pit, saving some coals for the lid of the pan. Place the skillet atop the bed of coals. Arrange the prepared pastry neatly on top of the plums,* tucking the edges into the sides of the skillet. Using a knife, cut several vents in the pastry lid so that steam may escape. Place the now-quite-hot lid on top of the skillet. Generously heap additional red coals onto the lid. It is important that the coals upon the lid remain blazing hot during baking. Should they cease to glow, heap on a fresh batch. Bake until the crust is golden and firm to the touch, about 20 minutes.

4. *Increase the heat of one's fire to high; Return the skillet to the cooking grate and let it simmer until the juices beneath the surface of the pastry begin to bubble thickly through the vents and take on a jamlike appearance, 15 to 20 minutes. Let cool 5 to 10 minutes in the skillet before slicing into wedges and serving, crust side up, or flipped, crust side down, onto a plate.*

MaDeiRa Cake

PROVIDES
6–8
PORTIONS

THERE IS, WE MUST ADMIT TO AVOID CONFUSION, NO MADEIRA IN THIS CAKE. IT IS MEANT TO BE EATEN WITH A DAINTY GLASS OF THAT FORTIFIED WINE. Madeira wine is so very pleasing, it can be a challenge not to drink it all at once. To halt such unsociable gluttony, some intrepid ancestral baker created a cake to divert one from one's cordial glass and slow the rate of sipping. The citrusy butter cake complements its namesake beverage nicely, but take care! Madeira cake is also superb with a glass of bubbly—and, as everyone knows, once that bottle of Champagne is uncorked, it must be drunk posthaste.

1. *Prepare a medium-high-heat fire, with the flames occasionally licking the grill grate. Let it burn steadily until glowing, ash-covered embers begin to form, about 45 minutes. Then use a coal shovel or other like implement to scrape a bed of embers to the side of the fire pit. Generously butter a 1-quart metal bowl and set it aside until you are ready to bake.*

2. *Drop the butter into a metal bowl and place it directly upon the grill grate. Allow the butter to melt, 1 to 2 minutes, and transfer the bowl to a resting place to cool slightly.*

3. *In a separate bowl, combine the flour, sugar, baking powder, and salt. When the butter is no longer hot, whisk in the eggs, lemon zest, and orange zest. Fold the dry ingredients into the wet until just combined. Scrape the batter into the prepared 1-quart bowl.*

4. *Place the baking stones or tea towel in the bottom of the Dutch oven. Rest the batter-filled bowl on top of the stones or towel. Pour enough water into the Dutch oven to reach halfway up the side of the bowl. Cover the pot and rest it on the bed of glowing embers. Shovel additional glowing embers on top of the lid. Allow the cake to steam for 40 to 50 minutes or until it is firm to the touch and a wooden skewer inserted in the center comes out clean. Allow the cake to rest in the pot, uncovered, for 15 minutes before turning it out onto a platter. Cut the cake into slices and serve.*

1 cup (2 sticks) unsalted butter, plus additional for the bowl

1¾ cups all-purpose flour

¾ cup sugar

1 teaspoon baking powder

¼ teaspoon kosher salt

3 large farm-fresh eggs

Freshly grated zest of 1 lemon

Freshly grated zest of 1 orange

4 smooth stones or a folded tea towel, for lining the pot

As the Bard of Avon mused, "All the world's a stage, and all the men and women, merely players; they have their exits and their entrances, and one man in his time plays many parts, his acts being seven ages." Is it any surprise, then, that man need only cast a cursory glance at the universe for evidence of the number seven's divine place within? Seven, our dear friends, deserves

THE SEVEN WONDERS OF THE S'MORE

a tribute. So it is with great pleasure that—in honor of Shakespeare and the Seven Wonders of the World, Romulus's Seven Hills of Rome and the Seven Sisters of the stars—we offer up these seven transcendent manifestations of the classic campfire confection commonly known as the s'more.

PROVIDES

4

PORTIONS

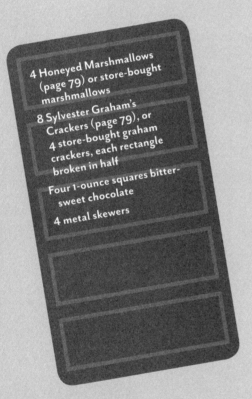

4 Honeyed Marshmallows (page 79) or store-bought marshmallows

8 Sylvester Graham's Crackers (page 79), or 4 store-bought graham crackers, each rectangle broken in half

Four 1-ounce squares bitter-sweet chocolate

4 metal skewers

CLASSIC S'MORES

1. Prepare a medium-heat fire, with the flames just under the grill grate. Spear a marshmallow on the tip of each skewer and distribute a skewer to each diner. Sitting or crouching a safe distance from the fire, hold the marshmallow just over the flame until it is heated to one's desired level of meltiness, 1 to 2 minutes. (Some prefer a charred marshmallow; others prefer a firmer candy puff.)

2. Place the marshmallow upon one graham cracker square, top it with the chocolate and then an additional graham cracker square. Eat whilst hot.

Honeyed Chocolate Orange

Drizzle a bit of wildflower honey on the graham crackers and top the chocolate with a paper-thin slice of orange.

White Chocolate & Strawberry

Spread a thin layer of strawberry jam on the graham crackers and substitute a square of white chocolate for the bittersweet.

Grasshopper S'more

Substitute a thin after-dinner mint chocolate for the bittersweet chocolate. Sandwich the toasted marshmallow and mint chocolate between chocolate wafer cookies, if desired.

Petit Écolier S'more

(for Swift Campfire Gratification)

Omit the graham crackers, omit the chocolate. Simply toast the marshmallow and sandwich it between two dark chocolate Petit Écolier cookies.

Creamy Peanut Butter Open-Faced S'more

Spread the bottom graham cracker with creamy peanut butter and omit the top cracker.

Dulce de Leche & Fleur de Sel

Spread a thin layer of dulce de leche on the graham crackers and sprinkle on a pinch of fleur de sel before topping with the toasted marshmallow and chocolate.

"WE CHERISH OUR FRIENDS NOT FOR THEIR ABILITY TO AMUSE US, BUT FOR OURS TO AMUSE THEM."

—EVELYN WAUGH

CHAPTER NINE

AFTER THE REPAST

AND NOW THAT THE DAY'S FEAST HAS COME TO AN END, NOW THAT DISHES HAVE BEEN CLEARED, DIGESTIFS HAVE BEEN DRUNK, TENTS PITCHED, BEDROLLS UNFURLED, AND LEFTOVER FOODSTUFFS HOISTED INTO THE BEARPROOF BRANCHES HIGH ABOVE, IT IS TIME FOR A NIGHT OF FIRESIDE ENTERTAINMENT. Ah, yes, these hours when the fire crackles for no other purpose than to transfix one's gaze can be so pleasantly meditative and restful. One might think it best to trundle off to one's tent—but we respectfully disagree. A bit of convivial storytelling or game playing, and a good many more fanciful flights of impudent imagination are called for before a night's sleep has been earned. However else will one be properly worn out, without some kind of late-night carouse? One is on holiday, after all; one needn't maintain the sober bedtime hours of the workaday world.

How fortunate one is when one's clever companions may add to the general merriment by reciting an excellent line (several lines, even) of verse! Or—still better fortune—when one is asked to amuse one's guests with an impromptu airing of one's skill on the harmonica or expert knowledge of the starry night sky. What could give greater satisfaction than to display one's accomplishments to an appreciative audience?

But fear not, gentle reader! If one is unsure what accomplishment one might display, simply peruse this chapter for gainful suggestions. In these pages, we shall reveal our secrets designed to make any after-dinner party extraordinary, whatever the proclivities of the firelit merrymakers. If one's brain feels too feast-addled for reciting verse, why not give voice to a haiku? (Yes, we'll provide instruction for composing one of these gemlike poems.) Try spinning a ghost story—or if a plot for a classic gothic tale eludes one, we'll describe how to hold a fireside séance. With luck, perhaps a real spirit will arrive, providing inspiration for frightening yarns during generations to come.

Unsure if holding a séance (even in jest) is the right course? Well, then, turn to our section on tarot cards, and shuffle up a deck to learn what the future holds. Of course, if one would rather debate the subject of free will versus destiny, do proceed to our section on philosophical ponderings. To put it in the shell of a nut: the nighttime fun may go on until one's guests begin to quarrel about whether the birdsong issuing from the forest is the work of the nightingale or the lark.

And if it is the lark trilling out its morning reveille, do fill a kettle for the fire. A strong cup of tea will set all to rights and put everyone in the ideal frame of mind to tuck in to another marvelous breakfast prepared over the open flame.

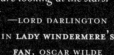

> *"We are all in the gutter, but some of us are looking at the stars."*
> —LORD DARLINGTON
> IN **LADY WINDERMERE'S FAN**, OSCAR WILDE

Adventuring is a vigorous affair. During the day, one's party might remain well-occupied scaling mountains, hacking through jungle growth, wading through brackish lagoons, and sailing across fathomless seas. In spare moments, one has botanicals to identify, game to hunt, camps to make, wood to collect, fires to light, and cocktails to shake. Not to mention a fair number of hammocks to swing. A staid sort of person might think this excitement enough for a lifetime, let alone a holiday. But true adventurers know that the art of exploration is never complete. And so, when darkness settles and limbs grow weary, we turn our attention to a more sedentary (but no less thrilling) means of discovery: stargazing.

Sailing the evening skies leads to any number of celestial pleasures. Novice astronomers will find no better place to begin than with a good peek into the heavens. Unlike a chemists' lab, where compounds are locked up tight behind sterile doors in tightly sealed test tubes, the astronomer's laboratory is plain to see and swirling with mysteries, including milky galaxies, hazy nebulae, meteor showers, and all those colorful planets noted in one's schoolbooks. Professional astronomers often rely on amateurs for new discoveries, so it is entirely possible that the budding Galileo among one's party might be the genius to settle the question of dark matter once and for all.

If the realm of Science is a bit too sober for one's magical weekend, then let us consider alternatives. Astrology, the art of telling one's fortune by the movements of celestial bodies in space and time, is anything but dull if the modern preoccupation with newspaper horoscopes is any gauge. As any farmer's almanac shows, stargazing can help determine when to plant or when to expect one's harvest, which can be useful in home gardening or even foraging. And if one is learned enough to identify the bright light of the North Star, one can faithfully navigate the way home if lost.

But, most of all, the simple constellations are a feast for the eyes in stargazing. The tragedies of the Greek gods are written there, and if armed with a sky map or astrolabe, a good set of eyes, and a curious mind, one might while away a perfect evening caught up in the melodrama of the ancients. To help one along, we have composed a guide to some of our favorites among the many constellations. First, some general advice:

Advice for Observing the Heavens

- If one is serious about astronomy, then a telescope is a wise investment, but make sure it is not so large and cumbersome that one will loathe dragging it outdoors. For dabblers, a good pair of binoculars or one's own peepers will suffice.

- Assess the daytime weather. If one has been blessed with clear blue skies, it is time to rustle the binoculars and maps from the trunk, for a clear, dark night is likely.

- Over dinner, or even over cocktails, hold an informal planning meeting. Unroll one's constellation map (see illustration, page 257), bring out one's pointer, and become visually acquainted with what the party hopes to observe. When night falls, all eyes will be primed for success.

🍂 While it isn't easy organizing one's adventures around the whims of the moon, it is ideal to set out for stargazing on moonless (or nearly moonless evenings). The romantic, lunar glow is strong enough to interfere with the view. Similarly, stargazing is best in rural areas devoid of streetlamps, headlights, and flashing signs. While we would never discourage urban-rooftop astronomy, one will spy a superior wealth of stars in the wild.

🍂 Unlike nocturnal animals, who can spot even the tiniest prey scurrying across the dark forest floor, humans are not naturally inclined to see well at night. Proceed with patience. As the sun goes down, the eyesight will improve bit by bit. One's night vision will not be at its best until two or three hours after full darkness.

🍂 Besides consuming carrots in excess, there exist other means of improving night vision. Don one's chicest sunglasses during the day to avoid sunlight, which weakens the eye, and don't stare too steadily into one's campfire. Take slow, deep breaths, which will send the greatest amount of oxygen to one's eyes, making them more likely to spy that shooting star. When using a telescope, we like to cover our observing eye with a patch between gazes, which also helps frighten away any marauding campers who may be scavenging for plunder.

🍂 If one fears complete darkness or is frustrated by an inability to properly consult one's star map, we suggest covering one's lantern with red tissue paper to diffuse the glow. The human eye is less sensitive to red light.

A Smattering of Constellations

The ancient Alexandrian astronomer Ptolemy catalogued forty-eight official constellations in the night sky; according to modern astronomers, one should be able to pick out eighty-eight (throughout the year and across the globe, as the positions of the stars are everchanging, and their visibility depends upon the time of year and which hemisphere one inhabits). Here we recall the mythology behind some of our favorites. For a picture of each, please consult page 255.

THE GREAT BEAR (URSA MAJOR) AND THE LITTLE BEAR (URSA MINOR)

This is the story of a tragic young beauty named Callisto. The great god Zeus spied her sleeping under a tree and thought her one fine filly. Before long, she was carrying his child. Understandably, Zeus's wife, Hera, flew into a jealous rage and turned Callisto into a bear as punishment for tempting her husband. Years passed. One afternoon, while hunting in the forest, Callisto's son, Arca, happened upon a lone bear, who, unbeknownst to the boy, was none other than his mother. Arca aimed his arrow at it, but Zeus swiftly intervened, preventing tragedy. He transformed Arca into a bear as well and then (to appease his jealous wife) flung both mother and son into the night sky, forming the Great Bear (Callisto) and the Little Bear (Arca). Ursa Major is most notable for its seven brightest stars, which line the bear's back and tail (we assume bears were scarce in ancient Greece, since it is common knowledge that bears haven't much of a tail); these stars form the ladle-shaped Big Dipper, one of the most easily recognized constellations. The tail and back of the

Little Bear form the Little Dipper, and the last star upon the tail, shining ever brightly, is Polaris, or the North Star.

CASSIOPEIA, PERSEUS AND ANDROMEDA

Not far from the Big Dipper, perched upon her regal throne, is the Ethiop Queen, Cassiopeia, a braggart type who told anyone who would listen that she was lovelier than any other woman, or even any goddess. Poseidon, god of the sea, was irritated by this boasting and snatched her daughter, Andromeda, as punishment. He lashed the innocent lass to a rock and set a ravenous sea monster upon her. Along came young Perseus, fresh from slaying the snake-haired Medusa. He rescued Andromeda and demanded her hand in marriage as a reward. Upon Cassiopeia's eventual death, the gods placed her in the heavens—but they turn her throne upside down for half of each night, presumably to muss her hair and mock her conceit. Perseus, too, eventually landed in the sky, holding the head of Medusa. The brightest star in the constellation of Perseus, Algol, is Medusa's eye. Andromeda can also be found in the heavens, arms outstretched to her gallant husband.

THE CRAB (CANCER)

Zeus's wife, Hera, was quite a troublemaker. Responsible for the sad fate of Callisto (the Great Bear), she also wrought havoc upon the Crab. When Hera's stepson, Hercules, whom she didn't much like, charged off to fight the multiheaded monster Hydra, Hera began plotting. Deciding that this was an ideal moment to snuff out Hercules, she sent a giant crab, Cancer, to distract him from battle. Poor Cancer had scarcely nipped at the ankles of the great warrior before he was crushed underfoot. Feeling a twinge of remorse, Hera placed Cancer in the sky

as recompense for his efforts, but his lights blink weakly, since she found his work unsatisfactory.

THE CHARIOTEER (AURIGA)

There are varying interpretations of the Charioteer, though perhaps the most common identifies him as an Athenian king who was possibly lame (or, alternatively, a lame man who was possibly king) and who invented the four-horse chariot. To honor him, the gods gave him a home in the stars. One cannot see the chariot in this constellation; instead one sees a man with, oddly, a goat wrapped around his neck. Although the Greeks are mute on the subject of the goat, Roman mythology suggests this is the goat who suckled the god Jupiter (yes, this confounds us, too). The brightest star of the Charioteer is Cappella. It is tucked into the body of the goat, and is the sixth brightest star in the night sky.

THE TWINS (GEMINI)

This constellation consists of two men, Pollux and Castor. Many variations of their story exist, but our favorite is that they were brothers. Both shared the same mother, but Pollux was yet another son of Zeus, while Castor was the son of a mortal king. When the brothers grew into men, they bravely headed off in search of the Golden Fleece, a Holy Grail sort of quest. When mortal Castor was killed in battle, Pollux became inconsolable and begged Zeus to kill him too. The god finally consented to allow the two brothers to reside together in the sky. Sailors and travelers have long looked to the Twins for protection, as they symbolize a roving, carefree life.

THE HUNTER (ORION)

Orion was a demigod, son of a mortal woman and

STRANGE CREATURES IN THE SKY

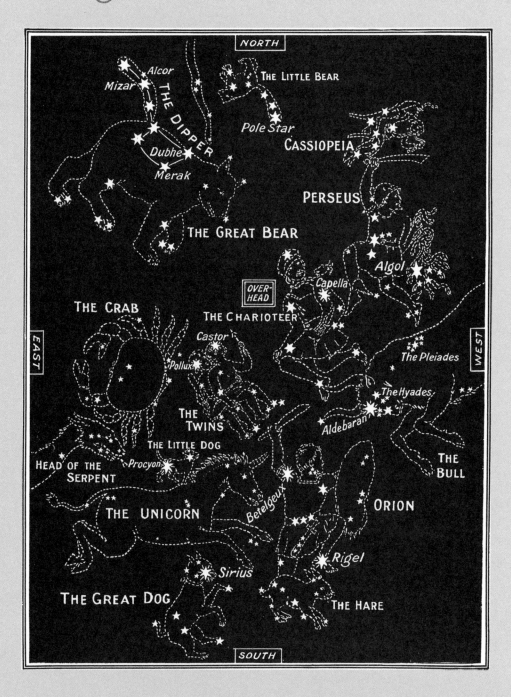

the water god Poseidon. He was a strapping, fine-looking giant, and women often fell for him; the goddess of the Hunt, Artemis, was no exception. Unfortunately, her brother Apollo disapproved of the budding romance. One fateful day, he sent a giant scorpion to attack Orion. Though Orion fought as well as he could, he was no match for the creature—the scorpion mortally wounded him. When Artemis discovered her lover's death, she placed him in the sky so that she would remember him always. The three closely arranged stars that form Orion's belt are among the easiest to spot in the sky.

THE BULL (TAURUS)

This constellation represents Zeus, who, ever lustful, turned himself into a white bull with golden horns in order to draw the attention of a beautiful young maiden, Europa. As soon as Europa took her place atop the bull, Zeus charged off with her to the island of Crete, where we suppose he intended to have his way with her. In the constellation one sees only the front half of the charging bull—the horns, head, and forelegs. We should also note that Taurus contains two beautiful star clusters (visible with a telescope or binoculars). The first, visible in the bull's head, is called the Hyades, and consists of over 150 multi-colored stars. The second, the Pleiades, is a cluster of stars nestled in gas and dust located in the bull's shoulder. The Pleiades represent the Seven Sisters, a group of sisters hotly pursued by Orion until Zeus saved them by turning them into stars (only six of the sisters are visible to the naked eye).

STAR CHART

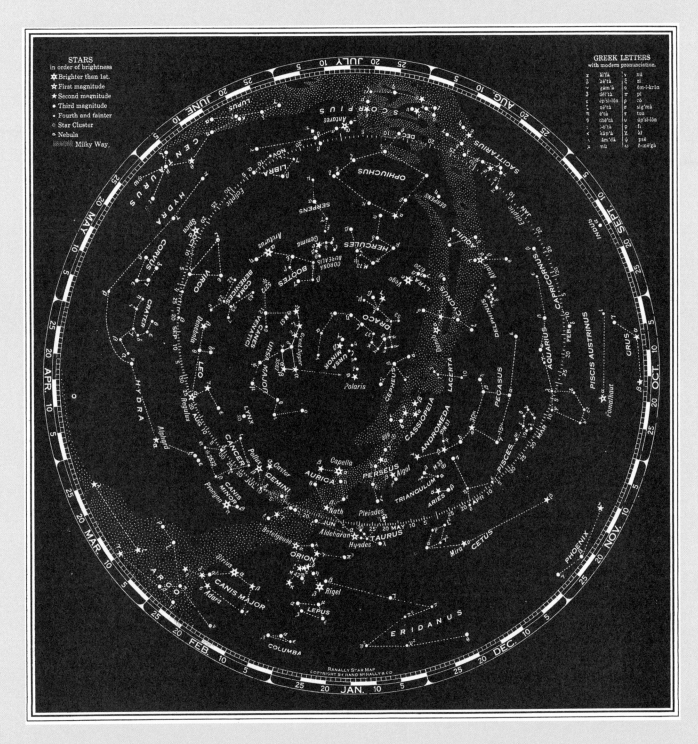

the art of the tarot, or, shuffling toward the future

If one feels, as we do, that the time after a festive meal is most advantageously enjoyed in a spirit of convivial reflection and wonderment, then one must remember to bring along a deck of tarot cards for a round of after-dinner divination. Indeed, witnessing one's companions' various reactions to a proffered tarot reading is an amusing diversion in itself.

We find our friends fall into one of two camps. The scientific-minded amongst them, aghast at our medieval affection for pictorial hocus-pocus, shun the very idea of the cards and proclaim no faith in fortune-telling other than in the logically parsed outcomes of cause and effect. Of course these devotees of reason are also motivated by curiosity and cannot refrain from asking for a reading, if only to scoff for its duration. One must not begrudge these naysayers their fun! They allow themselves precious little of it.

On the other side—and usually this second faction is populated by overly empathetic souls—are those eager romantics who cannot get enough of the tarot. They greet the sacred deck with rapid-yet-prim hand claps and (though they think no one notices) push ahead in the queue for a reading, asking a variation of the same query over and over ("Does my true love think of me?"). We recall only too well the evening when, after laying out the cards for just such a lonely-hearted darling, we were forced to tell the silly thing what the cards revealed: that the querent's object of affection frequently did think of her . . . and those thoughts came in the form of nightmares. Never let it be said that the tarot cards don't tell it like it is!

Somewhere between these polarities lies our own attitude. It is our strongly held belief that contemplation of the future ought to be a lighthearted endeavor, undertaken in the carefree knowledge that no tomorrow is set in stone and everyone may diverge from a present path simply by changing the mind. For where there is life, there is hope—no matter what the cut of the deck (fortunate or not), one's own free will is sure to be the trump card.

If one's mind is prettily framed with that cheery point of view, we heartily propose that one acquire a deck of tarot cards at a local curio shop. We will provide advisement on just how to go about reading the cards without further delay.

The aspiring tarot reader must begin by gaining an intimate knowledge of the deck. Toward that end, it is recommended that the reader sleep with the cards beneath her pillow. It may well be that a kind of psychic connection is formed whilst dreaming. In any event, this arrangement will certainly prevent one's cards from being stolen or otherwise abused whilst one slumbers.

Then, the reader ought to devote a stretch of time during her waking hours to examination of the pictures and the study of their meaning. The tarot is composed of the minor arcana, which foretell the kind of occurrences and foibles that may occur in day-to-day life (i.e., this career move will be a good one, that suitor's kiss will be one for the record books, or beware of slipping in the bathtub), and the major arcana, which speak of grander matters and esoteric influences of the sort that shape one's elemental journey on a spiritual plane (i.e., this career opportunity is a just reward for one's stellar performance in a past life, that suitor's kiss could change the course of one's life, or the soul-healing power of a thousand good, salty weepings may also be achieved by a spur-of-the-moment trip overseas).

One will see that the minor arcana is made up of numbered cards, with suits similar to those found in a standard deck of playing cards. The major arcana is represented by pictures and titles whose meanings may be open to more intuitive interpretations. Of course, every deck of cards has subtle differences (and, handily enough, comes with a booklet of instructions for further explanation), but here we offer a brief sketch of some of the broader definitions of the pictographs. We advocate the use of one's imagination to fill in any blanks.

Minor Arcana

SUIT OF PENTACLES

Some tarot decks depict this suit as coins decorated with a five-pointed star. This suit connotes events that take place in one's home or have to do with money.

SUIT OF SWORDS

Swords connote power and (sometimes) aggression. They speak of the mercurial nature of everyday emotion, often predicting outbursts of temper.

SUIT OF WANDS

Wands are all about one's career or avocation—the work one does out of passion, not simply a job one completes in exchange for financial reward.

SUIT OF CUPS

These cards are predictors of love and romance—everybody's favorite suit!

Major Arcana

THE FOOL

Right side up: A new beginning undertaken in the spirit of carefree naïveté. The universe favors all her beloved fools.
Upside down: A new beginning undertaken in the spirit of immature irresponsibility. The universe frowns upon idiocy.

THE MAGICIAN

Right side up: Like the pictured magician, the querent has everything at the ready to create whatever one might choose. He or she can have it all and is prepared for any circumstance.

Upside down: Warns the querent of trickery or perhaps self-delusion. More preparation is required before rewards are justified.

THE HIGH PRIESTESS

Right side up: Let one's intuition be a guide. Follow one's dreams—they may prove prophetic after all.

Upside down: A secret is about to be revealed!

THE EMPRESS

Right side up: One is upon the correct path; continue it for an abundance of good fortune in love and money.

Upside down: Too much of a good thing may smother; take a break from the pursuit of abundance.

THE EMPEROR

Right side up: The querent is metaphorically embraced by protective paternal love.

Upside down: An authority figure may become oppressive; too much love can feel imprisoning.

THE HIEROPHANT

Right side up: Divine inspiration is available; one need only open one's mind to its possibility!

Upside down: Guard oneself against too much striving for protection. One is only human, after all.

THE LOVERS

Right side up: Let go of the past in order to claim a new love.

Upside down: Love may be temporary—but it will be exciting.

THE CHARIOT

Right side up: Continue striving—one exerts greater control over one's destiny than can be imagined. Keep in mind the fun of the journey rather than the importance of the destination.

Upside down: Does one feel as if one's life has gone off the rails? Concentrate on small achievable goals; baby steps will bring about a journey's successful completion.

JUSTICE

Right side up: Justice in the truest sense—this card could foretell satisfaction or discomfort in equal measures, depending upon the justness of one's cause.

Upside down: Justice has gone awry, but do not blame oneself! It will right itself, if not in this life, then in the next.

THE HERMIT

Right side up: Self-knowledge and inner strength is paramount to reaping emotional reward.

Upside down: One's isolation may have been imposed rather than chosen. Make every attempt to enjoy the company of others, for that is the path to emotional contentment.

THE WHEEL OF FORTUNE

Right side up: A change in fortune is on the way! Dare to expect the unexpected.

Upside down: The upside-down wheel foretells a closure, the ending of one cycle of destiny. Fear it not—be glad the natural order and disorder of the universe is beyond one's control.

STRENGTH

Right side up: Passionate forces abound—greet them with the solemn strength of patience.

Upside down: Do not panic in the face of a force greater than one's own; one need only bend a little to conquer.

THE HANGED MAN

Right side up: The time has come to view one's life from a different perspective. Be patient and step away from strife; it will resolve itself.

Upside down: One may be feeling tethered to an unhappy situation or contract, but this is merely an excuse for inaction.

DEATH

Right side up: Move away from the familiar toward new opportunities, even if such a journey is frightening. It is simply the natural progression of life.

Upside down: Move away from old and familiar patterns. If one does not make the change oneself, it will be made for one. And nobody wants that.

TEMPERANCE

Right side up: Meditation and concentration are required to achieve a harmonious balance. Belief in one's ability to judge a situation adeptly is all that is needed.

Upside down: Imbalance and a tidal wave of trouble are approaching. Stop treading water and climb into the lifeboat while it is still possible.

THE DEVIL

Right side up: Guilt, fear, and out-and-out addiction may shackle one to an unsatisfactory way of being.

Upside down: Sensual temptation need not always be resisted.

THE TOWER

Right side up: A sudden bolt from above threatens all one holds dear. Fear not! One's foundation is sound.

Upside down: Disaster awaits, but it is yet avoidable.

THE STAR

Right side up: Creativity sparkles and inspiration abounds; good fortune in any inventive endeavor awaits.

Upside down: Starlight may bewitch! Rethink one's invention in the clear light of day to ensure its success.

THE MOON

Right side up: The world is cast in moon-inspired shadows. Life may be rendered topsy-turvy; rely on one's basest instinct to do more than survive.

Upside down: One may be enjoying the temporary respite of the night—but be wary of the danger of inaction.

THE SUN

Right side up: The heat of the sun warms all creation. This card signifies health, happiness, children, relationships, and true success. Huzzah!

Upside down: The gifts of the sun are just out of reach. But take heart—this card signifies delay, not defeat.

JUDGMENT

Right side up: Whether this card heralds new beginnings or final closure, events will move quickly. One will marvel at a faster pace of life.

Upside down: An important matter has been delayed. One must confront one's fear of change.

THE WORLD

Right side up: Energy and optimism surround one's aura. Now is the time to take a step into the wider world.

Upside down: One may have the feeling of being trapped in an ever-tightening circle. Break out of this cycle by breaking out of an established character and the world will open up again.

And now, to the ceremony of the tarot

The reader ought first to spread out a silken cloth upon which to lay the cards, for one's future should rest upon only the finest textile. Next, the reader will shuffle the cards, then ask the querent to shuffle them. It matters not the duration of the shuffle, only that the querent has an intuitive sense that the cards are sufficiently mixed up. The querent should cut the deck once and hand the cards back to the reader for placement.

The reader then places the cards on the silken cloth in the order in which they appear, drawn from the top of the deck in the following manner, which is known as the Celtic Cross:

Place the first card in the center of the cloth. Lay the second card, crosswise, on top of the first. The third card goes above the first card, the fourth card goes to the left of the first card, the fifth card goes below the first card, the sixth card goes to the right of the first card.

Then the reader will place the next four cards (card numbers seven through ten) in an ascending horizontal line just to the right of the cross of cards already laid out.

THE CARD POSITIONS HAVE THE FOLLOWING SIGNIFICANCE:

1. The task at hand
2. The opposition to the successful completion of that task
3. The querent's past
4. The querent's present
5. The querent's near future
6. The querent's distant future
7. The querent's attitude (important when one considers that our own thoughts are the creators of reality)
8. The energy or forces surrounding the querent
9. The hopes and fears of the querent (think of this as showing the querent what is most desired, as that is often what is most pushed away)
10. The outcome of the first card (the task at hand)

The cards should be left right side up or upside down and read as they appear to the reader (rather than the querent), with each one's meaning affected by its position in the layout. The reader may wish to keep a list of the meanings of each card handy to refer to during the session, but we discourage this practice. There is more fun to be had by glancing at the cards and then making things up. After all, the best psychic is really just the best guesser.

We find it a great tragedy that reading aloud seems to have fallen out of favor amongst all but the most exclusive literati. Why should the posh parlors of bluebloods remain the sole heir to the literary salon? To us, a good book of verse around a campfire is like a good box of bonbons—we cannot sit near a crackling flame without indulging in either (particularly if the poetic treats are printed on the pages of a first-edition, leather-bound tome, although those features are not essential).

It seems that poetry terrifies many an otherwise well-read soul, as if only an experienced cryptographer might crack its hidden code. We find such a notion to be rubbish. The ultimate value of poetry is like that of wine; it is directly proportional to the tastes of its consumer. Perhaps one scours a poem for political or historical significance, perhaps one is wallowing in a broken romance, perhaps one doesn't follow a single, godforsaken word, but finds the language lovely. As the great poet T. S. Eliot once wrote, "Genuine poetry can communicate before it is understood," which we think was his way of saying that people ought not worry about the meaning of poems because they are created to perplex.

As this is a book about adventure, and not, say, automobiles, we have chosen to share some read-aloud classics certain to draw out the derring-do in one's companions. These lines celebrate journeys and sallying forth with a good deal of moxie (which should overflow in the Great Outdoors). To inspire one's companions appropriately, take care to read confidently, varying the tone, volume, and pacing. A faux British accent also makes a valuable asset.

George Gray
By Edgar Lee Masters

I have studied many times
The marble which was chiseled for me —
A boat with a furled sail at rest in a harbor.
In truth it pictures not my destination
But my life.
For love was offered me and I shrank from its
    disillusionment;
Sorrow knocked at my door, but I was afraid;
Ambition called to me, but I dreaded the chances.
Yet all the while I hungered for meaning in my life.
And now I know that we must lift the sail
And catch the winds of destiny
Wherever they drive the boat.
To put meaning in one's life may end in madness,
But life without meaning is the torture
Of restlessness and vague desire —
It is a boat longing for the sea and yet afraid.

Excerpts from
"The Golden Journey to Samarkand"
By James Elroy Flecker

We are the Pilgrims, master; we shall go
    Always a little further: it may be
Beyond that last blue mountain barred with snow,
    Across that angry or that glimmering sea,
White on a throne or guarded in a cave
    There lives a prophet who can understand
Why men were born: but surely we are brave,
    Who make the Golden Journey to Samarkand.
Sweet to ride forth at evening from the wells
    When shadows pass gigantic on the sand,
And softly through the silence beat the bells
    Along the Golden Road to Samarkand.
We travel not for trafficking alone:
    By hotter winds our fiery hearts are fanned:
For lust of knowing what should not be known
    We make the Golden Journey to Samarkand.

There is no Frigate like a Book
by Emily Dickinson

There is no Frigate like a Book
To take us Lands away,
Nor any Coursers like a Page
Of prancing Poetry.
This Traverse may the poorest take
Without oppress of Toll;
How frugal is the Chariot
That bears the Human Soul!

"Courage"
By Johann Wolfgang von Goethe

Carelessly over the plain away,
Where by the boldest man no path
Cut before thee thou canst discern,
Make for thyself a path!
Silence, loved one, my heart!
Cracking, let it not break!
Breaking, break not with thee!

Sonnet 30
By William Shakespeare

When to the sessions of sweet silent thought
I summon up remembrance of things past,
I sigh the lack of many a thing I sought,
And with old woes new wail my dear time's waste:
Then can I drown an eye, unus'd to flow,
For precious friends hid in death's dateless night,
And weep afresh love's long since cancell'd woe,
And moan th' expense of many a vanish'd sight:
Then can I grieve at grievances foregone,
And heavily from woe to woe tell o'er
The sad account of fore-bemoaned moan,
Which I new pay as if not paid before.
But if the while I think on thee, dear friend,
All losses are restor'd and sorrows end.

No matter how much one adores one's avocation, there comes a time when staleness and inertia sets in, when despite all efforts, one's output remains as unmoving as lichen on a boulder. So it was with our poetry writing some years ago. Seeking inspiration, serenity, and a new silk kimono, we set off for the hushed peace of Mount Fuji. There, at a remote Japanese inn, we met an aging local poet, who forever altered our wordcraft. Each morning, after a spare breakfast of rice and salmon, we would wander the hills—across footbridges, along koi ponds, through rock gardens—while our master educated us. Japanese poetry is a vast discipline, and many a dawn we were certain our craniums would split, so tightly did we pack in poetic vocabulary, such as onji (phonetic unit), waka (Japanese verse written in Japanese) and kanshi (Japanese verse written in Chinese). At the end of our pilgrimage, we bid adieu to the Land of the Rising Sun and returned home, our writing plumes much refreshed.

In subsequent years, we have come to lean most heavily on two particular poetic forms: haiku and tanka. Both are well suited to composing verse in the outdoors, as they are traditionally concerned with matters of nature, love, and emotion, all of which abound at camp. They are also on the short side, structurally speaking, which leaves more time for merriment, than, say, the composition of a sestina, or even a sonnet. Let us examine each in turn:

The Japanese Haiku

A Japanese haiku is traditionally made up of seventeen onji, which is a sort of phonetic value for Japanese writing characters. It is similar, but not equal to, the English syllable. Thus, in English we do our best, keeping it structurally to seventeen syllables divided into three lines, classically of five, seven, and five syllables each. We should mention that if one is reading a Japanese poem that has been translated into English, this might not add up perfectly. For example, take this poem by seventeenth-century Japanese poet Masahide. In Japanese it is seventeen onji; in English it is only nine syllables:

Barn's burnt down—
Now
I can see the moon.

The second mark of a Japanese haiku is that at some point it makes a reference or two to nature. More specifically, it likes to infer a particular season through the use of word choice. For example, the above haiku's use of "moon" might imply autumn, when moon-viewing festivals take place in Japan.

Finally, although we do love a good rhyming poem, Japanese haiku poets do not, as they prefer to mirror the impenetrable mysteries of life, which seem diluted in rhyme. Thus, pairing "moon" with "baboon" would have been a grave misstep on the part of Masahide.

The Japanese Tanka

We rarely hear talk of tanka in the Western world, perhaps because it takes a quarter hour longer to compose than the succinct haiku. Tanka is like haiku in that it is bound to strict syllabic form and focuses primarily on nature; however, tanka is longer— thirty-one syllables altogether and five lines. The first three lines follow the form of the haiku, then two lines of seven onji (or syllables) each are added. We believe the way to go about crafting one is to write a line or two each day so as not to buckle under the sustained pressure of proving one's intellect. Tanka also tends to be more lyrical and emotionally complex than haiku. Here is one of our favorites, from *The Tale of Genji* by Murasaki Shikibu (translated by Royall Tyler). Again, do remember that, as a translation, its syllabic content does not add up precisely:

> Fireflies rule the night
> And it is sad to see them
> When at every hour
> One burns with the searing flame
> Of love now lost

Writing One's Own Poetry

We believe a poem should concern itself primarily with purity of invention and less so with form. For example, T. S. Eliot wrote a charming haiku that, frankly, flouted each of the Japanese rules:

> I grow old . . . I grow old . . .
> I shall wear the bottoms of my
>   trousers rolled.

So if adhering to a particular structure is just too rigid for one's soul, then write in free verse, or engage one's companions in a brisk round of renga (see Advisement). However, we confess that we enjoy puzzling out a proper haiku on our adventures. Perhaps one will find inspiration in a few of ours:

> Burning midday sun
> Leaves one wishing for aloe
> Or gin on the rocks

> Forest snow angels
> Should be made wearing long johns
> Not one's birthday suit

> When my love is near
> I feel heart's fire consume me
> But when love journeys
> Out of sight it only takes
> One blink—passion is forgot.

NIGHTCAP
JAPONESQUE JASMINE TEA WITH SAKE & GINGER

After a rousing round of haiku-making, we feel a cup of fragrant jasmine tea (known in the islands of Japan as *sanpin cha*) is just the thing to prepare our minds for the night's rest. Its soothing warmth and exotic floral aroma are treat enough for most—but to make it a proper nightcap, we like to swirl in a good amount of sake and a drizzle of ginger syrup. The tea heats the sake brilliantly and soothes our throats in anticipation of the next night's session of verse.

> PROVIDES **4 PORTIONS**
> 2 to 4 ounces *futsu-shu* sake (see
>   Advisement)
> Ginger Confectionery Syrup (page 77),
>   to taste
> 1 kettle brewed jasmine tea, piping hot

Divide the sake amongst 4 Japonesque tea cups, allowing ½ to 1 ounce of sake per cup, depending upon the wishes of each imbiber. Drizzle in the ginger syrup and top with the tea. Allow the brew to cool slightly before putting the cup to one's lips.

Advisement: *Futsu-shu* sake is the sort of sake one might use for everyday needs, similar to a *vin ordinaire*.

Advisement: Even the Japanese recognized that working out perfectly metered poetry was taxing work. Thus, a game was invented, whereby one poet would scribble the first several lines, then pass it along to a second poet, who would complete it. They called these linked poems renga.

Essential Philosophical Quandaries

FOR THE PONDERING

One evening in the wild, whilst intently engaged in discussion of the latest scandals and sensations of high society, we were interrupted by a tremendous crack just beyond the clearing, followed by a shuddering boom. Our party immediately dispatched a companion to investigate. The sleuth returned, relieved to report that the racket was nothing more than the falling of an old oak. Pleased as we were that no lumbering giant was headed into camp, the conversation was derailed. For we could not help but wonder: if the tree had fallen while we were not in the forest to hear it, would it have made a sound?

And so it was that we began an investigation into the ways of philosophical inquiry. At first it was a trifle embarrassing that we had gone so many years without even peeking at the pages of Plato, but before long, we realized that we were not alone, particularly after reading this bit from the great German philosopher Arthur Schopenhauer:

> How very paltry and limited the normal human intellect is, and how little lucidity there is in the human consciousness, may be judged from the fact that, despite the ephemeral brevity of human life, the uncertainty of our existence and the countless enigmas which press upon us from all sides, everyone does not continually and ceaselessly philosophize, but that only the rarest of exceptions do so.

While we appreciate Mr. Schopenhauer's passion, we must disagree with his pessimistic assertion that dimwittedness is a natural human trait. Out to prove him wrong, we have assembled the following ten philosophical dilemmas for our fellow adventurers. We hope they will serve as an excellent stepping-off point for an intellectual exploration of our physical universe, which is so beautifully on display in the Great Outdoors.

TEN PHILOSOPHICAL QUANDARIES

1

Is the universe infinite or finite—that is, is it eternal, or does it have a beginning and an ultimate end?

2

Does each being experience life in the same way, or do we each experience entirely different realities? If one lives a singular reality, does anyone else truly exist?

3

If the self does not exist, does love exist?

4

Is our perception of space and time real or illusory? Is time travel possible? Do parallel universes exist?

5

Is life self-determined or fated? To what extent can we control our life circumstances?

6

Do good and evil both exist absolutely, or is the nature of each a matter of historical, social, or personal perspective?

7

Which is more productive: dedication to personal happiness as a means to societal harmony, or dedication to societal harmony as a means to personal happiness?

8

If the world had to subsist on the knowledge of only one discipline—science, art, mathematics, philosophy, or religion—which should we choose? Which could we not survive without and why?

9

What is beauty? Is it an innate sensibility or is it culturally determined?

10

Is all self-expression, whatever the form, worthy of the term "art"? Is there a limit to what constitutes art? Where does that boundary lie?

For austere campers, chirping crickets might be a perfectly adequate orchestra for the evening fire. But, until owls manage to master harmony, we see no need for the regretfully tuneless music of the wilderness. Simply include a talented musician or two among the merry band of travelers; for although a bawdy joke might provoke a smile, the only certain means of increasing mirth, dance, and general abandon is a bit of live song.

Before one waltzes off to the nearest railway station in search of any scruffy busker collecting coins in an open case, let us review the instruments most appropriate to an outdoor holiday:

Accordion: Something of a one-man band, the squeezebox is particularly useful for a good old-fashioned polka, or for those wishing to capture the aura of a smoky Left Bank café.

Banjo: An excellent choice for pastoral types longing for frenetic bluegrass, or for those looking to resurrect old-fashioned barn dances. If one has failed to bring along a banjo, one might improvise with a pie tin, hunk of wood, and some tightly wound wire.

Fiddle: Any lively lad or lass will jump up for a reel about the campsite the moment a fiddler lifts his bow. If one's party is lucky (and not too demanding), a deft musician might even switch to Tchaikovsky in the morning for a serene breakfast melody.

Guitar: An evident classic at camp, one might use this for nearly any sort of musical pleasure. It is particularly useful for accompanying vocals. It has been well documented that simply carrying one around is sufficient to attract comely companions.

Harmonica: Ah, how this reed wind instrument is evocative of hobos, hillbillies, and idyllic antebellum living. It is said that Abraham Lincoln carried one in his pocket, which suggests it is a must-have for aspiring renaissance men and women. In good hands, it can perform melancholy blues, sweet jazz, and wistful folk tunes of yore.

Percussion: Do not be madcap—one cannot cram a full drum kit into a travel trunk. A pared-down jug-band approach is just right for percussion needs in the Great Outdoors. A washboard, for example, is portable and keeps a quirky, timely beat. Clack together a few clean spoons, which are easy enough to dig up from the dish bin. And since one has overturned the dish bin, employ an engineering-type companion to assemble a washtub bass with a large length of kindling and some string. Voilà—perfect percussion for jazz or ragtime ditties.

Ukelele: Despite its wee size, this stringed, lutelike instrument ought not be underestimated. Originally popularized in Hawaii by Portuguese immigrants, it quickly became a favorite of jazz icons, vaudevillians, and luau organizers the world over. We adore its Old World-meets-tropical-island glamour, and promise it will invigorate one's quickstep.

Voice: Do not forget that we each carry a portable instrument within. If one's knees are set knocking at the thought of offending companions with sour notes or inaccurate lyrics, rest assured that the others won't hear a thing over their own ale-sodden voices. If concern persists, we suggest the camp tradition of singing in rounds, a certain means of concealing musical transgressions.

A Selection of Tunes

Knowing which songs are guaranteed to set toes tapping is an art form, and fortunately, one we've mastered. To guide the uninitiated, we have helpfully assembled a collection of winning melodies.

THE MARCH (FOR INSPIRATION)

"It's a Long Way to Tipperary"
This song has all the vim and verve of soldiers going off to war, which is perhaps why it remains a favorite among military corps. In truth, it began life as a rollicking music-hall song; at some point, its catchiness spilled into the infantry lines. We find this tune particularly effective when rallying one's party for an exciting day ahead or when trying to unify companions after an unpleasant spat. It can even cure a short bout of homesickness. For inspiration, seek out the jumping rendition by big-band legend Artie Shaw, or a mellower version by blues artist Mance Lipscomb.

THE MUSIC-HALL SONG

"Night in the Woods"
Sometimes in the wild, when the velvet darkness of night falls upon us, we are reminded of the shadowy corners of our favorite burlesque haunts, where spirits were always high and entertainment fabulously eclectic. This tune, originally performed in French at the renowned Parisian hall, Les Folies Bergère, beautifully synchronizes the exotic mystery of both darkened forest and cabaret stage. If one has remembered to pack one's sequined headdress, this would be the moment for it.

THE ROMANTIC DITTY

"Moonlight on the Ganges"
Do we not all have moonlit memories of swooning upon a bridge above a river—be it the Thames, the Seine, the Amazon, or the Ganges—while some handsome companion crooned sweet nothings into our ears? This is a song of adventure, a song of romance, a song of daring: in short, a song for the Great Outdoors. Depending upon the camp musicians' tempo, it can be dreamy or danceworthy.

THE JAZZY FOXTROT

"Indian Cradle Song"
Although the title sounds like something of a Native American lullaby, this is actually an upbeat foxtrot, worthy of a dance partner or even a solo, haphazard jig. Our dear friend Louis Armstrong always performed this song to a thumping beat; it is an excellent opportunity to give a party's percussionists a moment to shine.

THE SENSATIONAL PARISIAN SUCCESS

Nights in the Woods

(Les Nuits du Bois)

FOX TROT SONG

English Lyrics by
ARCHIE BELL

Music by
HAROLD DE BOZI

GET THIS SONG
FOR YOUR PLAYER PIANO
OR TALKING MACHINE

In a shad-y bower, At the sun-set hour, Let us wait to-geth-er for the
Let us stroll a-long In this land of song, Lis-ten-ing to ev-'ry sound and

pale moon-light; There I'll show to you How all lov-ers true
try to learn What it is they sing— For each feath-er'd wing

Copyright MCMXXIII by Enoch & Co., Paris.
International Copyright Secured.
All Rights Reserved.
Printed in the U.S.A.

Sole Rights United States
and Canada
SAM FOX PUBLISHING CO.
Cleveland and New York.

Sole Rights British Empire
(excluding Canada)
KEITH PROWSE & CO Ltd
London.

Reservados los derechos para las Repúblicas Argentina y Uruguay Queda hecho el deposito que marca la ley.
English lyrics Copyrighted MCMXXIII by Sam Fox Publishing Company for all countries.

Seek-ing the qui - et woods at night,   Lis-ten to the leaves, Birds up in the trees
Has un-der-neath a heart like ours.   Let us put in words All we hear the birds

Whis-per-ing love mes-sag-es up - on the breeze. From a ti - ny throat,
Call-ing to their cho-sen mates in tones of joy, I will sing to you

Throbs a yearn-ing note — 'Tis a lov-er sigh-ing for a kiss;
As the oth-ers do When they meet the ones that they love best.

poco rall.

She will hear his song, And you'll see ere long How she soft-ly war-bles a re - ply.
Please do not de - ny, Try to make re-ply In the gen-tle syl - la-bles of love.

poco rall.

REFRAIN

Oh, these rare nights in the woods;— Let me take you by the
hand, Lead you to the mag-ic land Where all lov-ers un-der-stand How to love and
spoon. In this hour of sweet ro-mance, Let us steal a fleet-ing
glance Of a vi-sion that en-chants And breathe the word Love, Love, Love.

When the stars shine in the sky — Let us count them you and I, And it would not be a

miss If I stole from you a kiss As they bright-ly gleam. Sweet ca-ress im-

plor-ing, Al-ways you a-dor-ing — I would prom-ise to be true

As all oth-er lov-ers do In-spired by mu-sic of Nights in the Woods. Woods.

"It's a long, long way to Tipperary"

Written & Composed by
JACK JUDGE & HARRY WILLIAMS

Up to might-ty Lon-don came an Ir-ish man one day,
Pad-dy wrote a let-ter to his Ir-ish Mol-ly O',
Mol-ly wrote a neat re-ply to Ir-ish Pad-dy O',

As the street are paved with gold, sure ev-'ry-one was gay;
Say-ing, "Should you not re-ceive it, write and let me know!
Say-ing, "Mike Ma-lon-ey wants to mar-ry me, and so

Sing-ing songs of Pic-ca-dil-ly, Strand and Leices-ter Square, Till
"If I make mis-takes in "spell-ing," Mol-ly dear," said he, "Re-
Leave the Strand and Pic-ca-dil-ly, or you'll be to blame, For

Pad-dy got ex-cit-ed, then he shout-ed to them there:—
mem-ber it's the pen that's bad, don't lay the blame on me"
love has fair-ly drove me sil-ly— hop-ing you're the same!"

It's a long, long way to Tipperary 4

Its a long long way to Tipperary 4

The tradition of swapping ghoulish tales around a flickering campfire is long. This is hardly surprising when one considers the many frightening mysteries lurking in the woodlands after sunset. Have we not all been on an adventure or two when a perfectly commonplace night at camp is disturbed by an unidentifiable creak in the dark, a sudden chilly breeze, or a glimpse of some ghostly mirage between the shadowy trees?

We believe these moments of fright make a fine addition to the excitement of camp and try to cultivate more of them through the act of ghost storytelling. Ever since we spent a bloodcurdling night in a dank and gloomy castle in the Scottish Highlands, we have been partial to the gothic tradition. Certainly any folktale or urban legend, well told, will do a fine job of giving one's party the creeps, but the gothic tradition is marvelously dark. Born in the eighteenth century (possibly as an antidote to the sunny, fairy tale–strewn Romantic Movement), the genre quakes with familiar, eerie themes—brushes with the occult, haunted manors, murders, madness, and grotesque plots unfolding atop remote and windy cliffs. It is, in fact, a rather small feat to pull off a dreadfully frightening tale of this ilk, and one needn't dust off the old Ouija board for assistance.

How to Tell a Gothic Tale

Begin with special effects: No point in going overboard here, as one doesn't want to distract listeners from the story itself. Instead rely on a few choice props—perhaps a lantern held under one's chin, a squealing fiddle for the sound of a creaky door, or a red silk scarf pulled from the breast at the moment of a character's murder.

Command attention: The last thing a storyteller hopes to see is a row of companions nodding off, when the point is to ruin their chances for a good night's sleep. Take the role of storyteller as seriously as if one were a professional impresario. Practice the story a few times while out foraging or while dressing for cocktails. Focus on rhythm, intonation, and speed. For instance, we always tantalize our companions by slowing or pausing as we near climactic moments. Alternate between a soft, steady voice and a loud, frantic one. Stand while speaking.

Make eye contact: This works particularly well when one fixes a wide-eyed stare upon those who seem the most frightened. After all, the aim is to provoke a reaction, and fear tends to have a domino effect— terrorize one, and all fall to pieces.

Blend the iconic with the realistic: It doesn't matter if it is an oft-repeated image; a haunted house on a hill is always a bit scary. But to truly drain the blood from companions' faces, situate that fictional hill house down the lane from camp. A solid plot needn't bulge with twists and turns. A seamless blend of classic themes and familiar details works best.

Avoid the gory: It is surprising, but blood and guts rarely move an audience. One does better to strive for moments of terror rather than gruesome turns, for it is a story's unsolvable mysteries that set listeners' imaginations free. For example, perhaps the bellhop's paramour vanished inexplicably on her way to the chamberpot, instead of being cleft in two by an ax-wielding madman. One's audience will immediately begin to entertain a host of terrifying conclusions.

Suggestions for One's Ghost Story Library

For some, creating a gothic story from scratch is a pleasurable creative pursuit; for others, it is pure drudgery. If one hasn't the flair, we recommend investigating the following works by masters of the craft (see note page 283). They can serve as mere inspiration or at-the-ready campfire reading.

Ghost-Stories of an Antiquary (1904) *by Montague Rhodes James.* Slightly less gothic than his predecessors, James enjoyed writing spooky tales with a scholastic bent (expect plots to involve rare religious manuscripts, strange museum acquisitions, and architectural wonders). His stories are ideal for the Great Outdoors, as many take place in rural settings.

In a Glass Darkly (1872) *by Sheridan le Fanu.* A collection of horror stories built around the experiences of the fictitious occult detective Dr. Hesselius. The story "Carmilla," about a lesbian vampire, may have influenced Bram Stoker's *Dracula.*

The Moonstone (1868) *by Wilkie Collins.* An allegedly cursed Indian jewel disappears from an English manor. No characters are safe from suspicion in this spine-tingling novel.

The Short Fiction of Edgar Allen Poe: If one is lucky enough to happen upon his macabre anthology, *Tales of the Grotesque and Arabesque, Volume I* (1840), snatch it up—it contains the chilling short story "The Fall of the House of Usher." Otherwise, one's local

---

NIGHTCAP
CAMPFIRE GERMAN GLÜHWEIN

This heady mulled wine is absolute perfection when sipped in the dark recesses of the Black Forest—or any forest locality, for that matter—and can be of special assistance if one has developed a fear of the dark through exposure to gothic ghost stories. Just one gobletful of glühwein will give one enough of a glow to light the path to blissfully sunny dreams.

PROVIDES 6 TO 8 PORTIONS

One 750-milliliter bottle robust red wine, such as Malbec or Pinot Noir

¼ cup sugar

4 whole cloves

1 cinnamon stick

1 vanilla pod (seeds scraped and reserved for another purpose)

Zest of 1 orange, removed in strips, white pith trimmed away

1. Pour the wine into one's Dutch oven and stir in the sugar. Nestle the Dutch oven, uncovered, atop a glowing ember bed scraped to the side of the fire pit and allow the mixture to heat, stirring occasionally, until the sugar has completely dissolved, about 5 minutes.

2. Bundle the cloves, cinnamon stick, vanilla pod, and orange zest in a scrap of clean muslin cloth or tie them securely together using kitchen twine. Add the bundle to the brew and allow it to steep on the heat, taking care that the mixture does not come to a boil, until very fragrant, 15 to 20 minutes. Serve in goblets whilst hot.

Employing Classic Gothic Tropes

Creating a gothic tale from thin air is far less mysterious than it seems. One need only draw from a plentiful stock of typical themes. We recommend that novice storytellers employ the following chart to sketch out a plot. One can mix and match with whatever settings, characters, phenomena, or props feel most inspiring. The resultant yarn will be in keeping with the gothic tradition and yet entirely of one's own making.

SETTINGS	CHARACTERS	PHENOMENA & PROPS
Rambling mansion	Solitary old maid	Mysterious archaeological artifacts
Stodgy, ivy-covered university	Bewhiskered sailor	Candles extinguished without warning
Weathered, abandoned farmhouse	Woman in white	Banging shutters
Moonlit, labyrinthine garden	Band of pirates	Black cats
Run-down hotel	Lame servant boy	Discovered corpse
Gloomy castle	Creepy gardener	Reappearing bloodstains
Ancient, forbidden forest	Untrustworthy butler	Valuable missing jewels
Empty country crossroads	Cloak-shrouded horseman	Inexplicably skittish pets
Overgrown cemetery	Bumbling detective	Madness
Cob-webbed crypt	Mustachioed millionaire	Old, yellowed treasure map
Bat cave	Bespectacled professor	Ravens
Secret passageway	Off-his-rocker scientist	Bells tolling at midnight
Foggy moor	Glamorous starlet	Paranoia
Windswept cliff	Orphan sent to live with distant relatives	Poison
Sanatorium	Toothless gravedigger	Vampires
Campsite constructed over Indian burial mounds	Innocent governess	Ghost ships
Abandoned morgue	Wandering gypsy/fortune teller/magician	Egyptian mummies
Masquerade ball	Morose hitchhiker	Thunderstorm
Crumbling belfry	Craven shopkeeper	Werewolves
	Tragic lovers	Curses
	Escaped prisoner	Unspeakable past

bookshop will surely sell any number of other Poe anthologies. Look for those that include any of our favorite tales, such as "The Oval Portrait," "The Cask of Amontillado," "The Pit and the Pendulum," "The Tell-Tale Heart," and "The Gold-Bug."

The Turn of the Screw (1898) *by Henry James*. This novella recounts the tale of a young governess who senses that her new post is plagued by intrusions of a supernatural sort.

The Wind in the Rose-Bush and Other Stories of the Supernatural (1903) *by Mary Eleanor Wilkins Freeman*. This American writer's gothic-inspired tales are a refreshing take on the genre. Her stories brim with uncanny happenings in the New England countryside.

The Woman in White (1860) *by Wilkie Collins*. Collins's work is so well done that we believe he deserves two mentions. Star-crossed lovers, an asylum escapee, and a stolen inheritance converge in this classic mystery novel.

*Although space does allow us to mention specific works, one might also investigate the writings of Arthur Conan Doyle, Ann Radcliffe, Elizabeth Gaskell, and Daphne du Maurier for further excellent gothic reading.

spirit-awakening séances

If one's companions are seated comfortably in a circle around the fire, if it is a moonlit night with only the sound of the breeze whistling through the trees, and (more to the point) if everyone's glasses are topped off with spirits, then it may be an apt moment to join hands for a séance. Time was, séances were all the rage as after-dinner entertainment. Everyone who was anyone—skeptics and believers alike, from President Lincoln to Queen Victoria, Sir Arthur Conan Doyle to Harry Houdini—would have registered some alarm if a group dabble in the spirit world hadn't been proposed right along with the selection of digestifs. And though these kinds of spirit-awakening antics tend to be more readily found in the parlor rather than the Great Outdoors, we find an impromptu séance under the stars (especially when we know we won't have the option of sleeping with the lights on) too titillatingly spooky to resist.

First, everyone ought to clasp hands. Modern psychic intermediaries tell us that hand-holding is not necessary for communicating with the other side, but we like to do it all the same. As any disembodied spirit will be glad to remind one, life is short—and affectionate contact with fellow human beings is the chief sensation one will miss after crossing the river Styx.

Next, everyone should agree upon a spirit whom the group would like to contact. This will concentrate the general mind power and allow the departed soul to home in on the psychic signal. Choose someone everyone knows and can picture well in the mind's eye, such as Lord Byron or Oscar Wilde.

Then, the group should select a medium from amongst their party. This is the person with whom the spirit will primarily communicate. The medium ought to be the guest who exhibits the greatest flair for the dramatic, the most delicate attunement to the afterworld's vibration, and the largest appetite for

THE MAGIC LANTERN

If one wants to get really serious about one's fireside séance, consider making room for a magical lantern in the ol' kit bag. The magic lantern is a forerunner of the modern film projector, and it produces hazy moving images without the need for electricity. Though magic lanterns are no longer commonplace devices, one still might find these elegantly clunky pieces of machinery in better antiquarian shops. In the nineteenth century, these projectors were employed by merry-making spiritualists to add a little spice to their séances. They projected images of ghostly apparitions, fantastical demons, or scantily clad fairy folk to enthrall their (paying) guests. The ruse worked so well that many witnesses were convinced they had seen scientific evidence of the nether realm's existence. Some, such as that brilliant surgeon and spinner of mystery tales Sir Arthur Conan Doyle, were completely taken in by the flickering imagery. Conan Doyle would not recant his belief even after the hoax was revealed. His chum excused Sir Arthur thus: "I'm afraid the old boy's intellect is that of Dr. Watson much more than Mr. Holmes."

HYPNOTIC TECHNIQUES

Whilst enjoying a restful outdoor holiday, one may find that the less charming habits of one's companions are more difficult to overlook away from the distracting hustle and bustle of urban living. The crackling of the fire and the song of the cicada can only do so much to cover up the subtle-though-incessant cacophony of the next person's nail-biting, nose scratching, deep-sleep snoring, or worse. One needn't allow these irritating personal tics to spoil one's tranquillity. Simply employ these hypnotic techniques, giving general suggestions for more harmonious living whilst the subject is under mesmeric control. It may prove a useful and entertaining way to while away an hour or so by the fire. And if, after a bit of amateur hypnosis is attempted, offensive habits persist, perhaps one will consent to be put under at the next fireside gathering and to be given the hypnotic suggestion "live and let live."

First, determine that one's subject is open to hypnosis. It is said that those who have a rather wide-eyed look, laugh easily at jokes of the knock-knock variety, or openly weep at animated films of cuddly woodland creatures are likely candidates. Or one may ask, "Are you the sort that is open to hypnosis?" If they answer in the affirmative, carry on.

Next, provide a relaxing setting. Make sure the subject is seated near enough to the fire for warmth, but not too close, lest clothing be ignited by an errant spark. Speak to the subject in soothing and dulcet tones. Ask, at thirty-second to one-minute intervals, "Are you relaxed?" and wait for an answer. If the subject does not respond, he or she may be taking a snooze, in which case, true hypnosis is not possible.

Once a sufficient state of relaxation is achieved, take out one's fob watch and wave it rhythmically to and fro a few inches from the subject's eyes. Do this for ten to fifteen minutes, or until one's wrist tires.

Voilà! the subject is hypnotized. It is time to plant a suggestion into the psyche. Rather than expressing the suggestion in the negative (such as I will never bite my nails, scratch my nose, or et cetera again), state the idea in a positive way (Whenever I feel the urge to bite my nails, scratch my nose, or et cetera, I will instead sing an operatic aria). This way one will not only eliminate an impolite behavior, one will instill an artistic proclivity so that all one's companions may feel the benefit.

drink. In our experience with these matters, these attributes facilitate ghostly contact.

Once these details are organized, the medium might kindly request the spirit's presence, saying something like, "Dear Mr. Wilde, would ye care to join us for a fireside chat?" If nary a sound is forthcoming in response, one might add that a dram of whiskey and a plate of cookies could also be arranged. Having gone centuries without eating, spirits can sometimes be enticed by good food and drink.

Once all these steps have been taken, it is up to the spirit world to deliver the rest of the entertainment. One may experience the unexplained rustling of foliage or the eerie flickering of the fire; if one is very, very lucky, the spirit will speak to the party via the chosen medium. That is why it is a good idea to summon Byron or Wilde. If the medium starts to spout witty bons mots in a vaguely Anglo-Irish accent, then it is cinch to conclude that the séance has been a success.

shadow puppetry for one & all

We love the spellbinding simplicity of old-fashioned shadow puppetry. Unlike elaborate (and sometimes ghastly) marionettes, shadow puppetry uses the silhouettes of figures and scenery projected onto an illuminated backdrop to tell a story. Although one can present a shadow play anywhere, it is excellent for nights in the wild, where shadows are at home.

The art of shadow puppetry originated in ancient China, where it was often used at court to entertain royals. Naturally after performing this technique for thousands of years, Far Easterners have become quite sophisticated about the whole thing. Their puppets are exquisite and sophisticated puppets, and many characters flitting about the screen at once (we can only imagine the impressively limber contortions of the puppeteer backstage). Over time, French travelers returning from the Orient brought the puppets to Europe, and by the eighteenth century, Parisian puppeteers were becoming skilled in *ombres chinoises,* or Chinese shadows.

What we suggest for the Great Outdoors is a pared-down, primitive form of this puppetry. One needn't have intricate puppets or a perfectly prepared staging area to produce magical results. Although adventurers of every age enjoy the show, we have found this a wonderful nighttime diversion for children, particularly those who respond aversely to the telling of ghost stories.

ONE WILL NEED

- Thin, good-quality poster board
- Sharp scissors
- Box cutter, optional
- Paper fasteners, optional
- Dowels of assorted sizes (we find thicknesses of ⅛ inch to ½ inch work best)
- Sturdy sort of tape (duct, packing, or masking)
- White sheet or other large piece of thin material
- Length of heavy-duty, dark-colored fabric, optional
- Several river rocks or bricks
- A few bright lanterns

TO DO

1. Draw the form of one's characters and scenery onto the poster board. Anything makes a suitable character, including people, animals, or fantastical creatures; scenery might be a tree, a table, a castle, a window—whatever will help illustrate the story.

2. Cut out the forms using sharp scissors. As the edges of the puppet will be somewhat magnified when illuminated, take care to make them as clean as possible. If one is moved to create more detailed patterns or designs in the interior of the shape, we suggest cutting those away with a box cutter, which will yield a more polished appearance.

3. For parts that move, such as a bird's flapping wings or an arm that flails about, cut the pieces individually and join them with paper fasteners. Tape a long, thin dowel to the moving part for control during the show.

4. To support the figures and scenery pieces, tape a dowel or two to the back of them, with the stick protruding below the puppet to serve as a handle for the puppeteer (imagine a lollipop on a stick). Use as many dowels as needed to make the puppets sturdy.

5. In a traditional shadow play, the puppeteer's shadow is obscured by a platform of some sort. Because our wilderness shows are meant in good fun, we never worry about this. However, if one harbors a perfectionist producer within, one can sew or staple a strip of dark, heavy material to the bottom third of the sheet; the puppets will perform in the top two-thirds, where the light will light up the screen.

6. As showtime approaches and one must set the stage, we suggest moving a short distance away from the fire (keeping one eye on the flame for safety, of course); direct firelight tends to compete with the illumination of the puppets. Several means of hanging one's screen exist. One can (a) employ the hands of two companions to hold it during the show, (b) throw the sheet over a long tree branch, or (c) hang it over a rope strung between two trees. Whatever one's chosen method, it is important to keep the sheet as taut as possible to avoid distorting the puppet images. We like to weight the bottom end of the sheet down with a firm layer of river rocks or bricks. It is best if there is little or no breeze.

7. Arrange several lanterns behind the screen, adjusting their position and distance from the screen as needed until satisfied with the resultant image.

8. Situate the audience in front of the screen with the puppeteers squatting behind it, puppets in hand. Let the show begin! We find it helps tremendously to work out a storyline in advance. We often draw from personal experience, as it is remarkably therapeutic to reenact romantic capers or professional melodramas, but a favorite fable or Shakespearean soliloquy works well, too.

tableau vivant: the living picture

It is a certainty that gazing into a glowing orange fire is entertainment beyond measure. However there may be evenings when one's guests require an even more visually stimulating amusement. For those occasions, we propose putting on a living picture (what the French have so charmingly named a *tableau vivant*). And, truly, it is drollery of the highest order.

The tableau vivant was an elite parlor game popular both in the era of Charlotte Brontë (her Mr. Rochester used the game to provoke jealousy in the heart of spritelike Jane Eyre) and Edith Wharton (her tragic heroine Lily Bart played a part in a tableau and attracted all the wrong sort of attention from a society as unappreciative as it was high). In its old-fashioned form, players would dress themselves in elaborately detailed costumes to re-create scenes from major artwork, mythology, or history. Those involved in the scene would do their utmost to remain still as statues, in order to perfectly mimic the work of art they were portraying. The opposing players would try to guess which artwork (or moment in the history of gods and or men) was being depicted. Lest one think the participants were a tad stodgy or overly academic, rest assured that the true competition was not about the player who displayed the greatest knowledge of art or letters, but rather who came up with the prettiest, most attractively revealing poses.

We have seen this scholarly pastime lower the inhibitions of spinster maidens and confirmed bachelors much more readily than a simple cocktail ever could. Stiff-necked gentlemen of our acquaintance have doffed hats and shed ties in order to flex their muscles in robes of muslin—the better to convey Caravaggio's dramatic and quasireligious interpretations of antiquity. And more than one nearsighted librarian has been known to remove her spectacles and loosen her upswept tresses in order to embody the very picture of Diana on the hunt. In both cases, the tableaux were easily named, but the opposing players delayed their inevitable guesses so they could prolong such a comely view. Rascals, all! But when a bit of lechery is in the name of good fun, who can protest?

One may balk at hosting such an evening of tableaux vivants when one is away from home—how will one carry along the necessary costumes? If there is a general disinclination to bring the entire contents of one's wardrobe and jewelry boxes on a fortnight's sojourn, we humbly suggest another option (which requires far less space in one's steamer trunk).

We take inspiration from an example of the 1930s, a performance house in London known as the Windmill Theatre. Its specialty between, during, and for some time after the wars was entertaining lads in need of rest and recreation before returning to the front lines. And what entertains strapping young warriors better than the unconcealed form of the fairer sex? Unfortunately, the social restrictions and legalities of the era prohibited the theater from putting on shows involving naked ladies singing or dancing or even moving at all. So the Windmill got around this hurdle by presenting lovely performers in nude tableaux vivants. It satisfied the letter of the law and lifted the spirits of many a uniformed lover of the arts. In fact, the Windmill continued its merciful mission right through the London Blitz and beyond—its motto was "We never closed!" or, indeed, "We never clothed!"

One might perhaps follow the Windmill's lead and present an evening of tableaux vivants sans costume. It will free up room in the trunk for an extra bottle of Champagne, which is sure to come in handy. Do remember to save a little space for a box of body glitter, though—applied liberally, it adds so much vivant to one's tableau.

NIGHTCAP
TREE TODDY

Whilst enjoying an outdoor holiday, we celebrate the forest but never forget the trees. How could we, when they provide shade for our faces, fuel for our fires, and flavor for our hot toddies? On chilly evenings, we lift our steaming mugs to toast the bounty of our arboreal friends.

PROVIDES 4 PORTIONS
4 ounces good-quality Bourbon
4 ounces apple brandy
Hot water
3 tablespoons maple syrup
4 lemon wedges

Divide the Bourbon and apple brandy amongst 4 mugs. Pour in hot water from the campfire kettle and swirl in about 2 teaspoons maple syrup per mug. Garnish each with a lemon wedge and serve hot.

Conversion Chart

Weight Equivalents: The metric weights given in this chart are not exact equivalents, but have been rounded up or down slightly to make measuring easier.

Volume Equivalents: These are not exact equivalents for American cups and spoons, but have been rounded up or down slightly to make measuring easier.

AVOIRDUPOIS	METRIC
¼ oz	7 g
½ oz	15 g
1 oz	30 g
2 oz	60 g
3 oz	90 g
4 oz	115 g
5 oz	150 g
6 oz	175 g
7 oz	200 g
8 oz (½ lb)	225 g
9 oz	250 g
10 oz	300 g
11 oz	325 g
12 oz	350 g
13 oz	375 g
14 oz	400 g
15 oz	425 g
16 oz (1 lb)	450 g
1 ½ lb	750 g
2 lb	900 g
2 ¼ lb	1 kg
3 lb	1.4 kg
4 lb	1.8 kg

AMERICAN	METRIC	IMPERIAL
¼ tsp	1.2 ml	
½ tsp	2.5 ml	
1 tsp	5.0 ml	
½ Tbsp (1.5 tsp)	7.5 ml	
1 Tbsp (3 tsp)	15 ml	
¼ cup (4 Tbsp)	60 ml	2 fl oz
⅓ cup (5 Tbsp)	75 ml	2.5 fl oz
½ cup (8 Tbsp)	125 ml	4 fl oz
⅔ cup (10 Tbsp)	150 ml	5 fl oz
¾ cup (12 Tbsp)	175 ml	6 fl oz
1 cup (16 Tbsp)	250 ml	8 fl oz
1¼ cups	300 ml	10 fl oz (½ pint)
1½ cups	350 ml	12 fl oz
2 cups (1 pint)	500 ml	16 fl oz
2½ cups	625 ml	20 fl oz (1 pint)
1 quart	1 liter	32 fl oz

OVEN MARK	F	C	GAS
Very cool	250–275	130–140	½–1
Cool	300	150	2
Warm	325	170	3
Moderate	350	180	4
Moderately hot	375	190	5
	400	200	6
Hot	425	220	7
	450	230	8
Very hot	475	250	9

ACKNOWLEDGMENTS

CAMPFIRE COOKERY WOULD HAVE REMAINED NOTHING BUT A WISP OF AN IDEA WITHOUT THE ASSISTANCE OF A NUMBER OF EXCELLENT PEOPLE.

We wish to thank our literary agent Jenni Ferrari-Adler for seeing the potential in our eccentric little book. Thank you for helping us navigate the uncharted territory of first-time publishing. Thanks to Luisa Weiss for welcoming us into the wonderful world of Stewart, Tabori & Chang—*dankeschoen*! Thank you to our marvelous publisher Leslie Stoker and to our editor Natalie Kaire, who inherited this tome; we are so grateful for your unflagging enthusiasm and ever-present positivity. Thanks to Alissa Faden for her artistic talent and vision, and especially for indulging our design whims every step of the way. Thanks to Ana Deboo for her editorial eagle-eye, and to our wonderful managing editor, Ivy McFadden.

Thank you to the publicity and marketing crew at Stewart, Tabori & Chang—Lottchen Shivers, Kerry Liebling, Jennifer Brunn, and Jess Alter—for bringing our adventure to the people.

We're thrilled with the beautiful images in these pages; we owe that pleasure to the talent and hard work of photographer Tara Donne, prop stylist Heather Chontos, and food stylist Paige McCurdy-Flynn.

Several families were gracious enough to open their homes to a flurry of food and fire:

We are much obliged to Liz, Bob, Isabella, and Keifer Convertino for the use of their stunning Hudson Valley property for the photo shoot.

To the lady of the manor, Helen Jones—your hospitality is a continuing inspiration and your friendship a gift. Thank you for introducing us to Warwick and your lovely sprawling farm, where we learned how to split wood, tell ghost stories, and wait out the rain. Thanks are also due to Peter Jones, who warned us of the neighborhood bear and who mixes a wicked cocktail. To Molly Jones—thanks for your company around the fire whilst keeping a lookout for that dastardly redhead, Raymond Duvall.

Thanks to the wonderful Allon Azulai and his graceful daughters Daniella, Noa, and Shoshi for allowing us to set up camp in their Brooklyn backyard in the name of recipe development, all while offering us mugs of brandy-spiked cocoa, entertaining us with excellent humor, and raving (appropriately) about every dish.

We wish to thank each and every one of our nearest and dearest, including Ellen & Larry Huck; Kelly & Paul Huck; Kate, Todd, Lauren, & Davis Marschke; LaVora Karn; Jan Young; Minerva Young; and Maria & Joey Young for their love and support — it was needed and we are grateful for it. We'd like to especially thank a few of you who were near enough to smell the smoke: Victor Cirillo, Molly Killeen, Ronan Killeen, and Brian Malone for their steadfast friendship; Megan Gottig for her equipment expertise; and, of course, our faithful fire consultant Patrick J. Wessel—it's always a boon to have an Eagle Scout on board, especially when trails need blazing.

Last, but never least, to our dear friend and mentor, Melissa Clark: you've taught us pretty much everything we know about cookbookery, quite a bit about a healthy appetite, and oh yeah, a thing or two about life. Thank you.

Index